Democracy and the State
Welfare, Secularism and Development in Contemporary India

NIRAJA GOPAL JAYAL

OXFORD
UNIVERSITY PRESS

OXFORD
UNIVERSITY PRESS

YMCA Library Building, Jai Singh Road, New Delhi 110001

Oxford University Press is a department of the University of Oxford. It furthers the
University's objective of excellence in research, scholarship, and education
by publishing worldwide in

Oxford   New York

Athens   Auckland   Bangkok   Bogota   Buenos Aires   Calcutta
Cape Town   Chennai   Dar es Salaam   Delhi   Florence   Hong Kong   Istanbul
Karachi   Kuala Lumpur   Madrid   Melbourne   Mexico City   Mumbai
Nairobi   Paris   Sao Paulo   Shanghai   Singapore   Taipei   Tokyo   Toronto   Warsaw

with associated companies in   Berlin   Ibadan

Oxford is a registered trade mark of Oxford University Press
in the UK and in certain other countries

Published in India
By Oxford University Press, New Delhi

ISBN   019   565 6121

Typeset by Excellent Laser Typesetter, Tri Nagar, Delhi 110 035
Printed by Pauls Press, New Delhi 110 020
Published by Manzar Khan, Oxford University Press
YMCA Library Building, Jai Singh Road, New Delhi 110 001

This book is dedicated to

Kanta *and* Madan Gopal
who raised me on a Nehruvian vision of India

Rakesh Dhar Jayal
who has always shared that vision

and

Gayatri
in whose India there is alas little place for it

Acknowledgements

I have accumulated an enormous number of debts in the course of writing this book, and am happy to take this opportunity of expressing my gratitude to the many persons and institutions who have contributed to its making. None of them, I hasten to clarify, are culpable for its inadequacies or share any responsibility for its excesses of argument.

In its earliest incarnation, this book was a doctoral dissertation, and I am grateful to the Centre for Political Studies, Jawaharlal Nehru University which gave me leave of absence to pursue this research. I am especially grateful to colleagues who have contributed to it in many ways: Kuldeep Mathur, who supervised the study in its first avatar; C. P. Bhambhri who strongly encouraged its writing despite a well-founded suspicion that he would disagree with it; Aswini Ray and Sudipta Kaviraj who have, in their own very different ways, encouraged this enterprise.

Among those who have read and commented on parts of the manuscript, I am grateful to Manoranjan Mohanty, who has also most generously shared material on Kalahandi; Neera Chandhoke, whose friendly nagging has helped completion; Rukun Advani, who read this as a friend and not a publisher; and Bishnu Mohapatra. I thank the anonymous reviewer of the Oxford University Press, for extremely helpful suggestions as much as for emboldening me to allow this to appear in cold print. Some parts of this manuscript have also been presented at seminars at the Universities of Delhi and Sussex, at the Centre for the Study of Developing Societies, Delhi, and at the conference of the International Political Science Association's Research Committee on Political Theory at Harare, and I am grateful for comments received at these institutions.

I would like to thank many who helped me gain access to

research materials: Archana Mathur, Ashok Mishra, The Delhi Forum, J. S. Rana, Jyotsna Sahoo, N. D. Jayal, Nirmala Mitra, Rabindar Mahajan, Sanjay Kathuria and Virendra Dayal. Nitasha Devasar of OUP has been an exemplary editor, and it has been a pleasure to work with her. I am greatly obliged to Dr S. Srinivasan and Laxman Singh for their assistance with the computer.

My deepest gratitude is to my family, without whom this book would not have been possible. I thank Sachin, Nishi, Shagun, and Mandira and most of all, my parents who have cheerfully accepted the cares of grandparenthood much beyond the call of duty. For his insistence that it be written, as much as for sharing the travails of its writing, Rakesh must now share the blame for this book. Gayatri has contributed more than she will ever know.

Contents

Introduction

Fifty years after independence, many of the foundational principles of the Indian nation-state have been called into question, not least the very project of the nation itself. Among the goals of social transformation prioritized on the state's agenda at independence, at least three—secularism, welfare, and development—remain issues of central importance today, and inform what are arguably the most significant contemporary debates in the country. The project of secularism has increasingly been under threat as communal ideology and political forces have come to enjoy greater purchase in society and the polity. The project of the welfare state has been gradually undermined and discredited in the wake of the ideological struggle between the state and market, and the shifts in economic policy entailed by the process of globalization. The project of development has, finally, come to be questioned by the advocates of sustainable development strategies as well as by movements questioning the rationale of projects that contribute to the prosperity of some social groups even as they cause the large-scale displacement of others.

Although these projects of social transformation arose out of a deliberative–legislative rather than participative–democratic process, they were unquestionably the product of a consensus negotiated and evolved in the course of the movement for freedom. They were also quite unambiguously expected to be realized within the framework of a democratic polity, an aspiration that appeared at the time to be as non-negotiable as the agenda of social transformation itself. The idea of democracy was thus expected to inform, inspire, and cohere with the state's initiatives in the areas of welfare, secularism, and development. This study examines the relationship between state, society, and democracy in India over the past decade, by exploring the recent careers of these three goals of social transformation. The historical trajectory of each has, in no small measure, been impacted by democratic challenges, and in no period of post-independence history has this been more obvious than in the late 1980s, which is the broad time-slice in which this study is located.

The imperatives that informed the choice of these goals as central to the definition, the identity, and the ideological agenda of the Indian nation-state in 1947 do not require detailed description. In these three spheres, as indeed in many others, the odds appeared virtually insurmountable. If vast poverty, especially in the rural sector, was the imperative for welfarism, the absence of an industrial and technological base dictated the choice of development strategy. Secularism, in turn, was the state's response to the possibilities of conflict and divisiveness contained in a society marked by deep attachments to cultural identities such as those of caste, religion, and language.

It is also widely accepted that, though an outcome of the nationalist struggle for independence from colonial rule, these goals were not popularly derived. They were the goals set by a modernizing élite inspired by the ideas of British liberalism and, in some cases, by socialist trends within that tradition. The assumption, by the state, of welfare functions is possibly the best example of this. I shall however argue that the philosophy of state *welfare* in India was, from its very inception, grounded in ideas of charity, benevolence, and paternalism, and has therefore proved to be singularly unreceptive to challenges couched in the more egalitarian terms of claims to rights. The disjuncture between the location of rights to liberty in the justiciable Fundamental Rights chapter of the Indian Constitution and the location of welfare rights in the non-justiciable Directive Principles of State Policy not only reaffirms this perception, but has also haunted this project and impeded its realization. In this book, the theme of welfare will be explored through an examination of hunger in Kalahandi district in Orissa since 1985.

As the strategy of imitatively traversing a path rehearsed and charted elsewhere, the project of *development* was inspired by the happy if rather naïve image of a successful transition—institutional and ideological, economic as well as social and political—from tradition to modernity, eventually mirroring the Western experience. In the years since independence, development has been both *mantra* and myth, as thousands of crores of rupees have been ploughed into millions of projects, while the promise of prosperity has remained elusive not only for the 39 per cent of the population that stands below a rather sparely defined poverty line, but also for the 500,000 people displaced every year since independence by development projects of the central government alone. In this study, I focus on the Narmada Valley Projects, especially the Sardar Sarovar Dam, and the movement against it, to illustrate the contemporary challenge to the conventional paradigm of development.

Perhaps the single most important component of the Indian state's portfolio at the time of independence, was the task of constructing a unified national society out of a dauntingly hetero-geneous diversity of ethnic, religious, and linguistic groups. Stand-ing uncertainly on the threshold of a yet uncharted history, its most pressing and immediate task was that of holding itself together territorially, and maintaining civil order in a society badly scarred by the violence of a Partition justified by the principle of religio–political self-determination. Despite this recognition, by the demitting imperial power, of the legitimacy of religion under-writing claims to political self-determination, the young Indian republic was confident of being able to manage cultural differences. The formulaic rhetoric of nationalism had already projected communalism as the 'other' of nationalism and, after freedom, *secularism* came, almost by force of habit, to mean the principle of nationalism realized, actualized and enthroned by historical writ. Doctrinal secularism, however, proved to be a fragile plant, as communal challenges multiplied. Here, the problem of secular-ism and communalism will be explored through a discussion of the celebrated Shah Bano case, and the issues raised by the passage of the Muslim Women (Protection of Rights on Divorce) Act, 1986.

Even as each of these projects is in peril today, they continue to remain at the heart of the most lively and critical debates on the future of Indian politics and society. The emergence of a neo-liberal agenda in economic policy has discredited not only the 'socialistic' elements of the strategy of planned development, but with it also the need to provide the basic elements of social security for the poorest sections of Indian society. Declining investments in social services, including health and education, cohere with the change in the tenor of policy rhetoric as it professes the new faith of liberalization, globalization, and economic reform. The challenge to the welfarist orientation of the state has come from three distinct quarters, the first of which is represented by international agencies such as the World Bank and the International Monetary Fund and, linked to these by ideological persuasion, the arguments of the local enthusiasts of marketization. In an argument reminiscent of the critique of the welfare state in the Anglo–American world in the 1980s, they claim that welfarism has produced a flabby, overburdened, and inefficient state, able to achieve neither equity nor efficiency. The second challenge to welfare systems has sought, not to undermine the interventionist state, but to make it more amenable to selective redistribution. This challenge finds expression in the claims of groups to particular social goods, through reservations in educational institutions and public employment. Such groups are clearly not agitating for a rolling back of the state, but their defence of welfare is unequivocally non-universalistic in its scope, seeking to create categories of citizenship in relation to social resources, and therefore has the potential of sustaining a welfare state at the cost of fragmenting society into competing groups. Consequently, not only does the search for social justice come to be defined euphemistically, in rather partial and exclusivist terms, it also displaces altogether, from any foreseeable political agenda, the programme of distributive justice. Finally, there is the challenge of those who seek a redefinition of the development agenda, drawing attention to the fulfilment of basic needs and, therefore, by implication to the question of state responsibility for welfare.

It has come to be widely believed that the model of development adopted by India was thoughtlessly derivative, and has proved to be at once economically inequitous, environmentally unsustainable, and politically less than democratic in its denial of the rights of equal citizenship. In the formulation of development policy and the setting of development priorities, Indian planners have tended to interpret development exclusively in terms of economic growth. As a result, economic evaluation in the choice, design, and implementation of policy has enjoyed priority over the question of the appropriateness of policy which should ideally take into account cultural and social factors, provide space for debate on the normative aspects of policy and, above all, for democratic negotiation. The outcome biases of development have also been painfully obvious : even where successfully implemented, projects have notoriously tended to benefit politicians, administrators, and a variety of commercial interests instead of subserving the common good; when the implementation is faulty, it is blamed on leakages and the rent-seeking proclivities of the development bureaucracy. The regional and class imbalances that have resulted from the process of planned development have only served to further discredit the strategy of development.

Altogether appropriately perhaps, the interrogation of techno-cratic developmental policies has taken place at the level of political practice, rather than scholarly discourse, by mounting protest on questions of survival, against the displacement and alienation, by development projects, of people from their habitats, cultures, and ways of life. Deriving sustenance and power from grass-roots mobilizations, such movements have perceived the state as the embodiment of technocratic arrogance, of bureaucratically di-rected development, and of repressive intolerance towards dissent. There is a curious paradox in the fact that they simultaneously make claims *upon* the state and *against* it, sometimes appealing to the state as the putative provider of justice, and at other times appealing beyond it to meta-state agencies, such as international bodies. The first, intra-state dimension, expresses the conflict between the 'national interest' as defined by the state, and the interests of some sections of the citizenry. The second speaks to the problem of political obligation, seeking to balance the state's call on the loyalty of its citizens with the right of citizens to resist the state, if necessary by appeal to international organizations.

Finally, that the project of secularism had fallen upon bad times was most tragically symbolized in the destruction of the Babri Masjid in December 1992. It had become apparent, even before that event, that the secular state stood on rather shaky ground and, what is more disturbing, that the secularization of society or the creation of a secular public sphere, was far from being realized. The ideology of liberal neutrality adopted by the state proved to be hopelessly inadequate to the task of managing a culturally plural society. Resting upon a mistaken equivalence between interest and pressure groups, on the one hand, and cultural and religious communities, on the other, it offered an identical liberal pluralist solution for both. Recent history has demonstrated the state's own alarming vulnerability in relation to the politics of religion, its inability to contain or prevent communal violence, the complicitous involvement of its enforcement arm in the perpetration of such violence, and the cynical manipulation of religious 'issues' by the political élite. Meanwhile, the legacy of Partition has continued to haunt India, with claims to self-determination—including some for secession and autonomy—being grounded in a variety of social cleavages. It is a measure of the extent to which this idea has come to enjoy popular and intellectual currency that these demands continue to be judged as legitimate or otherwise primarily in terms of the primordiality or constructedness of the cleavage in question, as the definitive mark of its authenticity or otherwise.

The choice of our three cases, namely Kalahandi, Narmada, and Shah Bano, is far from arbitrary. They are comparable because they span approximately the same period. Each represents, in fact, an as yet unresolved issue: Kalahandi has continued to be, in 1996-7, in the grip of acute hunger; the Narmada Valley Projects continue to be contentious, even as the Supreme Court is yet to decide their eventual fate; and the issues raised by the Shah Bano case have markedly altered the terms of discourse as we see them today both in the renewed feminist debate on a Uniform Civil Code, as well as in the political pronouncements of right-wing political parties.

They are also comparable because they highlight different facets of the same Indian state, even at times of the same regime. This is a point of some importance in the scholarly debate on state–society relations, cautioning us against attributing to the state a fixed and unvarying nature in relation to society. While the highly differentiated nature of Indian society is too apparent to need any emphasis, a recognition of the differentiatedness of the state is equally important. It is widely accepted that the complexity of Indian society makes it incumbent on the scholar to take cognizance of its immense and taxonomy-defying diversity. Likewise, state differentiation provides clues to the understanding of the apparently contradictory responses to the same situation that issue from different wings of the state structure.

In trying to map the cultural landscape of the state-society interaction, we recognize another, third, similarity between our cases. This consists in the fact that all three cases are, in the ultimate analysis, concerned with a category that we might describe as doubly disadvantaged citizens. Both the Kalahandi and Narmada cases illustrate the interpenetration between tribal identity, structural poverty, and backwardness, expressed in the overlap between class and ethnicity, as the worst affected citizens in both cases are landless labour and tribals. The Shah Bano case illustrates the overlap between religion and gender, pointing to a category of citizens who are disprivileged as a result of both their minority status and their gender identity.

Finally, these cases are comparable because democracy is central to each of them. Indeed, each exemplifies a different democratic mode, thereby providing variety and range to the study. The first accounts of widespread hunger and starvation in Kalahandi were reported by the local press and then taken up in the legislative assembly. To date, it has not been the people of Kalahandi who have directly protested their hunger. It has been a quintessentially parliamentary mode of democratic protest through the legislature and the press. The Supreme Court's verdict in the Shah Bano case generated a controversy that became only more heated once the government's intentions of passing the Muslim Women's Bill came to be known. These agitations were conducted both within parliamentary institutions and without, and can therefore be accurately designated as examples of para-parliamentary protest. Finally, the mode of democratic protest adopted by the Narmada Bachao Andolan has been almost entirely extra-parliamentary, eschewing the institutions of formal democracy and even, on occasion, engaging in the boycott of these (e.g. elections).

Democracy, in this study, is not however limited to the formal institutions of procedural democracy. It encompasses the idea of a substantive content for the democratic project (discussed in detail in the next chapter) as also the dimension of discourse. It seeks to identify the claims about justice, rights, and equality that are invoked in each of the cases, as well as the discourse of the state as it responds to these various claims. The divergence between the claims and the response are significant as, for instance, when the demand for the redressal of acute hunger is rooted in a needs-based conception of justice, while the state's interpretation of welfare takes the form of charity. Sometimes, political exigencies enjoin a convergence between such claims and responses, as when the *ulema* demand protection for the rights of cultural community, and the state supports this demand, also incidentally helping to entrench patriarchal social relations. It does so by employing a discourse of protection that seeks to encompass equally minorities and women as entities in need of such protection.

In exploring some aspects of the discursive terrain of Indian politics, this book seeks, heretically for the discipline of political science, to effect a marriage between the concerns of political theory and those of empirical political analysis. It brings to bear upon what is jealously guarded as the preserve of the political scientist, the normative concerns of the political philosopher. This attempt is indeed not confined to the discursive aspects of the study, but encompasses also the way in which democracy and the state are understood. Underlying this attempt is the claim that it is important to recognize the values that are implicitly invoked when political principles such as democracy, rights, and justice are proclaimed, and that unpacking these value-assumptions of political activity is as important as making explicit value-slopes in empirical political research that axiomatically makes a virtue of eschewing these.

The next chapter carries further the argument about the importance of normativity in understanding what are customarily taken to be purely empirical issues. It recognizes, however, the limitations of any exercise that seeks to forge a link between these by assigning weights to normativity *vs* explanatoriness in the analysis of democracy and the state. The case studies are elaborated in the three chapters that follow. Each case study is presented in a similar format of narrative followed by interpretation and analysis. The conclusion reviews, in a comparative perspective, the findings of the case studies and attempts to tie these together to create a coherent picture of the larger question: the relationship between state, society, and democracy.

1

Prolegomenon to a Theory of State, Society and Democracy for India

I. THE STATE

The state enjoys a unique conceptual status in the study of politics, which derives not so much from its pre-eminence in political life as from its simultaneous location in two realms: the normative-theoretical and the descriptive-empirical. Belonging exclusively to neither, it straddles both. If the abstractness of the state has eluded the political scientist, its tangible institutional manifestations have been inconveniently obtrusive for the political theorist. The separation between these concerns decreed by academic convention has ill-served the effort to arrive at an adequate understanding of the state. The area where the normative and the empirical intersect has thus remained unillumined as theoretical purists have disparaged contact with it, and political scientists have shunned it for its irredeemably unscientific and value-laden character.

Even within non-behavioural political science, the neutral and essentially descriptive character of this concept has been largely taken for granted. As a result, differences have centred around the characterization of its role in society, its dependence on or autonomy from various types of social forces, and its centrality or otherwise in political explanation. In all this, a certain minimal agreement about the state is presumed; presumptions that serve to consolidate the argument for the facticity of the state and undermine the argument for its normativity. The case for the normativity of the state is indeed a difficult one to establish, because unlike concepts such as democracy, justice, and freedom, which are terms of political appraisal and judgement, the state is not demonstrably so. However, considered as a social arrangement within the framework of which these values may be realized, and as the source of legitimate rule in which people collectively concur, its normativity is in principle undeniable. Similarly, critiques of the state that invoke its failure to meet the test of moral adequacy, however defined, are surely appraisive. Indeed, the prescription of a role, interventionist, minimal, or any other, for the state is an ineluctably judgemental exercise. Above all, any view of politics as a transformative activity manifestly entails normativity, and specifies the role of the state accordingly.

Like several other normative concepts, the state too could be said to be an 'essentially contested concept' (Gallie, 1956). Such a claim is underpinned by the recognition that political theory acquires a practical, action-guiding character as it moves confidently between social conditions and political concepts, explicating the widely shared beliefs that are implicit in a given social order, and identifying in them the seeds of future social change. After all, shaping social and political concepts contributes in the long run to shaping social and political institutions (Miller and Siedentop, 1983: 2). Meanings and definitions of normatively significant political concepts, including the state, may be mandated by dominant usages in society and, as such, are reflective of societal interests. On the other hand, multiple and contradictory meanings may abound, indicating conflicts between the interests that have a stake in defining the concept, and legislating for it a social role (Alford and Friedland, 1990: 395).

Thus, concepts are contested not merely theoretically but also politically and empirically. As part of dominant ideologies, and even more as part of ideologies of resistance, they are imbued with meanings that are deeply political. As such, the theoretical and empirical context of a concept is crucial to an understanding of its meaning and role in a given society at a particular point in its history. In the western intellectual tradition, the emergence of the concept of the state has been linked with the evolution of the state itself. As Quentin Skinner has shown, the descriptive content of terms like *status, stato, etat*, and the state differed according to historical and political context, their meanings being significantly altered and extended over time, with older usages being revived at the political convenience of absolutist monarchs in the seventeenth century (1989: 103). Unsurprisingly, transformations in the concept of the state also effected changes in the meaning of related concepts such as citizen, subject, allegiance, obligation, treason, leadership, majesty, and so on (ibid.: 123–6).

The discussion of the historical relationship between the origin of the state itself, and the concept of the state, raises important questions for the understanding of non-Western states. Historians have provided evidence of state-like entities in the pre-modern period, suggesting that the absence of coevality between the history of the state and the concept cannot be taken as lack of evidence of its existence (cf. Kulke, 1995; Haldon, 1993; Claessen and Skalnik, 1978). Considering aspects other than the purely formal or functional in the study of the state, enables us to interpret it as a normative or symbolic order as well.[1] The separation between the public and the private spheres, which is a theoretical require-ment to speak of the state in the Western context, is inadequate in interpret the non-Western experience, leading scholars to advocate, in the context of Third World societies, a study of the state in terms of cultural processes, symbols, and rituals.[2]

If the uniqueness of historical trajectories encourages us to look beyond the purely formal attributes of the state to its cultural and symbolic specificities, its contestedness in the present nudges us towards an altogether different, but not for that reason any the less significant, kind of specificity. This is the recognition that the state is subject to contestation not merely as an empirical entity, but also as a conceptual and symbolic one. The struggles between social groups to control the state as an embodiment of power and resources, are also simultaneously struggles over the meaning and definition of the state and its proper role. That normativity informs all these exercises—theoretical, practical, and discursive— is the case advanced in this work.

---

[1] Nettl (1968) has specified 'stateness' in cultural terms, as an attribute of the extent to which individuals have 'generalized the concept and cognition of state in their perceptions and actions'. The European tradition of stateness, in his view, is both extra-societal as well as intra-societal, whereas in developing countries the state is primarily extra-societal, i.e. defined through its role as a unit in international relations, lacking the tradition and ideas of the European state.

[2] Cf. S.H. Rudolph (1987) on South Asia; D. Cruise O'Brien (1991) on Francophone Africa.

The view of the state adopted in this study is consequently one that seeks to encompass not only state institutions, but also and indeed substantially, state projects, practices, and discourses. These are examined in relation to democratic institutions, processes, and discourses. The empirical case studies that form the core of this volume highlight, to greater or lesser degree, various dimensions of the state: its internal organization and the division of powers within it, the mechanisms deployed for state intervention, the balance of social forces as reflected in the state system, and state projects and discourses that attempt to give the state a unity of endeavour.

It is possible to essay a fairly inclusive definition of the state without losing sight of the argument outlined in the first section, that any definition, by virtue of the epistemological and political assumptions it conveys, inescapably prejudices the task of determining the place of the state in political explanation. An inclusive, as opposed to a rigorously delimited, definition is deliberately chosen to let in as much empirical detail as possible towards a theoretically richer understanding. The formal definition of the state has rested upon its external aspect, as a unit in, and a member of, an international system of states, recognized by fellow members as possessing the sovereign power to speak on behalf of the population of a given territory. Regardless of whether the organizing principle of such a population is its common nationhood, or some other antecedent principle of commonality, it is the state that definitively determines citizenship.

Internally, the modern nation-state is defined both in terms of its apparatus and its relation to society, in terms of what it is and what it does. It regulates a territorially defined society and population by making and enforcing laws, to this end engaging also in the extraction of resources. Its claim to the authority to make laws, as well as its claim to a share of the social product, rest on its claim to represent the common interest or the common good, if not the general will of society. This also provides the basis of its legitimacy, as well as the basis of the distinction between the public and private spheres. In terms of its apparatus, the state is a set of institutions inspired by this set of common purposes, to which end they collectively enjoy a monopoly over physical force in society.

II. THE STATE AND SOCIETY

The distinction between state and society has its origins in the separation between the public and private spheres in Western Europe: the former being associated with *res publica* (public affairs), everything directly owned, organized, and administered by the state (Hall, 1984: 20); and the latter encompassing the personal and familial sphere of sexual and emotional relations as well as the independent sphere of economic transactions, private property, and the market. Together, this latter has been designated by the term 'civil society', which has come to enjoy much political and intellectual currency in recent years and covers all forms of voluntary association and social interaction not controlled by the state. In Third World societies, it is widely believed that civil society has not been the precondition of politics, but rather that the creation of civil societies has been the task of states and of politics. The existence of civil society in these countries remains a contentious question.[3] The existence of *society* is, however, not merely acknowledged, but also seen as crucial to an understanding of the effectiveness of the state. Thus, debates about the autonomy—relative or otherwise—of the state or its capacity to effect social and economic change are typically grounded in discussions of state–society relations, which in turn are ineluctably premised on the assumption that there is a boundary (however amorphous or clear-cut) separating these spheres. In the following sections, I examine some aspects of these debates that are relevant to my argument.

[3] With regard to India, it has been argued that civil society, in the sense of opposition to the state, is developed, while civil society, in the sense of associational groups, is not (Kaviraj, 1996). Implicitly drawing on the first meaning, Partha Chatterjee (1997b: 30–4) argues that civil society was the most important site of transformations in the colonial period while political society is the corresponding site in the post-colonial period. He sees an emerging opposition between civil society and political society in the latest phase of the globalization of capital. Meanwhile, a series of anthropological caveats (in the form of case studies) to the Western model of civil society are contained in Hann and Dunn (1996). These show that different human communities are concerned with establishing their own version of a civil society in their own differing ways, and therefore the search for the replication of a universalist (i.e. western) model of civil society all over the world should be abandoned (Hann, 1996: 20).

The Boundary Question

The state, it has been said, is both more and less than society. It is less than society in the obvious sense that it arises out of society, is significantly shaped and constrained by it, and excludes many aspects of it. It is, at the same time, more than society, as a member of the international system and as an institution with an extra-societal face, whose interactions transcend cultural and national boundaries (Jessop, 1990). The state is underpinned by society and cannot exist without it; but conversely, many social institutions bear the imprint of the state. As the legal monopoly of physical force in society, the state also has the capacity to intervene in society and shape it in significant ways. Thus, the state and society are recursively and mutually constituted, in a dynamic and virtually endless cyclical process of reconstitution.

It is a striking indication of the hold of geography over the modern mind that the state–society division has, more often than not, been comprehended in terms of spatial metaphor. In an early and influential work, R. M. MacIver ([1926] 1969: 482) described the state as 'the paved highway of social life, bordered by fields and cities'. The metaphor of the highway was useful in underlining the commonness and public character of the state, as distinguished from the more privately experienced aspects of social life. But while endorsing the need for a broader highway (i.e. a more interventionist state), he simultaneously emphasized that the highway is 'for the sake of the life that is lived along it and beyond it'. (ibid.: 483).

More recently, Bertell Ollmann has also resorted to a spatial metaphor to argue that there is no single answer to where the state ends and where society begins, because these are not 'neighbourhoods separated by broad avenues' (Ollman, 1992: 1015). It is changes in the interests of the ruling class, and consequently in society, that cause variations to occur in the functions of the state, accompanied inevitably by changes both in the boundaries that limit states as well as in the meaning of the concept. This is a complete reversal of MacIver's highway state.

If the boundaries of the state must be grasped in terms of spatial metaphor, perhaps the metaphor of sea and sand may be more effective. The receding of the waters at ebb-tide and the inundation of the beach at flow-tide captures the shifting and untidy nature of the boundary, even though it suggests a mutuality that is repetitive and regular. But its usefulness lies in suggesting the spatial and temporal transience of these boundaries, as also the vastly different nature of the elements in question. The problem with all these metaphors of spatiality, however, is that they posit boundaries as inert. Even the metaphor of sea and sand suggests activity on the part of only one element, while the other remains passive. Any attempt to metaphorically capture the boundary question in terms of its physicality is thus doomed to flounder to the extent that it fails to account for the mobility of boundaries, and the causes of such movement.

The transience of boundaries does not, however, preclude their existence. As such, this study is premised on the existence of boundaries, even as it accepts their shifting nature and elusiveness. Boundaries are here interpreted solely as provisional markers of identity, rather than as definitive lines of demarcation. Nor does the drawing of boundaries rule out the interpenetration of state and society. Above all, the most important aspect of state–society relations that would be the inevitable casualty of abandoning boundaries, is that of mediations. The negotiation of the relationship between state and society takes place, not merely at the behest of two essentialized actors, the state and society, but through the crossing and contesting of notional boundaries by mediatory processes such as those signified by democratic institutions and social movements.

The boundaries between the public and the private are not fixed, immutable, or settled in perpetuity. They are historically and socially constructed and, as such, are constantly being redrawn, frequently, and certainly more visibly, at the instance of the state, but sometimes also as an outcome of struggles and changes within society. The impetus for state-sponsored efforts at redefining boundaries and reconstituting the private sphere is generally inspired by, and seeks to legitimize, state expansionism within society. Ironically, however, the extension of intervention generally renders the state more dependent on the cooperation of other forces in society to give effect to its projects. This is so because an increase in the state's activities tends to increase its internal complexity, causing its powers to get fragmented rather than concentrated, thereby making the task of coordination between different centres of policy-making more difficult.

Viewing social and political actions exclusively as expressions of the voluntaristic agency of either states or societies, is thus limiting and even reductive of states and societies to the persona of unified, individual actors. Conflict—social and political—must be allowed admittance into the two-dimensional cardboard model of state–society relations. If conflict is secondary for statists in their emphasis on the unity represented by the state, it is primary to any analysis premised on the permeability, mutability and porosity of state boundaries. Such analysis thus recognizes both the mediations that cause boundaries to shift, as well as the conflicts internal to the state which is far from impervious to conflicts within society.

State Autonomy and Capacity

State capacity is widely assumed to presuppose state autonomy. In other words, the capacity of a state to act authoritatively and effectively is assumed to be grounded in its autonomy from societal pressures. There are two quite distinct categories of formulations on this subject, from the statist and the neo-Marxist schools respectively.

The strategy of 'bringing the state back in', announced with much fanfare in 1985, claimed to offer a dramatically new way of looking at politics. This approach entails viewing states as, firstly, organizations through which official collectivities formulate and implement distinctive goals, rather than the particular goals of groups and classes; and, secondly, as configurations of organization and action that influence the meaning of politics for all groups and classes in society (Skocpol, 1985: 28). As such, it assigns to the state, as always and exclusively the independent variable, the special role of leading actor in defining and determining the contours of politics. Consequently, the state is accorded a privileged status in political explanation and may be seen to be the decisive variable in a variety of situations, from the encouragement of ethnic conflict to the management of economic transformation (Evans et al., 1985).

Empirical studies undertaken to test statist hypotheses, however, sometimes generated evidence contradicting their conclusions, and demonstrating the inadequacies of the approach.[4] On

---

[4] On such studies of Latin America, see Cammack (1989).

India, for instance, Atul Kohli's (1987) study of poverty reform in three states accorded explanatory primacy to the state, even as his data indicated important ways in which state capacity to effect redistributive reform was constrained by social and economic factors. There were other studies, however, which showed the limitations of the statist approach in the context of the Third World, where it is the structure of society that determines the capacity or incapacity of states to implement social policies and mobilize the people (Migdal: 1988).[5] Thus, if Kohli finds the Indian state to be the prototype of the statist approach, Migdal finds its putative strength considerably restrained by a fragmented, heterogeneous society. An intermediate position is taken by Lloyd and Susanne Rudolph (1987: 13) who locate the Indian state on 'a shifting continuum between constrained and autonomous', and view it as a 'third actor', along with capital and labour.

When statist theorists redrew the battle-lines within the discipline in the 1980s, they unambiguously consigned pluralists and Marxists alike to the intellectual waste-paper basket that they labelled 'society-centred' explanation. This was ironical, for it was the Marxists—chiefly in the writings of Louis Althusser (1971) on the ideological aspects of power, and the spirited debate between Nicos Poulantzas (1975) and Ralph Miliband (1975)—who had all along retained a focus on the state. Other neo-Marxists also argued that while state power is not reducible to class power, its exercise occurs within particular class contexts that constrain and shape it. Thus, state power serves to strengthen the process of capitalist accumulation not because the bourgeoisie controls state managers, but rather on account of a complex set of factors, external and internal, that impel state managers to act so as to strengthen capitalism and make it endure. These include the importance of an expanding economy for a strong military base; international economic competitiveness; the imperative against damaging business confidence, given the critical role of capitalists in securing higher rates of economic activity; the control of capitalists over resources, whether to bribe state managers or to finance elections; the process by which state managers are impelled to regulate the market, thereby saving capitalism from itself; and the pressures to

---

[5] In his more recent writings, Migdal (1994) has favoured a 'state-in-society' perspective, not dissimilar from the approach of this work.

intervene to ameliorate the social strains produced by capitalism (Block, 1980: 230–2). Another important neo-Marxist contribution to state theory argued that state power can only be assessed relationally, because the state per se has no power. Its power is the power of various class and other forces acting in and through the state. However, as an institutional ensemble, the state is never neutral, and the extent to which it has a particular structural selectivity (in favour of class or gender or regional interests, for example) is to be established rather than presumed (Jessop, 1990).

More eclectic frameworks for the analysis of state autonomy and capability have also emerged. Michael Mann (1988: 5) suggests a distinction between the infrastructural and despotic powers of the state as a way of assessing state capacity. The despotic power of the state élite consists in the range of actions that it has the power to undertake without routine, institutionalized negotiation with groups in civil society. Infrastructural power refers to the state's capacity to penetrate civil society, and to implement logistically political decisions throughout its territory. By these criteria, capitalist democracies are despotically weak and infrastructurally strong, as the state has the power to penetrate and coordinate activities in civil society, but the state élite does not possess power over civil society. Likewise, imperial states have low infrastructural coordination, but high despotic power.

It is clear that state strengths and weaknesses are a function of other attributes of the state, such as the past historical experience of state effectiveness, and the degree of autonomy a state enjoys from various social forces and groups. A strong formal institutional structure may make repression easier to accomplish, but it is not in itself a sufficient condition for effective intervention.[6] Recognizing this ambiguity in state functioning also implicitly accords to

---

[6] The developmental record of some countries in East Asia, notably South Korea, Indonesia, and Taiwan, has given rise to a widespread belief that 'soft authoritarianism' is the optimal political form for a developmental state (Sorensen, 1993: 13–14). Such states are led by determined developmental élites which, like the state institutions they command, are insulated from special interests in society. Civil society in these countries is often weak, penetrated, or even smashed, by the state (for a discussion of these issues, see Leftwich, 1993). This model can be questioned from two vantage points: the first, normative argument would be unwilling to compromise with democracy even if this means risking the prospects of development, while the second would

society and social forces a significant role in determining the nature of the state. Conversely, the state's weakness in the face of pluralist pressures need not be interpreted to imply a corresponding institutional weakness in its formal structure. Authoritarian states may have fragile institutions which are nonetheless capable of exercising brutal physical force.[7]

Indeed, the state cannot be said to be *ab initio* strong or weak across all policy arenas. State strengths and weaknesses vary depending upon the policy area in question, the nature of the interests at stake, and the balance of social and political forces at any given time. Consequently, the state's capacity to effect change, or to resist societal challenges, also varies. As its forms of domination vary, so do forms of resistance to it. The state may be weak in relation to powerful social groups, but strong and repressive in relation to powerless, even if large, ones. Further, like society, the state too is highly differentiated, and not monolithic in its nature. The complexity of its structure means that there is no necessary coherence between the functioning of state institutions at the local, intermediate and national levels. Thus, the infrastructural strength of the state is not constant, but may vary relative to proximity or distance in the territorial distribution of power, and the centrifugality of authority which makes governance and control at some levels easier than at others.

It is, therefore, important to understand state autonomy in relation not only to strong groups in society, but also weak ones. It is equally important to understand state capacity not only in terms of what it can do, but also in terms of what it can evade. For to the extent that the state's capacity is predicated on its autonomy, we may find that its autonomy from powerless and unorganized social groups lend the state the capacity to honour its

---

suggest counter-examples of states that are effective in repression, but not in developmental intervention. India could, though controversially, be considered an example of this kind.

[7] The need to distinguish between types of strength and weakness is underscored by James Manor (1991: 308), who argues that 'strength can flow from the use, or the potential use, of coercive power, from a state's willingness to govern even-handedly, from its capacity to entice or co-opt key social groups by drawing them into transactional relationships.... A particular state or regime may possess one or two of these things but lack others—so that it is strong in some ways and weak in others.'

formal commitments only in the breach. The case studies that form the core of this book will show why we need to identify *not only the interests of which the state is not autonomous, but also those of which it manifestly enjoys autonomy.* This will help to specify *not only what the state has the capability to accomplish, but also what it possesses the capability to not attempt.* The process by which the state sets an agenda, and defines its goals, as also its success or failure in achieving its stated objectives, can only be revealed by defining these concepts—of state autonomy and state capability—in both positive as well as negative terms.

In the advanced industrial societies of the West, as much as in post-colonial societies, states have assumed many more functions than were conventionally assigned to them. From the minimalist tasks of maintaining internal order, fighting wars, and collecting revenue, states have come a long way. They are now involved in economic transformations, implicated in processes of capital accumulation and, at least since the Second World War, also in processes of distribution and welfare. In the West, states accumulated these various roles over a long historical period of state-building, but in countries like India the state took them on simultaneously. This is significant not only because it indicates the enormity of the burden shouldered by Third World states, but also because it hints at the historical sociology of the state in the West, where an expansion in its role was a response to, for example, the increased importance of the bourgeois class in one phase, and working class movements in another. In Third World societies, on the other hand, these tasks were reflexively assumed by nationalist élites, who built upon the inherited structures of the supervisory state, superimposing on it elements borrowed, often—but not always uncritically—from the West. In addition, these state structures were invested with the capacity to direct the process of economic development. Of course, in these neo-liberal times, we have come to recognize that what is important about state intervention is not the amount or quantum of it, but its quality and character.[8]

---

[8] Cf. Bardhan (1990: 5) for the argument that even when states command similar instruments of intervention and display similar extents of intervention, their abilities to pursue the same goals with similar policy instruments result in a different quality of intervention in different contexts.

III. STATE, SOCIETY AND DEMOCRACY

More often than not, the relationship between the state and democracy is believed to be a derivative of the nature of the economic organization of a state. The ubiquitous concern, in Western scholarship, with the democratic potentialities of the capitalist state, is an obvious example[9] (cf. Duncan, 1989). It is thus no accident that the transition from command to market economies in Eastern Europe corresponds also to a transition to democracy. In such situations, however, the clue to the fragility of democracy lies in the coincidence between incipient democratic institutions, on the one hand, and economic crisis, on the other. The dilemma facing these societies is 'how to create incentives for political forces to process their interests within the democratic institutions when material conditions continue to deteriorate' (Przeworski et al., 1995: 70). In some writings on Third World societies, the 'failure' of democracy has even been explained by reference to the 'pseudo-capitalism' of their economies which, it is argued, places structural limits on the feasibility of democracy. On this view, even in developing countries with competitive polities, open political coercion by the holders of state power and the existence of over-politicized states render all the conventional conditions of democracy difficult to achieve (Sangmpam, 1992).

The theory of liberal democracy has suffered from the limitation of interpreting democracy primarily as a regime form of the state or a principle of representative government, rather than as a way of constituting collective life in society. As Bhikhu Parekh (1993: 165) has argued, if liberalism has provided the theory of the liberal-democratic state, democracy has supplied only its theory of government. Trapped within the confines of liberalism, the democratic impulse has been kept in check by its dominant partner,

[9] The earliest major work of comparative historical research on the subject was, of course, that of Barrington Moore, Jr. (1966). More recently, Rueschemeyer, Stephens, and Stephens (1992), also in a comparative historical mould, have argued that the emergence and stabilization of democracy is a function of power relations, encompassing (1) the balance of power among different classes and class coalitions; (2) the structure, strength and autonomy of the state apparatus; and (3) the impact of transnational power relations on both the former. Cf. also the articles by Bardhan (1993) and others in the 'Symposium on Democracy and Development' in the *Journal of Economic Perspectives,* vol. 7, no. 3, Summer 1993.

liberalism. On the other hand, the Marxist assumption that the problems of power and domination, as well as of participation, would automatically get resolved in socialism has been called into question in theory and belied in political practice, leading to the recognition that modes of domination need to be accounted for independently of, and in addition to, the mode of production.

In the orthodox versions of both these frameworks, then, the emphasis on the facticity of the state is closely paralleled by the attempt to capture democracy by enacting it institutionally. But democracy is self-evidently an appraisive concept. It must therefore encompass both (a) the formal aspect of democratic procedures and institutions; and (b) a critical–evaluative aspect that underpins claims for a more participatory and substantive form of democracy, which would be manifest in the consequences of the democratic process, rather than in its procedures alone. If the first inheres in representative institutions and decision-making procedures, the second may be seen to permeate all aspects of social and political life. Imbued with normativity, this second conception necessarily encompasses related political values and ideals, such as rights, equality, freedom, and justice.

There are broadly two types of arguments that theorize the necessity of a link between the state and democracy. The first is the argument that without an effective state, there can be no democracy. Hence, democracy is seen to require the state, because the state alone can create the conditions for the effective exercise of citizenship, provide and sustain the framework within which the rights and obligations of citizens can be respected and guaranteed, and arbitrate and resolve disputes about these. This argument is countered by the second which suggests that it is states, and not societies, that destroy democratic institutions (Weiner, 1983: 55). States being notoriously willing to curtail democracy, therefore, society, and preferably a strong civil society, is needed as a bulwark against these potentially authoritarian tendencies.

Both these arguments about the relationship between state, society, and democracy—(a) that an effective democracy is impossible without the state, and (b) that societies protect citizens and democratic institutions from states—underscore my earlier argument of the mutuality between state and society, as they constitute and transform each other. Clearly, democracy is hard to sustain without effective state institutions. Nevertheless, since civil society is needed as a protection against a potentially tyrannical state, in countries where civil society is still in an incipient stage of formation or weakly developed, and democratic institutions are likewise newly established or fragile, the tasks of democratization are that much more difficult to accomplish. Secondly, it is equally important to remember that even if societies do not generally destroy democratic institutions, powerful groups in society may hijack these institutions, divert or bend them to serve particularistic ends. This also occurs when groups articulating particularistic demands and interests use democratic institutions to gain sectional advantages, at the cost of other citizens. In this case, clearly, what is needed is added strength for the universalistic criteria of citizenship. It is, thus, possible to identify powerful constraints on democracy in both the realms of state and society.

Democracy and the State

At the institutional level, two types of factors may be seen to inhibit democratization. Some of these are *external* to the state, in that they define its relationship to different areas of social life; while others are *internal* to state institutions. Of the first category, we may identify three factors, foremost among these being the way in which the realm of the public is defined, placing certain areas beyond the reach of state action. Part of the struggle between the state and society has surely been the constant negotiation of this agenda, and the bringing into the public sphere of issues hitherto considered 'private'. Thus, the state's role in legislating on women's issues, such as reproductive rights or rights in personal law, may be questioned. Likewise, the attempt to give formal constitutional recognition to rights of cultural community is a way of protectively defining the 'private' against possible invasions by the state, thereby placing limits on the 'public' sphere. Secondly, it is well known that the state is dependent on the process of capital accumulation for an efficient and optimal extraction of revenue. This is paralleled by the dependence of state personnel on capital, which possesses the resources with which to finance the election campaigns of the political élite, as well as to bribe state managers. Guarding the long-term interests of capital cannot but, under the circumstances, be a matter of priority for state personnel. Thirdly, the decline of political parties in both developed and developing countries has also been an institutional factor limiting democracy.

The second category of constraints is *internal* to the state, and three factors of this type may be identified. The first of these is the more than self-evident one of the increasing concentration of power in the executive branch of government. This has been partly a consequence of the transference of legislative powers, and partly the result of the establishment and expansion of powerful and unaccountable policy-making apparatuses like the Prime Minister's Office. The centralization of decision-making in these apparatuses has taken place at the expense of more legislatively accountable administrative departments and ministries. Secondly, there has occurred an increasing fusion of the executive, legislative, and judicial branches of government that exemplify a concentration of powers, even as increasing state interventionism takes the form of a multiplication of policy networks and a fragmentation of implementing agencies. Finally, an expansion of the law and order machinery of the state has marched hand in hand with a contraction of its welfare functions. The rolling back of the state has, in many countries, signified a dwindling of welfare services even as outlays on policing and surveillance mechanisms have registered an increase.[10]

The six factors identified above—three internal to the state, and three external to it—combine with the limits on effective participation in civil society to suggest a variety of obstacles to the realization of democracy. They are all present to a greater or lesser degree in the Indian experience, though the individual case studies here will illuminate some more than others. These constraints notwithstanding, it is important to underscore the point that an effective democracy is virtually unrealizable outside suitable

[10] In India, social sector expenditure (including health, education and agriculture) has declined considerably as a percentage of GDP, during the period 1990–1 and 1994–5, from 6.1 to 4.6 per cent. The population below the poverty line, on the other hand, has been steadily increasing. This study will argue the point that welfare whether in the context of the tribals of Kalahandi or those of the Narmada Valley, or in that of indigent divorcees, is not the primary preoccupation of state agencies. Outlays for development projects, for example, tend to make relatively small provision for the rehabilitation of those displaced, and implementation priorities tend to conform to this pattern.

institutional arrangements. However, institutions cannot exclusively and by themselves ensure democratic performance in the actual functioning of a polity, and are substantially limited by the social and cultural context within which they subsist. Thus, it is not unusual for multicultural societies to witness conflict over institutions themselves, because institutions have distributional consequences and groups claiming to represent ethnic, religious, linguistic or caste groupings often compete with one another for control over these (Przeworski, 1995: 49).

Democracy and Society

On the societal front, the limits on effective democracy stem from a combination of (i) inequalities in social relations, and (ii) the logic of democracy itself. Inequitous social relations may derive not only from economic inequalities, but also inequalities based in, for instance, gender or caste. The concentration of social power is not reducible to, and can be as undesirable as the concentration of economic power, and indeed we know that the institutions of society are frequently undemocratic, as they actively neglect or subordinate weaker social groups. Social relations of domination and subordination tend to distort democracy, such that the voice of the powerful gets expressed (through interest groups, for example) while the powerless go largely unrepresented, except in the formal and ineffectual sense of periodically participating in elections.[11]

The impact of an unequal distribution of social and economic resources is complemented by the 'logic of democracy' itself which, even as it creates channels of political participation, limits their

[11] Political scientists have, since at least the 1960s, demonstrated the correlation between economic performance and the longevity of democracy. That democracies are highly sensitive to income inequalities is now a widely accepted idea. Economic resources are prone to translate into political resources (Hadenius, 1994: 76), but while greater individual resources (of wealth or education) do not translate into higher participation, those who are disadvantaged under-participate, and do not succeed 'in compensating for their weak economic position by raising their political voices' (Parry and Moyser, 1994: 54). In recent years, studies have also related social and economic inequalities to *attitudes* about democratic politics, with surveys showing that more educated people in Spain, Brazil, Hungary, and Poland believe that democracy is better than dictatorship (Przeworski et al., 1995: 37).

targets and controls their impact (Alford and Friedland, 1990: 431).[12] As participation expands, democratic institutions themselves contribute to the undermining of democracy. In the Indian context, for instance, Kaviraj has suggested an incompatibility between the institutional logic of democratic forces and the logic of popular mobilization, such that the realization of one part of the democratic ideal undermines the other part. Extensive democratization makes democracy less sensitive to the secular democratic principles on which the nationalist élite sought to ground the state. Thus, 'high politics...are coming under pressure from the alphabet of the lower discourse' (1991: 73). The political mobilizations of recent years by the backward castes are an obvious example.

In this work, the Kalahandi and Narmada cases will illustrate the link between socio–economic inequalities and the democratic process, while the Shah Bano case will highlight the obstacles to democratization in a society marked by cultural cleavages and identity-based politics. It will thereby become possible to identify and bring together, in an interactive framework, elements in state and society as they (a) impact each other to create challenges for the democratic project, or (b) are mediated by democratic institutions and processes.

In the ultimate analysis, and in real terms, what these processes achieve is the effective disfranchisement of large sections of the citizenry. All our cases have, at their core, categories of citizens who, despite being constitutionally equal participants in the democratic polity, are nevertheless severely handicapped in the enjoyment and exercise of the rights of equal citizenship.

Citizenship may be undermined in at least two ways, the first of which is the absence of public enforcement of a universalistic legal order (and, complementary to it, the injunction that state officials are equally subject to that legal order). This mode of undermining citizenship can take several forms: the state may fail to ensure the enforceability of the constitutionally guaranteed rights of citizenship; state personnel such as the police force may fail to protect citizens from privately perpetrated violence; or they

---

[12] This has not merely political, but also economic, implications. As Atul Kohli (1993: 684) has argued, democratization creates expectations that cannot be easily satisfied without sustained economic growth and some redistribution.

may themselves engage in the violation of citizens' rights. Different sections of the citizenry may be differentially protected by the state, the rule of law may apply to some but not to all, autonomous spheres of power may emerge that inflict injustices on weaker groups in society, and so on. Examples of all these abound in India, but the case studies will provide only a very few illustrations of these.

It is the second way in which equal citizenship is undermined that is exemplified by this study. This relates to the absence of the social conditions that make possible the effective exercise of citizenship. Negatively defined, the presence of sharp economic disparities and inherited social inequalities is a countervailing factor. But in positive terms, such social conditions may include welfare provisions like education and public health. These may be considered steps towards creating an informed citizenry, which has access to information, and is capable not only of exercising its political rights (such as voting or other forms of participation) in an enlightened manner, but also calling its democratically elected government to account.

Placing citizenship at the heart of the democratic project, and even making it the test of democracy is, of course, a normative exercise. The normativity of democracy, and its character as a contested concept, is more easily established than the normativity of the state for which a case was made at the outset of this chapter. If state discourses, as well as discourses of resistance to the state, are worthy of study, so too are discourses of democracy emanating from the state, as also from other sources. The discourse of democracy encompasses a variety of allied concepts, including rights, justice, freedom, and equality. These are, more often than not, invoked by groups mounting protest against or making claims upon the state, but they are also sometimes invoked by groups to enlist the assistance of the state in controlling their own members. Thus, the tribal people of the Narmada Valley have been protesting the construction of the Sardar Sarovar Dam by invoking their right to their centuries-old habitat and style of life, as also the claims of justice in the matter of their rehabilitation. On the other hand, in the aftermath of the Shah Bano case, Muslim community leadership is seen to claim protection for their rights of cultural community in order to deny Muslim women equal access to certain provisions of the Criminal Procedure Code, otherwise equally applicable to all citizens. State discourses about democracy are frequently manipulative, ranging from the expedientally majoritarian (Shah Bano) to the cynically utilitarian (Narmada). The discursive terrain that we traverse in the course of the case studies, will attempt to show how the recursive relationship between state and society is not only mediated by democratic processes, but frequently also by discourses about both democracy and the proper role of the state.

The preceding pages have attempted to set out the theoretical terms of reference adopted by this study, which is quite substantially empirical in character. A case has been advanced for normatively interpreting not only democracy but also the state. This, it is believed, makes it possible to understand these concepts, in the Indian context at least, not merely in terms of their facticity, but also as representations of, on the one hand, the moral claims to legitimacy conveyed by state institutions and, on the other, the moral claims made by citizens to democratic values such as rights, justice, or equality. Just as a view of formal democratic institutions, such as legislative assemblies or electoral rule-books, is inadequate and even impoverished, a formalistic view of state institutions is also arguably insufficient. States, as I have argued, are moral orders that make moral claims not merely when they command the allegiance of their citizens, but also when they seek legitimacy on the basis of their role as providers of welfare and directors of development for the societies they control. Likewise, it is clearly impossible to speak of a substantive notion of democracy, to give content to the ideal, without defining it in terms that are inescapably normative and prescriptive. Too long has the division of labour between political theorists and political scientists prevailed, resulting in arid institutional studies that can, at best, comment upon gaps between the promise and performance of states and democratic institutions in particular country-contexts, without going into the question of how and on what basis those promises came to be defined in the first place, or how the performance of institutions is impacted by factors external to both but located in society.

In so bringing together state, society, and democracy under one explanatory umbrella, I have argued thus far that states and societies are separated by boundaries that are not easily specifiable or demarcated clearly and for all time to come. States and societies are mutually constituted and have a relationship of recursiveness in their impact upon each other. The boundaries between state and society are continually being negotiated, and this is a process that knows no historical full-stops. The impact of the state, therefore, varies across different policy and social arenas, as does that of society. If state capacity is, as is widely accepted, premised upon the autonomy of the state from society, then that autonomy must be defined both in positive as well as negative terms, to encompass not only which social forces compel the state to act in particular ways, but also those of which the state is manifestly autonomous. Its capacity, too, therefore is to be defined positively as well as negatively, to cover not merely what the state has the ability to accomplish, but also what it does not have the ability to do or even attempt.

It has further been argued, that the state–society relationship is mediated, among other things, by democratic institutions and processes. Democracy is not merely a political, but also a social project, and the case for its normativity is therefore further consolidated. On the one hand, an effective democracy is impossible to sustain without a state, but on the other, a vibrant civil society is necessary to curtail a potentially tyrannical state. If states pose dangers to democracy, so do societies, especially when powerful social groups seek to divert democratic institutions to serve particularistic ends.

Democracy, whether interpreted as institutions or as movements of resistance, is not however our independent variable, authoritatively determining the relationship between state and society. The claim being advanced here is much more modest. It is that, even as democratic institutions and processes mediate the state–society relationship and contribute to the negotiations of boundaries as well as mutual impacts, they are themselves constrained in significant ways by factors emanating from both the realm of the state as well as that of society. Thus, we identified six factors which, at the state institutional level, serve as powerful constraints inhibiting the fulfilment of the democratic project, of which three are external to the state (summarily, the way in which the public realm is defined; the dependence of state personnel on capital; and the decline of political parties) and three internal to it (namely, the increasing concentration of power in the executive branch of government; the increasing fusion of the three branches of government; the expansion in the law and order machinery of the state accompanied by a contraction in its welfare functions). Likewise, we identified two factors, social inequalities and the logic of democracy, to show how the societal realm also places difficulties in the way of the accomplishment of democracy.

The project of democracy, procedural or substantive, political or social, cannot be said to have been accomplished till such time as the effective exercise of the rights of citizenship is achieved and guaranteed to all. This in turn is a combined function of the enforceability of constitutionally guaranteed equal rights and of the social conditions that make their effective exercise possible. The discourses of democracy, emanating in the state and in society, are powerful symbolic indicators of this, and we shall therefore make a modest attempt to reflect upon these towards the end of each case study.

2

The Welfare State

Welfare tasks were pre-eminent on the agenda of the Indian state at independence, and the removal of want was indisputably central to these. The persistence, after the passage of half a century, of widespread endemic hunger and malnutrition are in themselves symbolic of the extent to which the Indian state failed to achieve its welfarist objectives. But equally, if not more, stark is the dismal record, despite a variety of policy measures, of acute, often seasonal, hunger sometimes even resulting in starvation deaths. Acute hunger is a moral commentary on a state which, at independence, charged itself with the task of removing want, and of providing for its citizens through the strategy, first, of planned development, and later of poverty alleviation.[1]

The focus of this chapter is the problem of hunger as experienced in the Kalahandi district of Orissa since 1985. I shall examine hunger in Kalahandi, and establish its existence chiefly through official policy documents, legislative committee reports, and judicial pronouncements, seeking to assess the adequacy of relief policies in this framework. I shall also, secondly, investigate the question of the effectiveness of democratic institutions in requisitioning state response. At one level, the Kalahandi story is a perfect

[1] I have argued elsewhere (Jayal, 1994: 20–1) that the Indian state could be more appropriately characterized as an interventionist state (with a developmental thrust) than a welfare state. The developmental initiatives of this interventionist state were largely directed to the so-called modern, dynamic, industrial sector. Its welfarist initiatives, on the other hand, were directed substantially towards the redressal of inequalities generated not by the market, but stemming from inequalities in the ownership and use of land. Thus, poverty alleviation programmes were compensatory in nature. They were also negative in character (as they aimed at ridding rural society of poverty), instead of seeking to enhance, much less maximize, welfare.

copybook instantiation of the public action model.[2] It shows how the press and the opposition in the legislature turned the spotlight on starvation deaths in Kalahandi, provoking a response from the central government. This is, however, an unwarrantedly optimistic reading of the situation, for this model employs a rather restrictive notion of democracy on the basis of which to raise the hurrahs. A second look at Kalahandi reveals the stunning passivity of the people themselves, who have now endured acute hunger and even near-starvation conditions, on and off for over a decade. Even the response of the state to hunger in Kalahandi has been marked by a curious duality: on the one hand, the official denial of starvation deaths and acute food crisis and, on the other, the repetitive and escalating demands for relief expenditure. This duality was, it will be argued, rendered possible by the politics of nomenclature, which entailed converting the discourse of hunger into the discourse of drought, impliedly shifting the blame from the state to nature, and thereby reducing the responsibility of the state for its mitigation.

The problem of hunger speaks directly to the modern state as an imperative that cannot be ignored, least of all by states that define themselves in terms of their welfarist orientation. Most often, the creation and alleviation of hunger are a direct result of state policies, in one or more of the following areas: agricultural production; food distribution and food security; inequitous structures of land ownership; and famine relief. While state intervention may be optional in the matter of combating endemic hunger, no state can be a silent witness to the phenomenon of starvation deaths in a famine situation. In such circumstances, state intervention clearly becomes a moral imperative, invoking important political values such as the right to life and survival, as well as the demands of equity and justice.

David Arnold has argued that:

the fortunes of the state, whether in Europe or in Africa or Asia have long been closely bound up with the containment or prevention of famine and, more generally, with provisioning the populace. Protecting its subjects from starvation and extreme want has for centuries been one of the primary

---

[2] Drèze and Sen (1989) have, in a comparative study of hunger in India and China, argued that India's greater success in combating famine is attributable to its democratic institutions, chiefly a free press and adversarial politics. Thus, 'public action' is instrumental in provoking a policy response.

functions of government and one of the principal public expectations of the state. So central have been ideas of the ruler as the ultimate earthly provider that notions of kingly or state legitimacy have often hinged upon this responsibility...famine was invariably a testing time for states as well as for people [1988: 96].

Hunger could trigger revolt and, as it rendered subjects incapable of being taxed, could deprive a greedy ruler of both revenue and legitimacy. On the other hand, a state that provided in times of need was rewarded by enhanced legitimacy, and the longevity of the Confucian state in China has been attributed to its paternalist concern for the material well-being of the famine-affected peasantry (Hsiao, 1979).

The present case raises several questions, among them why there has been a manifest absence of *popular* protest against the recurrent scarcity conditions in Kalahandi? How did the press and legislature succeed in putting the national spotlight on this issue? Was there a difference in the response of the national state, the regional state, and the local state? Was there any manifest connection between the pressures placed through the institutions of formal democracy, namely the legislature and the media, and a more concerned or efficient response by the state? An examination of the formal institutional mechanisms of democracy—as they are used to recall to the state its professed and avowed commitment to the material welfare, or at least the subsistence, of its citizens—is not allowed to obscure the voicelessness of those citizens themselves.

I. THE STATE AND HUNGER

Imperatives of State Intervention in Famine in Colonial India

In pre-colonial India, there are countless examples of monarchs providing free kitchens and gratuitous relief in times of famine, as also tax remissions and loans (Alamgir, 1980: 54–6).[3] The conception of welfare underlying these policies and state action is clearly

---

[3] The writings of the Mauryan strategist Kautilya (1987: 130) contain passages instructing the emperor on methods of counteracting the effects of famine in his kingdom. These include the distribution of food and seeds on concessional terms; sharing of the royal food stocks; commandeering private stocks for public distribution; shifting populations to other regions, and even encouraging temporary migration to friendly neighbouring kingdoms.

one of welfare as monarchical munificence, but it is interesting that the chief ways of combating famine, namely food provisioning and migration, have remained virtually unchanged through the centuries. In colonial India, famine relief was an important aspect of state policy, though ironically distinguished by an obsessive horror of state intervention. The intellectual and ideological basis of this approach is easily explained by reference to two important contemporary debates in Britain, on (a) policies of laissez-faire, and (b) the Poor Law. Two institutional factors provide additional clues. Firstly, the necessity for imperial control over the landowning classes, as well as considerations of revenue, impelled the colonial state to pay serious attention to the implications of famine in terms of immiserization. Secondly, the history of famine relief policy is closely interwoven with a variety of political and bureaucratic pressures, including conflicts within the civil service.

The most popular explanation for the colonial response to famine locates it in the intellectual influence of the classical economists, especially Adam Smith, whose doctrine of laissez-faire prescribed non-interference in the grain trade, and forbade the state from attempting to fix prices.[4] The other influential argument that militated against the provision of free relief by the state emphasized its undesirability on the grounds that it encouraged people to become lazy, indolent, and dependent on the state, besides interfering with wage levels and employment.[5] Both these arguments—

[4] In his *The Wealth of Nations*, Smith ([1776] 1937: 493) observed that the famine in Bengal had actually occurred because the East India Company had attempted to regulate the pricing and movement of foodgrains. For Smith, a rise in food prices was an essential incentive for traders, whose income suffered in years of good harvests, and who could therefore earn the rewards of their enterprise only in lean years. If government intervened, the import of food supplies from surplus to deficient areas was discouraged, acting as a disincentive for grain merchants.

[5] This argument was also earlier encountered in the debate in England on the New Poor Law of 1834, which introduced the concept of 'less eligibility', according to which the able-bodied poor would be assisted only within a workhouse, and to a level lower than that of the lowest-paid independent labourer. The rationale of this provision was to discourage low-paid labourers becoming a burden on the relief system, by not making available to the lazy among them a less strenuous alternative. The less eligibility principle was finally abandoned when the Fabian socialist Beatrice Webb joined the Royal

the defence of laissez-faire policies and the argument that relief discourages people from hard work and offers an incentive to idleness—are echoed in the colonial response to famine in India.

From the early to the mid-nineteenth century, non-interference with the grain trade was an article of faith with the government which argued the desirability of high prices as a disincentive to excessive consumption.[6] In Madras (1811), in the North-Western Provinces (1861), and in Orissa (1866) alike, official statements applauded the policy of restraint and inaction followed by local officials, even in the face of popular outrage, which was firmly suppressed so that merchants could be ensured the freedom to trade with confidence. Both the import of grain by the government and attempts to fix its price were thus deprecated, though some state responsibility for the economy was not altogether denied. The state's self-perception of its role has, in the context of the food scarcity in Madras in 1918, been described as follows:

Neither master nor servant, the state was to be like a powerful and generally sympathetic neighbour: it came to help in time of crisis; it firmly but quietly reproved a selfish action which adversely affected the interests of others.... Free food and cash doles were rarely given: the needy were expected to labour to earn the money to buy essential commodities from traders. The works closed as soon as the minimal wages paid ceased to attract, and the government was at pains not to supplant the private trader. It reset an adjustable screw, oiled the moving parts, and withdrew to let the economic machinery run by itself [Arnold, 1979: 136–7].

It is significant that, despite recurrent famine in virtually every part of the subcontinent, exports of foodgrains continued apace. Indeed, the government's anxiety to protect the export trade could well have been the reason for its discouragement of food imports into scarcity-affected regions. The net outcome, in any case,

---

Commission on the Poor Law in 1905. Her Minority Report is considered the earliest statement of the principles of the welfare state (Jayal, 1987: xviii).

[6] In 1876, the Madras Government had been severely reprimanded by the Government of India for having arranged with a private dealer to stock up on a small amount of 30,000 tonnes of foodgrains as a buffer against distress. (Alamgir, 1980: 70) Bhatia (1967: 108) has however argued that the government's reluctance to depart from the principle of laissez-faire was due less to ideological dogma than to its fear of the costs entailed in providing relief for a vast population.

whether or not intended, was the protection of mercantile interests, as also the interests of the land-owning classes.

The argument about gratuitous relief being a disincentive to hard work, and a provocation to idleness, is also reflected in colonial famine policy, though in documents of a later phase. 'Indiscriminate charity' in a government, it was officially stated, was even more reprehensible than indiscriminate private charity, the evils of which were well known (Bhatia, 1967: 90). The debilitating effects of relief were described thus:

We regard this tendency with much concern, for, in truth, the fault is not a venial, but a very grave fault, being akin to that most dangerous popular vice—the disposition to force the Government to grant public charity [Report of the Famine Commission, 1901: 45].

Colonial policies of famine relief were, however, a complex admixture of ideas and institutions. Apart from the two policy ideas discussed above, two institutional aspects can also be identified, namely the revenue policy of the government and the interplay of policy and personality within the bureaucracy. Aware that famine conditions rendered poor peasants extremely vulnerable to indebtedness, the First Famine Commission recommended abstention in revenue collection, as well as low-interest lending for cultivation and maintenance, while those who could pay without borrowing should do so (ibid.: 85). The use of coercion for the extraction of revenue nevertheless continued, in complete disregard of the Commission's suggestions. Indeed, provincial governments were wont to be especially boastful of their revenue collection achievements in times of famine, justifying resort to coercion as unavoidable. Between 1881 and 1891, the remissions granted in land revenue were less than 2 per cent of the total (Bhatia, 1967: 191).[7] Nationalist critiques of policy, by contrast, pointed to the extortionate—in extent as well as form—revenue demands as causes of poverty and famine (Dutt, 1985: 19; Naoroji, n.d.: 208–16). The absence of any earnest efforts at tax remission,

---

[7] Some revenue officials, such as Sir Edward Buck and Sir Denzil Ibbetson actually took the position that agrarian poverty and indebtedness were encouraged by low-pitched revenue demands rather than high-pitched ones. Low revenue demands, they believed, encouraged improvidence and careless farming, thereby rendering farmers more vulnerable to indebtedness, and reducing their capacity to resist famine (Stokes, 1989: 138).

let alone structural reform of the agrarian situation, meant that inequalities in the rural social structure were accentuated: while the landowning classes, traders and moneylenders flourished, small and poor peasants became increasingly subject to famine (Bhatia, 1967: 307) .

By the 1870s, however, a subtle but discernible shift had occurred in famine policy, in the direction of greater state intervention. It is certain that the frequent recurrence of famine and the heavy toll of human life and loss of revenue that resulted from a manifest confusion of policy, contributed to the shift. So, apparently, did the political and parliamentary criticism of the Conservative government of Benjamin Disraeli, as well as the grumblings of the so-called 'crotchets' (old India hands) who were pressing the Secretary of State for India, Lord Salisbury, for the development of railways and irrigation systems as a means of preventing famine. It is also possible that the utilitarian legacy— of authoritative and efficient government, rather than of liberty— contributed to the change, as did nationalist opinion.

The first Famine Commission was established in 1878, and two contentious issues engaged its attention: (a) the departure from policies of laissez-faire; and (b) the organization of relief works. A minority within the commission suggested experimental storage of grain by the government to supply food to inaccessible districts in times of scarcity. It also proposed that the weak and the infirm be given gratuitous relief, or very light work, in their villages, making for a more economical approach, which would preserve the fabric of village life and also save lives by not forcing weak people to traverse long distances to relief works. The minority view was strongly attacked and defeated by the majority, and the policy orthodoxy went largely unchallenged.[8] Nevertheless, the 1880 report of the Famine Commission did herald the beginning of a new era, of the assumption of some responsibility by the state for its famine-affected subjects, even if it was concerned more with the amelioration of famine, rather than its prevention (Zurbrigg, 1996: 5). It at least admitted, for the first time, the need for a

---

[8] The establishment of the Famine Commission was intended to be a political exercise culminating in a favourable report, rather than a measured response to the problem of famine. Brennan (1984) has documented, in some detail, the bureaucratic manoeuvring that influenced both the composition of the Commission, as also its eventual recommendations.

coherent policy on famine, as opposed to the confused and ad hoc moves that had hitherto characterized the administrative response.

Meanwhile, nationalist opinion had begun to express itself, in the writings of Dadabhai Naoroji and R. C. Dutt, as also in two resolutions on 'Poverty, Famine and Remedies' of the Indian National Congress in its Calcutta session of December 1896 (Bhatia, 1967: 272). The resolutions blamed famine on poverty, and poverty in turn on the drain of wealth from India for the upkeep of an extravagant state. These opinions found a sympathetic echo in the writings of the British socialist H. M. Hyndman, who enthusiastically joined the Anti-Famine agitation in England with his old friend Dadabhai Naoroji. Another such association, formed in London, was the Indian Famine Union, which counted among its members prominent nationalist sympathisers like Sir William Wedderburn, and the famous political philosopher of the 'new liberalism', Lord Hobhouse.

In 1896 and 1899, two widespread famines demonstrated the manifest inadequacies of the system of relief organization devised in the 1880s, and two subsequent Famine Commissions (1898 and 1901) further refined these arrangements in a more humane and practical mould.[9] But, while some improvements were effected in the administration and system of relief, and investments were made in famine prevention measures such as the extension of irrigation facilities, the government persisted in its stubborn refusal to interfere with food supplies or prices. The most disastrous outcome of this policy of non-interference was the Bengal famine of 1943, when the government was forced to intervene, but its intervention was so belated as to be ineffectual.

It was thus an indifferent record of managing famine, crowned by a completely inept handling of the terrible 1943 famine, that was brought to a close in 1947. With the imperial power demitting, and a nationalist government assuming control over the affairs of state, it was reasonably expected that the post-colonial order would be sufficiently sensitive to the problem of want. The Karachi resolution of the Congress (1931) had already signalled this, in its redefinition of 'swaraj' as including not just political freedom, but

---

[9] The 1901 report, Zurbrigg argues, suggests that the authors had 'finally placed themselves in the shoes of the starvation-vulnerable, thinking through the specific question "How do they eat?"' (1996: 17).

also the 'economic freedom of the starving millions' (AICC, 1969: 3–4).

The Welfarist Imperative: Need or Right?

The tenor of the Constitution adopted by independent India, as well as a series of official documents on planning, exemplify the welfarist orientation imparted to the Indian state by the patron saints of its movement for national self-determination. It is, however, significant that the rights enshrined in the chapter on Fundamental Rights in the Constitution are essentially those concerning liberty. Welfare rights are consigned to the non-justiciable Directive Principles of State Policy, a charter of the state's good intentions on a number of matters, including socialism. There is a clear disjuncture between rights to liberty and welfare rights in the Constitution, and the official approach to want and hunger, I shall argue, is strongly overlaid with altruism. Thus, the philosophy of welfare adopted by the Indian state adhered to a needs-based conception of justice in theory, but was in practice based on ideas of charity, benevolence, and paternalism. The idea of a right to welfare or justice was clearly precluded, possibly on account of the Fabian intellectual influence on early policy-makers (Bose, 1989: 65), and the problem of hunger has thus rarely been articulated in the vocabulary of rights.

Politico–ethical issues are surely central to the question of hunger, whether it is endemic or brought on by the occurrence of famine. The recent history of world hunger, as imprinted in the western consciousness by satellite television images of the famine situation in Ethiopia and Somalia, for instance, has unequivocally rebutted the conventional view of famine and hunger as inextricably linked to natural disasters. Does hunger interfere with the human right to subsistence, and is it therefore a candidate for compensatory justice provisions? Does such evidence of human need generate rights that place corresponding obligations on states? What is the relationship between hunger, poverty, and development? Is there a necessary incompatibility or even a disjuncture between the political and ethical issues involved, i.e. is relief in the form of charity and beneficent action precluded by political struggle or vice versa?

The moral necessity of state intervention is linked to the idea of basic needs as a starting-point (Plant et al.,1980: ch. 2). From the recognition of basic needs as requiring redressal by public authority, it is but a short step to the articulation of these needs in the form of rights. However, the assertion of a moral or natural or even human right is not as practically efficacious as the assertion of a legally enforceable right.

Unless obligations to feed the hungry are a matter of allocated justice rather than indeterminate beneficence, a so-called right to food, and the other 'rights' of the poor, will only be manifesto rights   [O'Neill, 1986: 101].

The assertion of a moral right to subsistence in order to secure a statutory right to food implies that the content of basic rights goes beyond the rights to liberty conventionally awarded to individuals by liberal theory to include welfare rights as well. The larger value that these conceptions of needs as well as rights appeal to is, of course, the architectonic value of justice.[10] In the context of hunger, social and political conceptions of justice may appear to be incomplete in the absence of material justice. Indeed, neither is adequate by itself: a situation where material needs are met, but social and political forms are coercive or deceptive is not to be preferred over one where non-coercive and non-deceptive social and political structures obtain, but material needs remain unmet. Theirs is a necessary complementarity (ibid.: 154).

The reason why ethical issues are central to the political discourse on hunger is thus implicit both in a needs-based conception of justice, as well as in theories of rights and obligations.[11] Indeed, I argue here that these provide two alternative groundings for a philosophy of welfare. Unpacking the assumptions underlying particular conceptions of welfare in terms of such justifying principles is essential to any understanding of state intervention in situations of famine. This is so because within a needs-based

[10] While concerns of distributive justice have been central to all major works of political theory over the past few decades (cf. Rawls, 1972; and Nozick, 1974 for a contrary view), the problem of hunger does not figure in these discussions, betraying the Western origins and orientations of these theories.

[11] From altogether different premises, Amartya Sen has argued the centrality of food provisioning as an issue in general social ethics. Food and freedom are, in his view, inextricably linked: the freedom to lead a decent life depends upon freedom from hunger, while freedom may also causally influence the success of the pursuit of food for all (1995: 90).

approach, state action as institutionalized charity adequately meets the requirements of justice, and there is no room for rights-based individual or collective action. It is sufficient for the state to be the grand philanthropist, bestowing largesse.

A rights-based approach, on the other hand, demands that states recognize the moral imperative, if not legal obligation, of bearing responsibility for their citizens, or else risk their legitimacy and authority by failing to do so. This latter approach may, of course, countenance state inaction, in the absence of articulated challenges by individuals or social groups. While both needs and rights appeal to the foundational value of justice, there is an important difference between them. Rights carry with them the mandate of enforceability. Needs may, but do not necessarily, create rights; nevertheless, they appeal to the idea of justice in seeking recognition, if not enforceability. The distinctive feature of such rights and needs is that they belong decisively to the public sphere, and appeal unambiguously to public authority for redressal.

The idea of need can in fact provide the basis not just for a conception of justice, but also for the notion of charity, bringing about a congruence between these two apparently dissimilar ideas. While both charity and the needs-based conception of justice appeal centrally to the idea of need, and are non-obligatory and unenforceable in nature, there are two important differences between them. The first pertains to their moral foundations. Within the framework of justice, needs—and especially basic needs—can morally require fulfilment (Singer, 1972). Within the framework of charity, it is virtuous to help the needy, but there is no moral requirement to do so. Secondly, while needs-based principles of justice appeal to public authority, the idea of charity generally belongs to the private sphere, appeals to philanthropy, but places no obligation on individuals, institutions, or governments.[12]

---

[12] Liberal philosophers have lately tried to rescue the idea of charity from its roots in the Christian tradition in order to restore it to a central place in liberal theory, on the premise that charity and justice are incompatible, and that the availability and exercise of welfare rights causes the virtue of charity to disappear (Den Uyl, 1993). John Locke ([1764] 1963: 206) also endorsed the idea of charity in terms closer to obligation than to right. More recently, the idea of charity has underpinned notions of welfare in public policy, as in the writings of Richard Titmuss (1987) on the 'gift relationship', which is the mark

Even in a country like India, with a long and tragic history of experiencing famine, the right to subsistence remains unrecognized as a right that can generate obligations for the state, or endorse popular action against an unresponsive administration as legitimate. While the existence of democratic institutions creates new possibilities for placing on the agenda a right to subsistence that is not already there, it has remained the prerogative of the state to redress want through measures that it may consider practicable, affordable, or expedient.

Policy on Food Security

The policy on food security of the fledgling Indian state had two essential components: the policy of increased agricultural production and the policy on food distribution systems. The first was clearly a vital component of the modernization agenda of the Indian state, though it also expressed an anti-imperialist impulse in its rhetoric of self-sufficiency and self-reliance. The second was more unambiguously a part of its welfarist orientation. Clearly, while increased agricultural production and an efficient public distribution system are important components of an overall strategy against food insecurity, they do not, indeed cannot, exhaust the potential of the state in combating hunger, whether persistent and endemic, or seasonal.

It is a commonplace today that the planning process in India has concentrated on bringing Green Revolution technology to irrigated areas, and in doing so, has neglected the problems of rainfed agriculture even this accounts for 70 per cent of the land under cultivation in the country, and contributes only 43 per cent of the value added in the agricultural sector (Bhatia, 1988: 370). These areas are also more vulnerable to ecological degradation, through the over-exploitation of available natural resources such as forests, cultivable land, and groundwater. Thus, when

---

of the social as much as exchange relationships are of the economic sphere or the market. Similarly, the sociology of relief in refugee camps also conceptualizes the relationship between the refugees and their benefactors as that between clients and patrons, of the giving and receiving of gifts (Harrell-Bond et al., 1992). Clearly, what distinguishes a right to welfare from charity and altruism is the differential nature of the obligation as well as that of initiative for political action.

deviations occur in the normal rainfall pattern of these regions, drought results, compounding the problems of poverty, ecology, and low productivity (Mathur and Jayal, 1993: 26).

The public distribution system has also suffered from an unmistakably urban bias, with 85 per cent of PDS supplies going to urban areas, which support approximately 30 per cent of the population. 51.60 per cent of the country's poor in the five states of Bihar, Madhya Pradesh, Uttar Pradesh, Orissa, and Rajasthan together get only 18.90 per cent of PDS supplies (Public Interest Research Group, 1993: 64–5).

The policies on drought and famine relief are also critical components of state policy on food security. Unfortunately, however, public policy on drought has been handicapped by a short-term, relief-oriented perspective, enabling it to act only when drought and/or famine conditions manifest themselves. It has rarely engaged with the long-term concern for drought-proofing and hunger mitigation, despite injunctions to the contrary by a series of committee reports from the Planning Commission. State policy on hunger can only be assessed in a composite context of policy on agricultural production, policy on public distribution, and policy on drought and famine relief. Even these, however, do not sufficiently account for the absences and silences of policy, and especially policy neglect of backwardness and poverty. The abysmal failure of land reforms is an important contributory factor, but problems of backwardness and underdevelopment have social, cultural, and economic roots and ramifications. They also have distinctly identifiable political implications. Thus it is that the occurrence of drought is most frequent in the backward regions of the country,[13] and also, that popular mobilization against drought is more likely to occur in better developed regions like Maharashtra, and less likely in backward regions such as Orissa (*Economic and Political Weekly*, 2.11.1985: 1855–60).

While it is true that India is no longer as vulnerable to famine as it has historically been, and perhaps even that India's record in preventing famine has been better than that of China (Drèze and Sen, 1989: 211), there is less cause for sanguineness than is generally supposed. Firstly, famine has not been wiped out; it continues to

---

[13] For details on the correlation between drought, backwardness, and instability in agricultural production, see Hanumantha Rao, et al. (1988).

recur periodically. In addition to frequent droughts, there have been at least two instances of acute food crisis which many have chosen to describe as famine: Bihar in 1967 (with a recurrence in Palamau district in 1993), and Kalahandi, Bolangir, and Koraput in Orissa since 1985. Secondly, in the account offered by Dreze and Sen (ibid.: 126) India's greater success in combating hunger has been attributed to its open polity. Adversarial politics and a free press are seen to act as triggers that enable the government's crisis management mechanisms to quickly and efficiently come into play. While these were precisely the political institutions that were brought into play in the case of Kalahandi, we shall note the inadequacy of the state's response to the recurring situation of scarcity there.

Protesting Hunger

While democratic institutions do theoretically create new possibilities, not available in a colonized society, for the articulation of rights and for mobilization for welfare claims, these have remained largely unutilized in India. Surprisingly, evidence of protest against food scarcity is more easily available for the colonial period. Indeed, while the survival strategies and coping mechanisms of famine victims have received much scholarly attention (Chen, 1991), there is little evidence of popular protest and no academic notice of its absence.[14] Why is it that citizens of a democratic welfare state do not protest the spectre of starvation, while subjects of a colonial state sometimes do? The answer to this question cannot be limited to the political sphere alone; it must necessarily also encompass the social, cultural, and economic spheres.

It has been argued that in pre-colonial times, the 'moral economy' of reciprocity ensured a certain minimum entitlement of food to the rural poor, the price of which was their disenfranchisement and possibly even bondage. Marketization and political enfranchisement however have witnessed a corresponding decline

---

[14] There is, for example, evidence of riots having occurred in Kerala and West Bengal in January–March 1966. In Bengal, in particular, these were violent disturbances, in which public buildings were burnt, buses, trains and railway stations were set on fire, and police stations were attacked. Several people were killed in police firings at Calcutta, and in Basirhat, Baduria, Krishnagar, and other places.

in entitlements, as the traditional moral ties that enjoined landlords to be responsible for their clients have been eroded (Appadurai, 1984: 495).[15] Paul Greenough's study of Bengal does suggest that while famine relief was traditionally regarded as an obligation in the paternalist *zamindari* ethic, British rule introduced a new model of prosperity that privileged self-interest and maximization over benevolence and redistribution. In the 1943 famine, the traditional *annadata* (providers)—the father, the *zamindar* and the provincial government—reneged on this obligation, abandoning their *posya*s (those dependent on them). Authoritative males conducted themselves in accordance with the new self-interested model, disregarding the dictates of traditional morality. The absence of revolt is attributed to the Bengali adaptation to famine, which took the form of violence inward and downward, against clients and dependents, rather than, as in Europe, upward and outward, against landlords, merchants, and officials (Greenough, 1982: 265 ff.).

There is, on the other hand, some evidence in colonial history for protest in the form of rioting, looting, and violence in times of famine (Arnold, 1979, 1984; Ludden, 1985). Arnold's investigation of two such episodes, both in Madras Presidency, though thirty years apart, suggests that when peasants did revolt, it was not an act inspired by nationalist sentiment, but rather a demonstration against the greedy hoarding and profiteering in grain by merchants, and the government's stubborn refusal to intervene in controlling food supplies and prices. Arson and looting were intended only to punish profiteers, not to take away their stocks; sometimes, promissory notes were left behind in exchange for food taken (Arnold, 1979: 126-7). Nor was the rioting intended to challenge or overturn the class structure. Its politics were far from revolutionary, intended only to remind the superordinate classes—

---

[15] This argument leans heavily on James C. Scott's work (1976) on the moral economy of the peasant, which in turn draws upon E. P. Thompson's influential study of food riots in eighteenth century England. Thompson had argued that rebellion expressed not only the acuteness of deprivation, but also moral outrage at illegitimate practices (in marketing, milling and baking) from a traditional paternalist perspective of social norms and obligations within the community (1971: 79). In relation to modern India, Torry (1986: 14) argues that the subsistence insurance once available barely functions now, and emergency food sharing covers only the family.

landlords, merchants, and moneylenders—of the responsibility that accompanied their power and command over resources (Arnold, 1984: 85). In times of crisis, thus, the 'normal' relationships of power, of subordination and superordination, were questioned, though when 'normalcy' returned, the subordinate classes lapsed quiescently back into the old order of power and domination.

Thus, the known instances of violent response to dearth are few, limited to the colonial period, and apparently directed not at the state, but at classes that visibly stood to gain from the suffering of their compatriots. In the post-colonial period, there is almost no reference to popular protest in studies of the Bihar famine of 1967 (Singh, 1975; Brass, 1986). Do the victims of famine then fail to protest only because the identifiable target, the state, is also the provider of sympathetic rhetoric, visits from Prime Ministers, and announcements of largesse as relief assistance? Does the inadequacy or failure of state response not create a crisis of legitimacy in the political system?

II. THE HUNGER OF KALAHANDI

A Short History of Kalahandi and of its Trysts with Famine

Located in the south-west of Orissa, Kalahandi district came into being in 1948, when the former princely state of Kalahandi was merged with Orissa. Kalahandi came under Maratha domination in the mid-eighteenth century, and when the Nagpur kingdom lapsed to the British, that suzerainty was also naturally extended to Kalahandi in 1863. The rajas of Kalahandi enjoyed a relationship of amiable subordinacy with their British superiors, who helped them to suppress revolts, such as the famous Kandha rebellion against the Kulta cultivators in 1882. Unsurprisingly, there are few traces of nationalist activity in Kalahandi. Its ruler resisted amalgamation with Orissa, and was the last to sign the merger in V. P. Menon's presence on 15 December 1947, complaining to the last of coercion.

The history of underdevelopment in Kalahandi can be traced back to the days of princely rule. The Report of the Orissa States Enquiry Committee (1939), headed by Harekrushna Mahtab of the Congress Party, described it as a vast, inaccessible state with extensive jungles and a largely aboriginal population. 'The system of administration', the Committee reported, 'is almost of a primitive nature. The Ruler is all in all.' (Orissa States Enquiry Committee, 1939: 195.) The report drew attention to the conditions of 'virtual serfdom' that prevailed under an absolute ruler who ran a privatized and lucrative system of justice and exploited his subjects. Taxation was oppressively high, and even landless people were liable to pay a cess called 'Sukhabari'.

As in other parts of Orissa, the *gauntia* system prevailed in the *khalsa* areas (state controlled land, as opposed to *zamindari*s). The *gauntia* (mostly belonging to the brahmin or *kulta* castes) designated by the ruler, was responsible for collecting the revenue on behalf of the king from the cultivators of the village or group of villages. In return, he received land—generally the most fertile, sometimes extending to whole villages—for personal cultivation. The subjects enjoyed no rights over land (including forests and other common resources), were not allowed to sell their produce outside the state without permission, and were liable to pay a forest cess or *nistar* and a grazing fee.

Historically, the tribal population of Orissa's hill regions had suffered a dual domination—that of the local *gauntia*s and upper castes, on the one hand, and of the migratory coastal officials, including teachers, clerks and traders, on the other. Belonging mostly to the brahman and *karan* castes, these classes came to dominate society and economy in all parts of Orissa after 1947, enjoying a virtual monopoly over the bureaucracy and education. In Kalahandi, they were the new middlemen between the local tribal population and the coastal élite, with a decisive voice in, and naturally personal profit from, the development resources and programmes that were devised for the tribals. The other dominant caste group since independence has been the *khandayats*—the middle and rich cultivating castes—who have provided the social base of both the major parties, the Congress and the Janata.[16] To this combination of brahmans and *karan*s, on the one hand, and

---

[16] Given that voter participation, partisan voting, and competitiveness have been lower in the former princely states as well as in tribal constituencies (Weiner and Field, 1975: 40, 117), it is not surprising that brahmans, *karan*s and *khandayat*s have also been preponderant in the legislative assembly, in ministries, and even in the distribution of important portfolios in the state cabinet (Mishra, 1984). The local leadership of the important political parties in any case remains in their hands.

*khandayat*s on the other, is generally attributed the persistent underdevelopment of the state of Orissa. These castes, it is argued, have been too deeply rooted in the old agrarian structure[17] to be able to free it from its pre-capitalist moorings. Nevertheless, they have assisted the forces of capitalist development in India in the exploitation of the rich mineral resources of the region. This brahman–*karan* middle class has not however generated a surplus that could give an impetus to industrialization or even capitalist agriculture, and the resulting backwardness has ensured that the marginalized classes of landless labour and poor peasantry are kept struggling for subsistence, quite unable to pose any serious threat to the domination of these castes (Mohanty, 1990).[18]

The regional imbalance between the coastal plains and the hills of the inland regions is evident not only in levels of economic development, urbanization, literacy, and the like, but also in political consciousness.[19] The social charisma of the erstwhile raja

[17] With superior lands, more sophisticated implements, and access to scarce irrigation facilities, they also remain the principal creditors of the small peasantry (Mohanty, 1990).

[18] Despite the reservation of legislative seats for the Scheduled Castes and Tribes, and despite the fact that the tribals constitute the largest single social group among members of the Legislative Assembly, they have been remarkably passive participants in the political process, and have been content to have only a minor say in the distribution of development resources. The passivity of the tribal politicians of Orissa is in striking contrast to the assertiveness of those in the neighbouring state of Bihar. This difference is attributed to several factors, including the sharp divide between the coastal, developed eastern region and the hilly, backward western part of Orissa; the subservient position to which *dalit* and tribal politicians have been relegated by all political parties in the state; and the absence of education. In Bihar, the tribal areas have been regions not only of mining and industrial activity, but also areas in which Christian missionaries have been active in providing education, and where facilities for higher education have therefore developed. The few universities in western Orissa, by contrast, are not located in the tribal belt. (M. Mohanty, Personal communication).

[19] In his celebrated study of Orissa in the 1950s, F. G. Bailey (1963) noted the difference in political consciousness between the people of Mohanpur (a village of the coastal plains) and Bisipara (a hill village). While the political agenda in Bisipara centred around taxes, access to forest produce, and policy on caste, especially untouchability, that in Mohanpur reflected a greater awareness of power, politics, and state-level issues such as flood relief and the mismanagement of rehabilitation funds.

has tended to endure,[20] and Kalahandi has, for much of its political history, elected candidates belonging to the Ganatantra ,Parishad and its ideological successor, the Swatantra Party. In this respect, until the 1980s when we find a convergence between the patterns of voting in the state as a whole and in the district of Kalahandi, the latter consistently voted against the current in Orissa state.

Between 1801 and 1943, Orissa twice experienced acute famine, in 1865–6 and 1888–9. Ironically, in the five years preceding the 1865 famine, Orissa had exported 33,000 tons of rice, almost double its annual average export for the past five years. However, when the rains failed in 1865, and grain became both scarce and expensive, the government remained truculent in its refusal to import food into Orissa on account of the huge expenditure that this would entail.[21] Imports were finally allowed when, in 1866, police reported widespread looting of grain, but by this time the famine had already claimed 1.3 m lives (Bhatia, 1967: 65–9) Kalahandi was among the affected areas, but little is known about the impact of the famine there, except that relief centres were opened to supply cooked food (District Gazetteer, 1980: 140), and that the traditional social code that obligated landlords to provide for their cultivators in times of distress was observed to have broken down (Bhatia, 1967: 79).

When, in 1888–9, another scarcity occurred, induced by crop failure and continuing foodgrain exports, the government moved

[20] The former maharaja, P. K. Deo, represented the Kalahandi constituency in the Lok Sabha for five consecutive terms from 1957 to 1980. His son B.K. Deo has represented Kalahandi in the state Assembly, and was the Lok Sabha candidate of the BJP in the 1998 general election.

[21] In his autobiography, *Atma Jivana-Carita*, the first autobiography in the Oriya language, Phakirmohana Senapati [1917] (1985) described the terrible conditions in Orissa during the famine of 1866. He wrote about the distress sale of gold, and brass in exchange for rice; of the physical deterioration and debility wrought by the famine; of the migration that separated children from their parents, and husbands from their wives; and above all, of death. 'Early each morning from around the relief centres and from elsewhere on the highways and byways about the town sweepers picked up the previous day's dead, piled them on carts and tipped them into the river. For a month to six weeks I saw sweepers take three or four cart-loads to the river each day' (ibid.: 31). In an episode strongly reminiscent of the 1980s, he described the Commissioner consulting the court clerks about the possible course of action, and was told by them that there was sufficient paddy stored in the homes of *zamindars* and traders to last a year (ibid.: 28–9).

in more quickly to set up relief works in addition to extending loans and advances, and providing gratuitous relief. The administrative investigation that followed showed that the greatest burden of destitution had fallen on the hill tribes, who were originally cultivators, but were now increasingly joining the ranks of landless labour (ibid.: 169). This was inevitable as the highlands came under the plough cultivation of higher castes from the plains, as also because the colonial forest laws denied the tribals access to the natural resources that were the basis of their subsistence. Famine recurred in 1897, when famine deaths were reported at the rate of 81 persons per mile (Rao, 1995: 240). The severity of the next famine in 1899 is indicated by the fact that the land revenue suspension that year was in the region of Rs 8.5 lakhs. Milder scarcity conditions visited the area again in 1902–3, and partial scarcities in 1922–3, 1925–6 and 1929–30.

After independence, Kalahandi suffered drought in 1954–5, and more severely in 1965–6, along with many other parts of the country, including Bihar, Gujarat, and Rajasthan. The District Gazetteer informs us that the landless agricultural labourers who constituted the bulk of the population of the district were rendered unemployed, but that 'the worst sufferers were the landed gentry, who because of the drought could not reap a harvest nor could they (sic) take to manual labour to which they were never accustomed' (1980: 142). It is not difficult to surmise in what proportion the benefits of the Rs 1.37 crore loans and advances would have been distributed. Indeed, it has been estimated that in 1965, 55 per cent of the population was dependent on free kitchens. Kalahandi was again visited by drought in 1974–5, when the Drought Prone Areas Programme was launched there, though with little material evidence of success in drought-proofing.

Kalahandi: A Contemporary Socio–economic Profile

The population of Kalahandi, according to the 1991 Census,[22] was 1,591,984, showing a decadal growth rate of + 18.88 per cent since 1981. Though higher than the decadal growth rate for 1971–81

[22] The statistics available in the 1991 census pertain to Kalahandi district, before its Nuapada *tahsil* was constituted as a separate district in April 1993. This, however, presents no methodological problem for this study, for the events with which we are chiefly concerned, as also the period when the census data were gathered, pertain to the undivided Kalahandi district.

(+ 15.06 per cent), this is still appreciably lower than the state and national growth rate average of 19.5 and 23.5 per cent respectively. The child mortality rate is correspondingly higher: 148, which is the same as the Orissa average, while that of Punjab is 94, and of India as a whole 123. The infant death rate in Kalahandi also shows a virtually unmitigated increase, from 4.44 per cent in 1981 to 7.02 per cent in 1987 (District Statistical Handbook, 1990: 24–5). The sex ratio is high, especially in the rural areas (1005), which may be indicative of the rates of male migration in search of employment.

Conventional development indicators suggest the low levels of development in the district. The total literacy rate is 25.31 per cent, 75 per cent of which is accounted for by men. Of the total enrolment in schools during 1986–7, only 6 per cent was at the High School level, 15.3 per cent at the Middle School level, and 78.7 per cent at the primary level (District Statistical Handbook, 1990: 1–2) It is significant that of the 19,455 persons registered with the Employment Exchanges in the district in 1987, over 10,000 were educated below the level of matriculation, and only 1536 were graduates or more (ibid.: 52). District statistics for 1992–3 indicate that there are a total of 434 beds available in the allopathic medical institutions in the district, while less than 15,000 people are serviced by banking facilities.

Much of the population of Kalahandi is rural (93.47 per cent according to the 1991 Census), of which 15.76 per cent belongs to the Scheduled Castes and 31.28 to the Scheduled Tribes. Together, these groups account for almost half the entire population of the district, and for much of its rural population, as 76.81 per cent of the urban population is not from these groups. The rates of urbanization of the Scheduled Castes and Tribes are also substantially lower than the state and national averages. Thus, in 1981, the rate of urbanization for Scheduled Castes was 5.79 per cent, against an Orissa average of 9.40 per cent and an Indian average of 16 per cent. The urbanization trends for Scheduled Tribes, likewise, showed an average of 1.35 per cent against a 4.61 per cent state and 6.20 per cent national trend (Nayak and Mahajan, 1991: 26–7). The home of the tribal population of Kalahandi is predominantly in the hill ranges of the Eastern Ghats, which cover virtually the entire eastern and southern areas of the district, and remain largely inaccessible to this day.

The numerical strength of the Scheduled Castes and Tribes is, unsurprisingly, not reflected in the pattern of landownership, which reveals that the percentage of marginal and small landholdings increased from 46 in 1970 to 64 in 1985, as the agricultural labour force also expanded (ibid.: 30). Indeed, 45 per cent of agricultural labour is from the Scheduled Castes, while about 39 per cent is from the Scheduled Tribes. Only 15.58 per cent of the Scheduled Castes and 10.10 per cent of the Scheduled Tribes are literate. The dropout rate of Scheduled Caste and Scheduled Tribe students in Kalahandi is also very high (Lok Sabha Debates, 27 April 1987: 241–2).

There is hardly any industrial activity in the district, though the region is richly endowed with minerals, and the production of granite and quartze, for instance, does take place. There were, in 1993–4, 32 working mines, employing 106 workers, the value of their output being only Rs 14 lakhs. In 1985, 32 registered factories were reported to be functioning, providing employment to only 880 workers (District Statistical Handbook, 1990: 2), while the value added by manufacture in 1982–3 was only Rs 70 lakhs (Nayak and Mahajan, op. cit.: 41). In 1992–3, 16 registered factories were reported to be in existence, with a total of 537 employees, of whom 413 were workers. The value added by manufacture was Rs 50 lakhs. (District Statistical Handbook, 1993.)[23]

Agriculture, then, is by default the principal occupation available, and in 1991, approximately 84 per cent of the working population of Kalahandi was dependent on it for a living, with 45 per cent of these being agricultural labourers. The agricultural labour force expanded from 35.59 per cent in 1981 to 38.52 in 1991, of which the percentage increase for women was higher than that for men. Thus, women agricultural labourers increased from 61.16 per cent in 1981 to 64.67 in 1991, while the corresponding figures for men are 30.52 (1981) and 31.67 per cent (1991) (1991 Census Supplement, Provisional Population, Orissa: 189). By contrast,

---

[23] Members of Parliament have frequently raised questions in the Lok Sabha, asking for Kalahandi to be declared a 'No Industry' district, to encourage industrial investment through incentive schemes (Lok Sabha debates, 7.5.86: 327–8; 4.3.86: 540–1). In 1994, Chief Minister Biju Patnaik inauguarated a Rs 60 crore factory of the Western India Sugars and Chemical Industries Limited. There are some doubts about the viability of this, given the low levels of sugar cultivation in the district.

while 86 per cent of the work force was engaged in agriculture in 1971, only 37 per cent was dependent on agricultural wages (Nayak and Mahajan: 29). Even the figures of only those seeking employment through Employment Exchanges have been registering dramatic variations, with annual increases of between 2 per cent (1986–7) and 42 per cent (1984–5) since 1981. In 1987, only 418 of the 19,455 such persons on the rolls, could be found placements (District Statistical Handbook, 1990: 52).

Agriculture is not highly developed, and only 16.97 per cent of the net area sown is irrigated, the lowest for any district in the state (Government of Orissa, Economic Survey 1992–3: 210). Operational landholdings are mostly small: in 1985–6, only 31 holdings were 10 ha. and above, while marginal (below 1 ha.) and small (1 to 2 ha.) holdings between them constituted 64 per cent of the total number. But, simultaneously, the semi-medium (2 to 4 ha.) and medium (4 to 10 ha.) landholdings, while fewer in number, accounted for 34.6 per cent of the area (ibid.: 158). The average size of operational landholdings is 1.94 ha. The use of modern agricultural practices and mechanization continues to be limited, though the area under high-yielding varieties of paddy in Kalahandi has increased from 7,199,000 ha. in 1986–7 to 11,622,000 ha. in 1990–1 (ibid.: 156), as has the consumption of fertilizers from 1.8 kg/ha. in 1986–7 to 7.2 kg/ha. in 1990–1. This, along with an increase in the use of mechanized agricultural implements (cane crushers, oil engines, and tractors) signifies the emergence of an affluent section among the peasants (Lokadrusti, 1993: 6).

Although the district headquarters of Bhawanipatna had a diesel power house installed in 1925, electricity is available today in only 40 per cent of the inhabited villages, and, of course, in all the five towns of the district, of which only one, Bhawanipatna, is a Class II town, and all the others are Class IV towns. The consumption pattern of electricity is also significant: in 1986–7, agriculture and irrigation used only 6.65 per cent of the total electricity generated, with even domestic consumption being five times higher (ibid.: 58). Thus, agriculture remains dependent on low quality inputs and primarily on rainfall. Hunger in Kalahandi may be a function more of the backwardness of agriculture than of variations in rainfall. In the years since 1986, parts of the district have had to be repeatedly declared drought–affected. Officially described as drought, and correlated with rainfall variations, the condition of Kalahandi has been problematized as such. The politics of this diagnostic will be discussed in a later section of this chapter.

Hunger in Kalahandi since 1985

When the Orissa Legislative Assembly (henceforth OLA) opened for its budget session in July 1985, the issue of the sale of a baby raised on the first day developed into a stormy debate on the drought in Kalahandi as the session progressed. Only repeated grilling by the Opposition in the Assembly forced the Congress (I) revenue minister, Jugal Kishore Patnaik, to visit the district on 13 July, and five days later he informed the House that there was no cause for concern. The Chief Minister and his revenue minister refused to acknowledge the occurrence of, let alone accept any responsibility for, the alleged starvation deaths. The opposition moved an adjournment motion demanding a debate on the subject: the revenue minister stayed away, and the Speaker postponed the debate to 29 July, two days after the proposed visit of the Prime Minister. When the motion eventually came up for discussion, the government stated that the deaths were due not to starvation, but to diarrhoea and gastroenteritis. Meanwhile, on 27 July, Prime Minister Rajiv Gandhi visited Kalahandi district, where, in a famous episode, Phanas Punji confirmed to him that she had sold her fourteen year old sister-in-law, Banita, for forty rupees for the survival of her two children and herself. She later told press reporters that she would not yet sell her three year old daughter, but would wait till the child was older and could fetch a higher price.[24]

In a letter to Chief Minister Janaki Ballabh Patnaik, the PM urged the state government to equip the poor with adequate resources to help them tide over such scarcities, and to expedite irrigation projects. In effect, the administration's neglect of backwardness and poverty were underlined, and even in the edited version released to the press, critical references to widespread

[24] P. Sainath (1996: 325–38) has documented how this focus on the 'sale' obscured the underlying realities. Banita, the girl who was 'sold', is married to Bidya Podh who is far from being the old, blind, exploitative landlord that the media made him out to be. He was, in fact, young, landless, out-of-work, with some sight-impairment. The perception of the actors in the drama is far removed from that of the national press: they see it as a marriage, not a sale, and all of them continue to maintain their bonds of marriage and family.

poverty could not be altogether expunged. On 31 March 1986, the Committee on Estimates presented to the Legislative Assembly its Thirty Fifth Report (Interim) on the Drought Situation of Kalahandi in the Year 1984–5.[25] It sanguinely stated that 'there is no drought situation at present in none (*sic*) of these Blocks and the same has been combated by the State Government,' forecasting further that a bumper paddy crop was expected in 1986 due to sufficient and balanced rainfall (OLA, Committee on Estimates, 1985–6: 2). It documented, however, the complete exploitation of labourers, and the failure of the Labour Department to enforce the minimum wage. The importance of this Report lies in the evidence it provides of the collusion between contractors, government officials, and engineers in holding up construction activity on roads and irrigation projects. It highlighted, for instance, the irregularities in the ultilization of funds for the Sunder Medium Irrigation Project, which was started in 1972–3, but remained incomplete while contractors refused to work and owed large sums of probably irrecoverable money to the State exchequer (ibid.: 2–3). Similarly, on the Palasada-Boden Road, the Committee blamed six Executive Engineers of the district for the inordinate delay and considered their explanation 'extremely unsatisfactory'. 'The progress of work of Khariar-Boden Road', they concluded, 'was held on intentionally' (ibid.: 5).

Meanwhile, reports and photographs of starvation, the distress sale of babies, the eating of roots and leaves, widespread malnutrition, and loss of eyesight continued to appear in the press, both local and national. The death toll by the end of July was unofficially estimated at about one hundred. Migration and abandonment, the survival strategies typical of both drought and famine, were also reported on a considerable scale. The desertion of wives and children by husbands and fathers was commonplace. Many men left to work as bonded labourers, mostly in Madhya Pradesh. But as the labour market in neighbouring Raipur began to shrink, the local population became hostile towards the migrants, even attacking them. Some men went to far away Pathankot where they were given earthwork for twelve hours a day, minimal food, and no wages (*Sunday*, 11–17 August 1985: 25). Women and

[25] The Committee had begun its investigations into the subject in August 1985, and visited Kalahandi in October 1985, and again in February 1986.

young girls were commonly sold to brothel owners in Madhya Pradesh and elsewhere.

Opposition legislators, like the press, kept up a sustained campaign on Kalahandi. One MLA claimed to have personally witnessed the offer of Rs 1500 to the family of Ulhas Meher (a forty-one year old woman who had starved to death within a month of her husband's death in similar circumstances) by a government official, to cover up the matter. Bhakta Charan Das, the young MLA from Bhawanipatna, went on hunger strike, demanding immediate and large-scale relief measures, but met with little response. In the Assembly, at the end of a four and a half hour debate on Kalahandi, this self-confessed follower of Jayaprakash Narayan hurled his microphone at the Treasury benches.

The people of Kalahandi, meanwhile, were quite overwhelmed by the visit of Rajiv Gandhi, and fell at his feet as they had apparently done when Indira Gandhi visited them in the 1966 drought, bringing promises of prosperity and plenty in the shape of irrigation and other development projects. The passivity of this response is in marked contrast to that of the tribal people of Jhabua, Kalidevi, Dutteygaon, and Lokshi (all in neighbouring Madhya Pradesh) who resorted to looting and plundering when faced by food scarcity (*Illustrated Weekly of India*, 26 Jan. 1986: 9–10). Even as widespread hunger and migration in search of employment continued unabated, the State government persisted in insisting that starvation deaths had not occurred. Drawing attention to the state's negligence, Kishen Pattanayak and Kapil Narain Tiwari filed a writ petition in the Supreme Court, invoking Article 32 of the Constitution.[26] The petition stated that the people of Kalahandi were being compelled by penury into distress sales of their crops, land, and labour leading to the exploitation of landless labourers by landlords. This took the form variously of bonded labour, and landlessness caused by the mortgage of lands by moneylenders, and the eventual transfer of tribal land to non-tribals. There were also, the petitioners stated, cases of people averting starvation deaths by selling their children. The Court responded to this petition only in 1987, by which time another

---

[26] *K. Pattanayak and others* v. *the State of Orissa*, Writ Petition (Civil) No. 12847 of 1985, admitted by Justice Bhagwati (cf. Currie, 1996 for a detailed account of the petitioners' submissions).

public interest litigation had also been filed, and eventually decided both petitions in January 1989.[27]

Meanwhile, Kalahandi continued to remain officially in the grip of drought. In 1984–5, 830 villages under 156 Gram Panchayats in 17 (of a total of 18) blocks in Kalahandi district were declared drought-affected. The official criterion for such a declaration is the assessment, in percentage terms, of the extent of crop damage suffered due to monsoon failure, and villages included in the drought-affected category are those which have suffered 50 per cent or more crop damage, with many of them showing damage of over 74 per cent. In the following year (1986), 11 of the 18 Blocks of the district reported damage of over 50 per cent to the *kharif* paddy crop, with 779 villages under 139 Gram Panchayats affected. In 1987–8, these figures registered a dramatic increase, as over 50 per cent crop loss was reported in 1109 villages (of a total of 2812) in 128 Gram Panchayats (of a total of 249) in 15 Blocks.

The Government of Orissa, however, maintained its ostrich-like position, firmly denying the existence of starvation, much less the occurrence of starvation deaths, which increased in number but continued to be blamed on old age, dysentery, and meningitis. In March 1987, the first reaction of the Revenue Minister to these reports was not to investigate them, or to rush food supplies to the affected areas, but to say that he had not yet received a copy of the newspaper that had reported these![28]

A Janata Party sponsored motion seeking a probe into the situation was defeated by 59 votes to 42 in the Legislative Assembly, even after 19 Congress (I) dissidents voted with the opposition.[29] The Chief Minister visited Kalahandi, promising the district special attention in the form of health care, school hostels, and drinking water, and developmental measures for tribal people.

[27] The other petition was Writ Petitition (Civil) No. 1081 of 1987, forwarded to the Court by the Indian People's Front, a Maoist group from Bihar.

[28] When directed by the Speaker of the Assembly to visit the district, he said 'I will go when I find time'. (*Indian Express*, 3.3.1987) Dissatisfied with the government's report on the situation, the Speaker asked the minister to personally make an on-the-spot study of Karduljhar village.

[29] The dissidence was not, however, strictly on account of the drought situation. J. B. Patnaik's government, though serving its second term, was in any case plagued by factionalism and intra-party differences.

In the meantime, the ruling Congress (I) also partially conceded the demand for an investigation, and on 9 April 1987 a ten-member House Committee was set up, headed by the Speaker, P. K. Dash,

to look into the problems concerning drought and other natural calamities in order to suggest short-term and long-term measures to the Government [Motion adopted by Orissa Legislative Assembly, 9.4.1987].

By this time, the word Kalahandi had become synonymous with death and destitution throughout the country, and Patnaik himself described it, with heavy sarcasm, as a village with an international reputation. Kalahandi was hardly ever absent from the columns of newspapers, even at a time when 267 districts of the country were reeling under the impact of the severe drought of 1987. The symbolic importance of Kalahandi perhaps explains the press conference held in Delhi by the Orissa Chief Minister on 12 June 1987, in which he claimed that he had personally, in a three-day, door-to-door tour of the district, ascertained that there had not been a single case of starvation death, and that such allegations were a canard put out by the Communist Party of India (Marxist), and the opposition Janata leader, Biju Patnaik. Even as he accused the opposition of 'mean politicking', J.B. Patnaik had already, in an infamous newspaper interview, claimed that the people of Kalahandi habitually ate a mixture of red ants, white larvae, and *haldi* (turmeric), and that this was, in fact, a 'type of delicacy for them' (*Sunday Observer*, 29.3.1987). Now, detailing state charity in the form of subsidies for rice and saris, he claimed that there was adequate relief available in terms of employment and feeding centres, and no resource constraint.

This latter claim is surprising, because Orissa had delayed the preparation of its memorandum requesting Central financial assistance for relief measures, and by the time it did put up a demand for Rs 60.5 crores on 3 August 1987, the Centre had already sanctioned Rs 250 crores for other drought-hit states. On the eve of the Central team's visit to the state, the Orissa government hastily cobbled together a first supplementary memorandum asking for additional assistance of Rs 155.46 crores. The Central team visited Orissa from 22–6 August, assessed the crop loss at 50–8 per cent, and eventually made provision for Rs 39.75 crores for drought relief in Orissa, of which only Rs 85 lakhs constituted non-plan expenditure. It also approved an additional Rs 11 crores for completing or expediting irrigation projects in drought-prone areas. When the Ministry of Finance made it clear that the State government's margin money would be set off against the Central assistance, the Government of Orissa submitted a Second Supplementary Memorandum on 31 December 1987, seeking an additional Rs 13.5 crores. Following this, another Central team visited Kalahandi and four other districts in January 1988, and sanctioned a further Rs 8.61 crores on 3 February 1988, for the five severely drought-affected districts. Of this, Rs 95 lakhs comprised non-plan expenditure for gratuitous relief for emergency feeding programmes. (White Paper, March 1988: 2–3.)

It is notable, and fairly typical, that the state government was reluctant to declare a scarcity, and even when it did so, was concerned to repeatedly deny starvation deaths. None of this, however, precluded it from making claims for ever-higher amounts of Central assistance. This is a characteristic feature of administrative response to famine, which is stoutly denied to the local populace, and magnified to donor agencies such as the Central Government. It is also a fairly typical aspect of administrative response to such crises that dusty and largely forgotten development programmes as well as relief activities are pulled out of bureaucratic cupboards, and paraded as evidence of humanitarian state intervention to mitigate hardship. In Kalahandi, too, the collector, Chinmay Basu said that almost 50 per cent of the villages of the district had emergency feeding centres, each feeding about 45,000 people a day. This was in addition to the 'normal' feeding programme for 2.12 lakh children, mothers, and expectant mothers. Similarly, the Joint Secretary for Rural Development in the Union Ministry for Agriculture said that there was no shortage of jobs under various rural development schemes. Food too was not in short supply as 38,723 tonnes, the government claimed, were released by the Central Government in 1986 for distribution at concessional prices in the Integrated Tribal Development Project areas of Orissa. The Central Government's foodstocks, at this time, stood at a surplus of 29 m. tonnes and the idea was even mooted in Delhi that since India was now a surplus grain-producing country, grain should be increasingly replaced by cash crops!

Among the more active responses of the state government was a disinformation campaign, of the sort that is habitually sponsored by defensive regimes. The Orissa Government put out quarter page advertisements in all the major national newspapers (in English), entitled 'Changing Landscape of Kalahandi', which attempted to project Kalahandi as a most inviting and promising area, standing on the very threshhold of great prosperity. It was not mentioned that during the first four months of the year, the bulk of the annual Plan allocations for tribal and Harijan welfare for 1987–8 had remained unutilized, with only 6.21 per cent (as against a 25 per cent target) of the outlay having been used. Similarly, the department of agriculture and cooperation only used 16.25 per cent of its outlay during the same period.

While the government remained trapped in the confusion of how much scarcity could be admitted to garner financial assistance, without compromising itself politically, the West Bengal units of the CPI and the CPI(M) were engaged in voluntary relief operations through their Orissa units. The hostile host government subjected to testing the supplies of medicines brought in by these parties, as the West Bengal Congressman Priya Ranjan Das Munshi issued public warnings against accepting the 'spurious' medicines being distributed by the Communists. But the Left parties forged a six-party combination with Nandini Satpathy's Jagrat Orissa, the Lok Dals (A) and (B), and the Forward Bloc to launch a sustained movement for Kalahandi and Koraput. On 30 August 1987, the parties organized a joint demonstration in front of the Secretariat in Bhubhaneshwar, held meetings at various places, and chalked out a programme for joint rallies throughout Orissa, culminating in Kalahandi. The Janata Party organized *padayatras* in 930 villages, and twice observed a Kalahandi *bandh*. During the *bandh* of 19 February 1987, 1000 persons were detained by the police, of whom it was claimed 800 belonged to the Scheduled Castes and Tribes (Resolution of the Janata Party National Executive, 29–30 March 1987).

On 8 September 1987, the Committee of the House on Drought and Other Natural Calamities, tabled its Interim Report on Kalahandi and Koraput in the State legislature.[30] Despite the fact

[30] Before the Report was tabled, the Committee had in July 1987, apprised the concerned government departments of its observations. In a meeting on 3 August, it noted with dismay that the compliance reports furnished by different departments showed inadequate attention to the Committee's suggestions on the part of the Special Relief Commissioner and the Revenue Secretary, and a consequent delay in preparing the memorandum for Central assistance.

that the majority (six out of ten) of the Committee's members belonged to the ruling Congress (I) party, it confirmed the worst fears of the administration which had strongly resisted its establishment. The Committee's report pointed out that the alleged starvation deaths had not been properly inquired into in accordance with the requirements of Section 39(i) of the Orissa Relief Code. Since the medical officers in charge of the primary health centres had not inquired into the cause of death in cases reported between November 1986 and February 1987, it was now clearly difficult to ascertain the actual reasons for the 214 deaths reported, of which 79 occurred before intensive care by the Medical Officers. Perplexed as to why the 'Revenue Department and Special Relief Commissioner did not give proper guidance to the Collectors in time' (Orissa Legislative Assembly, House Committee on Drought, 1987: 17), the Committee asked the Government to ensure, in future, that the cause of death was ascertained within 48 hours of such allegations being published in newspapers. The report also suggested the revival of the earlier system in which all deaths, including those occurring during epidemics, were reported by the village chowkidars/*gram rakshi*s at their weekly parade at the police station.

One of the most significant points made by the Report was its observation that the government's assessments of crop loss, prerequisite to a declaration of drought, considered only *kharif* paddy crops. In so doing, it ignored the damage to crops like *jowar, ragi,* and other millets that are grown in over fifty per cent of the cultivable area of Kalahandi district, and are the staple of the tribal population. 'The food habits of these people have also to be taken into consideration while assessing any distress on account of drought,' said the Committee (ibid.: 1), for rice is consumed mostly by the affluent people of the district. Thus, relief through the Public Distribution System takes the form of subsidized rice and wheat, wholly ignoring the requirements of the poorer sections of the people, the Scheduled Castes and Scheduled Tribes (ibid.: 9). Likewise, labour-intensive relief works were not organized so as to enable the tribal people to obtain employment within a five kilometre radius of their homes.

The Committee also unequivocally asserted prima facie negligence on the part of the Special Relief Commissioner, for delays in starting the emergency feeding programmes and allotting labour-intensive relief works.[31] It recommended the enhancement of irrigation in the area, greater efforts at afforestation, crop restoration measures such as second-cropping, and the discontinuance of grain distribution through contractors in the Food for Work Programme.

Meanwhile in neighbouring Koraput district the Sub-Divisional Officer of Gunpur, A. M. Dalavi was suddenly transferred as he submitted a report confirming 67 starvation deaths in his subdivision. Though Dalavi had been posted there for only a year, he had earned the wrath of local Congress (I) leaders by reopening land ceiling cases against some landlords, for refusing official transport to the Congress chairman of the *panchayat samiti*, and for his zeal in seizing hoarded stocks of rice.

By and large, relief measures were being put on special display for VIP visits, when fair price shops would suddenly become better stocked. It was argued, by some, that the contractor–local official–politician nexus was responsible for the siphoning off of both relief funds and foodstocks, and this view was lent credence when, in April 1987, an assistant civil supplies officer of Koraput district was apprehended by vigilance officials, while accepting a bribe of Rs 500 from a rice dealer for the release of seized rice (*Times of India*, 9.5.1987). Rations were finding their way into the black market on an unprecedented scale through the public distribution system. This was a strange contrast indeed to colonial practice, where prices shot up because of the refusal of government to intervene in private grain trading. Here, in the welfare state of independent India, the public distribution system was being hijacked for the private profit of not merely merchants, but also public officials and elected representatives of the people.

In September 1987, Prime Minister Rajiv Gandhi made a second visit to Kalahandi and other drought-affected districts. Not straying from the metalled roads, he was again shown the fairest face of test relief works and well stocked fair price shops. There was still no visible sign of Operation Salvage, the programme he had announced

[31] Whatever the inadequacies of other local officials, health officials in Kalahandi were displaying quite exemplary zeal. Not only did they exceed the family planning targets for 1986–7, by forcibly sterilizing 761 persons against the required 337, but among these 70 men and 89 women were in fact childless.

on his first visit in 1985.[32] A television newsmagazine broadcast a feature in which the Prime Minister was seen asking a labourer how much he earned, the labourer replied three rupees, and the Chief Minister translated this, for the PM's ears, as six rupees. This only confirmed the findings of the Estimates Committee which had, in 1986, drawn attention to the fact that labourers were ruthlessly exploited by contractors and departmental agencies alike, being paid only Rs 3 as a daily wage, instead of the statutory minimum wage. In a significant development in October, the Health Minister, Niranjan Patnaik admitted in the Assembly, for the first time, that 30 people had died due to 'lack of adequate food' in Keonjhar district of Orissa.

Starvation deaths and large-scale migration continued to be reported, through 1988 and 1989, in several districts of Orissa, including Kalahandi, Koraput, Ganjam, and Phulbani. On 22 March 1988, the Revenue Minister presented to the Legislative Assembly his department's 'White Paper on the Drought Situation in Orissa', 1987–8, an update on the White Paper tabled on 10 September 1987. Nowhere in this 18 page report is there any mention of the extent of area and population affected by the drought. The White Paper also showed that the suggestions of the House Committee (op. cit., 1987) had remained unheeded. It confirmed that Committee's concern that the administration's view suffered from an excessive emphasis on rice as the sole criterion for assessing crop damage (White Paper, 1988: 8), on the basis of which drought could be declared. Likewise, it commented on the bias towards rice in the public distribution system, and in crop restoration schemes (ibid.: 5). The Orissa Government's request to the Central Government for the Public Distribution System was aimed specifically at enhancing its quota of subsidized rice. The state government of Orissa claimed that its drought relief measures had considerably alleviated the effects of drought, and among these it listed the supply of subsidized rice and wheat in 118 Blocks of the Integrated Tribal Development Programme category (ibid.: 10). Similarly, in the compensatory supply of seedlings and plants, paddy, wheat, and pulses figured prominently, and millets not at all (ibid.: 5).

[32] In 1987, the District Collector Chinmay Basu said in an interview 'I am personally not aware of Operation Salvage' (*Illustrated Weekly of India*, 26.4.87: 14)

Thus, when the House Committee on Drought presented its Second Interim Report in September 1988, it again lamented that non-paddy crops were not covered in crop-cutting experiments, and that 'the present system had adversely affected cultivators in the interior and hilly areas' (Orissa Legislative Assembly, Second Interim Report , 1988: 2). It also criticized the practice of diverting funds allotted for drought relief to other developmental works, including irrigation projects that could not conceivably be completed with these funds (ibid.: 8). In the outlays for employment generation works, for lift irrigation points, and for soil conservation, Kalahandi was the single largest beneficiary district, which indicates the implicit concurrence of the state government in the seriousness of its condition, and simultaneously indicts the administration for its failure to pull the district out of the morass for years together.[33]

Both the White Paper and the Second Interim Report of 1988 mention the existence of Committees with elected representatives. The White Paper mentions the setting up, by Government, of Block Level Committees to get non-officials and representatives to actively participate in the drought effort. These Committees were to be chaired by the local Member of Parliament, and included, amongst their members, other MPs (such as those whose constituency fell within the Block); the resident member of the Rajya Sabha; local members of the Legislative Assembly; the Chairman of the Panchayat Samiti; the Block Development Officer; and two nominees of the Collector. It is not difficult to see, in the composition of these ostensibly democratic bodies, the continuing stranglehold of the dominant local notables. It is also unclear how, if at all, these Block Level Committees were expected to relate to the already existing District Level Committees on Natural Calamities which, the House Committee observed, were not meeting regularly, or at frequent enough intervals. (Second Interim Report, 1988: 12.)

One democratic forum, in particular, remained curiously impervious to the distress of Kalahandi: the Lok Sabha. Between 1985–8, there were a total of fourteen questions on Kalahandi, only two of which were about drought and the Drought Prone Areas

[33] Cf. White Paper, March 1988: 14 for Tables on employment works; Second Interim Report, 1988: 3 and 11 respectively, for Tables on lift irrigation and soil conservation.

Programme in Orissa as a whole. Nine of the questions were asked by Jagannath Patnaik of the Congress Party, Kalahandi M. P. from 1984–9, and of them seven relate to the possibility of sub-divisional postal and telephone offices being set up in the district; the progress of rural electrification; and the need to foster medium industry in Kalahandi, indeed to declare it a 'No Industry' district. Of the remaining two questions asked by the member, one points to the need to check the spread of epidemic diseases, and the other to the necessity for setting up a Special Development Board in the district. The party affiliation of the member (Congress (I), the same as the ruling parties at the Centre and in the State) perhaps discouraged him from putting more penetrating questions. There is however no evidence of Opposition members raising the issue either, as was the case in the Orissa legislature and the press.

It is notable that until 1991, the principal focus of the debate on the distress of Kalahandi, was on the question: were there starvation deaths or not? The role played by the national press in drawing attention to these was undoubtedly critical.[34] But, apart from the role played by the press (especially the English language press) in highlighting the inadequacies of government response, as well as in combating criticism by the state government, another aspect of this issue merits attention. This is the fact that the problem was essentialized in terms of its factual existence or otherwise. If starvation deaths could not be proven, there was no case for government culpability; and if they were claimed to have occurred, government, as the custodian of mortality statistics and

---

[34] N. Ram of the *Hindu* later described some journalistic interventions as overstatements with propaganda overtones that transformed 'a widespread drought into an unprecedented famine', but conceded that these efforts did influence public opinion as well as 'impervious official hides' (1990: 178, 184). Chief Minister Patnaik also sought to draw strength and credibility from press reports in refuting the charges of starvation deaths. In this, he particularly depended upon some reportage in *India Today* (October 1987) according to which, while there had been a large number of deaths on account of the drought, these had been caused by malnutrition, rather than starvation. They were specifically caused by the eating of improperly stored, and therefore fungus-ridden mango seeds, causing death by dysentery which was not medically treated. The question of why the people were resorting to the consumption of such foods at all was not an issue raised either by the press or the government. In any event, J. B. Patnaik found this report extremely useful as a handle with which to silence his critics.

reports on public health, and as the monopolist proprietor of such information, could without undue exertion establish that this had not been the case.[35] For the most part, however, while opposition leaders, activists, and the press shouted themselves hoarse in the legislature, in the field and in the newspapers, about starvation, some relief measures continued as drought was officially acknowledged, even though famine was officially denied.

In December 1989, after a record tenure of ten years in office, J. B. Patnaik resigned the chief ministership, succeeded by Hemanand Biswal, also of the Congress (I). In the Assembly elections of February 1990, the Janata Dal won a record 123 seats (out of 147), and formed a government led by Biju Patnaik. J. B. Patnaik's populist promises of an economic boom had not travelled further than the four coastal districts, while western Orissa continued to suffer from drought. The peasantry as a whole was now alienated from the Congress, as the absence of infrastructural facilities like water, electricity and fertilizers undermined the traditional link between the rich peasantry and the Congress (I) (Pati, 1990: 375).

In 1991, the Mishra Commission's report (discussed in the next section) conclusively established the occurrence of some starvation deaths. Continuing reports of starvation from Kalahandi provoked the new Prime Minister P. V. Narasimha Rao to send his Minister of State for Agriculture, K. C. Lenka to review the implementation of various development programmes in the district. The Minister suggested the revival of ADAPT (Area Development Approach for Poverty Termination) in all 18 Blocks of the district, which had lapsed when the Janata Dal Government came to office in March 1990. The Union Minister's visit apparently inspired the Orissa Panchayat Raj Minister, Dr Damodar Rout, to rush to the district, charging Mr Lenka with politicizing the issue. Dr Rout claimed that the foodgrains stock available with a former Congress (I) minister from the district could alone feed the entire population of Kalahandi for ten days. He also alleged that the bulk of the Rs 8.5 crores spent under ADAPT had been misutilized by the former

---

[35] Control over information is an important aspect of the exercise of power, which governments sometimes choose to justify in benevolent terms as, for example, in April 1993, when the Government of India informed Parliament of its unprecedented decision to withhold the preliminary forecast of the monsoon, to preclude speculative hoarding and inflationary activities (*Economic and Political Weekly*, 17 April 1993: 728).

Congress government of the state. Thus, both the Congress (I) government at the centre, and the Janata government at the state level, were engaged in extracting maximal political mileage from the destitution of Kalahandi. This was not surprising in view of the fact that the *gauntia*s and businessmen controlling the economy of the district have powerful representatives in all the major political parties. The familiar federal handle came into play, with the Congress government at the Centre blaming the Janata government in Orissa (as in Bihar, which also witnessed severe drought conditions in 1992–3), and vice versa.

In subsequent years, Kalahandi, along with many other districts of Orissa, has continued to suffer from severe drought conditions, sometimes followed by heavy rains and floods. Such, for instance, was the situation in 1992 when Orissa was ravaged by a cyclone and the sudden retreat of the monsoon resulted in drought in eight districts, including Kalahandi, Bolangir, Koraput, and Keonjhar. By October 1992, all 18 Blocks of Kalahandi district were declared drought-affected. Central assistance was solicited, and a crore of rupees sanctioned from the Prime Minister's Relief Fund. The expenditure on 'pure relief' from the Calamity Relief Fund alone added upto Rs 1339.65 lakhs, with an additional Rs 806.53 lakhs being allocated for drought mitigation measures.

In 1996 again, Kalahandi, Bolangir, Nuapada, and Sonepur districts have suffered extreme drought conditions, with over 90 per cent of the *kharif* crop being damaged. In Bolangir, there were allegations of at least one starvation death. Large-scale migration— some estimates suggested 200,000 people from the four predomi- nantly tribal districts—was recorded. The Government of Orissa responded with a variety of documents, including a fresh White Paper, an Annual Action Plan for 1996–7, and also a Long-Term Action Plan for the KBK Districts[36] (from 1995–6 to 2001–2). Apart from these, several non-governmental organizations were also active in advocacy and information-gathering work on the situation. In Kalahandi alone, 13 Blocks and 2205 villages are said to have been affected in the 1996 drought. Resources have poured in, even as central government teams consistently point out the low rate (30–5 per cent) of utilization of development funds given

[36] The KBK region, officially defined, includes 8 districts: Koraput, Rayagada, Nawrangpur, Malkangiri, Kalahandi, Nuapada, Bolangir, and Sonepur (Long-Term Action Plan, Government of Orissa: 1).

under centrally sponsored schemes. The reports of starvation deaths have been investigated by a team of the National Human Rights Commission, whose findings will be discussed in the next section.

Hunger in Kalahandi Investigated

Apart from the legislative committees that investigated the scarcity conditions prevailing in Kalahandi, some important judicial inquiries were also instituted. While the argument that these present evidence to substantiate the public action explanation (Currie, 1997) is contentious, it is nonetheless true that it was only these inquiries that provided compelling evidence of the acuteness of the situation. The two Special Commissioners appointed by the Supreme Court, Ambika Prasad Guru (a retired district and sessions judge of Sambalpur) and Shyam Sundar Das (a social worker), in response to the Writ Petition mentioned earlier, had been rendered incapable of functioning by the State government's stalling tactics, and the Supreme Court therefore replaced them by the serving district and sessions judge of Kalahandi, Pratap Chandra Panda, in whom not just the petitioners, but also the Kalahandi Bar Association (in a meeting at Bhawanipatna on 20 July 1987) expressed their lack of confidence.

Panda decided that nobody, specifically the petititioners, should accompany or follow him during his 14-day visit to the affected areas in July 1987. In three letters addressed to Kapil Tiwari (no. 3473(3) dated 16.5.1987; no. 3787 dated 16.6.1987; and no. 3860 dated 20.6.1987), Panda contradicted himself repeatedly, first asking only for the petitioners and State government representatives to be present, then asking only for the names of places where starvation deaths, child sales, and migration had occurred, and finally insisting that 'As this is a fact-finding enquiry, nobody should follow me to any place of inquiry'. In his reply, dated 25.6.1987, Tiwari stated 'it appears to me that you are going to have the enquiry behind my back, as a result the said enquiry would be unilateral....'[37] These events further delayed the inquiry report which Supreme Court Justices Venkataramiah and K. N. Singh had asked for by 30 April 1987.

[37] This correspondence is reproduced in Currie (1993), App. 8.1–8.4: 384–8.

On 9 January 1989, Justices M.M. Dutt and K.N. Saikia of the Supreme Court delivered a joint judgement (1989 Supplement (1), Supreme Court Cases 258) on both the writ petitions cited earlier, namely *K. Pattanayak and another* v. *State of Orissa*, as well as *Indian People's Front through its Chairman, Nagbhushan Patnaik* v. *State of Orissa and others*. The second writ petition related to the distress in Kalahandi and Koraput districts, accusing the Government of Orissa of 'utter failure to protect the lives of the people'. The state government, in its two responses of 160 and 181 pages respectively, attempted to prove that it had implemented social welfare measures in Kalahandi. Subsequently, P. C. Panda, the District Judge who conducted the inquiry as instructed by the Supreme Court, confirmed the Government's standpoint in a 361-page report, in which he argued that the Government had provided sufficient funds and loans to help those in distress, but the people themselves were idle and failed to take advantage of the opportunity provided to produce food and generate income, often choosing to spend it on liquor instead (Currie, 1996: 8). Echoing the nineteenth century debate on gratuitous relief, he said that it worked as a disincentive, making people dependent upon the state, and disinclined to work towards their own welfare for which the Government of Orissa was making much effort. The Court, however, stated that

Although the learned District Judge's report is against the alleged starvation deaths, we are of the view that the happening of one or two cases of starvation deaths cannot be altogether ruled out [1989 Supp (1) Supreme Court 258: 260].

As a solution, it directed the Government of Orissa to nominate, within a month, five persons belonging to recognized voluntary organizations such as the Sarvodaya Gandhi Peace Foundation and the Ramakrishna Mission, to the Natural Calamities Committees of the districts, which should meet at least once every two months. The Court clearly interpreted the problem as one of *legitimacy*, and as such attempted to resolve it to the satisfaction of the petitioners by creating more space for social workers and activists. On government policy, the Court declared itself quite satisfied, as it approvingly cited the respondents' statistics about emergency feeding, irrigation facilities, foodgrains stocks and purchases, and the ADAPT programme.

Meanwhile, the Orissa High Court, taking *suo moto* cognizance of a press report 'When Will the Exploitation End?' (published in October 1988 and sent to the Court by one Bhawani Mund) initiated a case, O.J.C. No. 3517 of 1988. At about the same time, Anukul Chandra Pradhan, an advocate, submitted to the Court a report based on his visits to several villages of Kalahandi district. This led to the institution of another public interest litigation, O.J.C. No. 525 of 1989. On 2 March 1990, a retired District Judge, Baidyanath Mishra, was appointed to conduct an inquiry into the matter. Mishra prepared his report by 16 March 1991, and the Revenue Department of the State Government was then given time to respond to it. Its Objection was filed on 4 November 1991, and on 12 February 1992, Chief Justice B. L. Hansaria and Justice B. N. Dash of the Orissa High Court delivered their judgement for the two cases, awarding cash compensation of Rs 25,000 to the families of the dead.

The Mishra Commission Report established that at least five starvation deaths had taken place in Kalahandi district: Sukha Jani, a Scheduled Caste person of Deypur village; and four tribal persons of village Sindhibhadi, namely Pamuli Sabar, Musila Sabar, Parbati Sabar and her husband Bandaki Sabar, all of whom died within the space of ten days in February 1989. The Report pointed to administrative negligence at every level, starting from the Tehsildar's report to the Collector—'palpably a distortion and travesty of truth'—which nervously attributed the four deaths in village Sindhibhadi to 'loose motions'. The Tehsildar did, however, include in his report a telling account of the conditions of poverty and unemployment that prevailed in the village, which indicated that of the 266 persons in the village, 115 were being sustained by Government feeding programmes. Only the previous year, the Bamboo Corporation, which provided some employment in the area, had closed down, and

the labour class public were facing much difficulties to arrange their 'minimum meals' and so he moved the Collector to provide immediate work to help the public for their 'minimum earn'. This clearly reveals that a major part of the population of the village which includes the dead and ailing *had actually no earning and hence no food* [Emphasis added, Mishra Commission Report, 1991: 39.]

The Commission also authenticated the distress sale of assets, including property, for want of food, though it did not confirm any allegation of the sale of children due to food scarcity. The District Administration was not only charged with apathy, but was also accused of collusion with the moneylenders who exploited the illiterate tribal labourers whose lands they would mortgage in exchange for loans, and refuse to return these even after the loans had been repaid with interest. Government officials and the police, the report said, appeared to 'help the Mahajans in such exploitation by not entertaining complaints, and also harassing them at the instigation of Mahajans' (ibid.: 2). Many cases of land-grabbing, encroachment, and the illegal and *benami* transfer of tribal lands, were recorded by the Commission, including one by a Scheduled caste moneylender. This provoked both the Commission and the Orissa High Court to remark upon the poignancy of the exploitation of tribals, even by *dalit* persons. The Commission also commented adversely upon the failure of the district administration to implement the Orissa Land Reform Act.

The reports about mass migration from Kalahandi were also investigated by the Commission, and these included villages visited by Prime Minister Gandhi, on the supposition that they would be better provided for. Mishra found that even the owners of good and sizeable pieces of land had migrated, suggesting that those with poorer lands or no land would perforce leave in search of employment (ibid.: 25-6). The Report recorded, further, that migrations had begun only in 1985 (ibid.: 35) and continued apace thereafter. Efforts to ascertain first-hand information about these migrations showed that they were surreptitiously organized by labour contractors and local contact men who, for fear of detection by the police, instructed the emigrants to conceal their true identities. One such emigrant was the owner of 20 acres of land who, when interviewed on a visit home, stated that his family laboured on construction sites in Surat, Gujarat, on a daily wage of Rs 20. This was roughly equivalent to Rs 5 in Kalahandi, but since he was unable to procure a Rs 5 wage here, he was compelled to leave his village (ibid.: 36-7).

Having established the extent of distress leading to starvation deaths, migration, and the sale of assets including property, as well as the exploitation of the rural especially tribal poor, the Mishra Commission examined the development performance of the Government in the district. It recognized that both the Central and State Governments had provided for large sums of money for the district, but wondered why, despite this, the small population of the area should live in such pathetic conditons of economic misery. According to Government statistics, 50 per cent of the population below the poverty line in Kalahandi should have been brought above the poverty line, as 1,97,468 beneficiaries of various poverty alleviation programmes were identified. But this claim was described as 'fantastic' in view of the judge's observation:

I saw people living hand to mouth and in the houses of landless and labour class inhabitants, a morsel of grain could not be had for next day meal [ibid.: 70].

Of the beneficiaries under the Integrated Rural Development Programme, a sample of 158 was interviewed, of which 54 per cent discontinued the scheme halfway. 29 per cent dropped out due to the death of animals; 8 per cent due to diversion of the loan for other purposes; and 5 per cent out of sheer poverty. Likewise, 44 per cent of the sample beneficiaries of the ERRP scheme were also found to have discontinued before long (ibid.: 65). The Commission argued that while the beneficiaries of these schemes were landless persons, the holdings allotted to them were marginal and uneconomic, requiring further financial assistance for cultivation. Large sums of money were provided without any effort to see how they were utilized. Hasty expenditure, without planning, and the faulty execution of projects of water harvesting and soil conservation, resulted in wastefulness. The Report insinuated that corruption, fraud, and leakages were in all probability taking place, in addition to the usual non-use and misuse of development funds. In an aside, it even noted that 'it was the year when election took place, and this is significant' (ibid.: 67).

The Commission's strictures on the district administration were thus severe and harsh. Baidyanath Mishra complained about the lack of cooperation he encountered in his task: 'I am handicapped due to failure of Government to post an experienced officer to assist me' (ibid.: 42). The Collector promised him every assistance except posting an officer to assist him in the inquiry. He assigned, instead, the District Development Officer to help the inquiry judge in his task. On the illegal transfers of tribal lands the Administration was not, the Commission noted, inspired to act by a sense of duty: it took cognizance only when the problem was brought to its notice by a voluntary organization AWARE.

The most serious lapse on the part of the Collector was clearly his inaction in the face of reports of starvation deaths. He did not, the Commission said, act as required by the Orissa Relief Code, which enjoins upon him the duty of immediately inquiring into such deaths, reviewing relief measures, and taking further steps to alleviate distress in the area. Thus, despite the report of the Tehsildar of Sindhibhadi, the Collector did not bother to visit the village, let alone report this to the Government as required by Rule 39 of the Relief Code. The Collector, said the Mishra Commission Report, 'has failed in his duties, and the Government is vicariously responsible for his apathy and inaction' (ibid.: 41).

The district administration was thus charged with laxity and slackness in the enforcement of the Orissa Land Reform Act and other social legislations such as the Orissa Money Lenders' Act and the Bonded Labour Act. It was charged with wastefulness and mismanagement in the utilization of resources provided for development in the district. It was charged with corruption and connivance with the rich and powerful ex-*gauntias* and moneylenders of the area, allowing them to exploit and usurp the lands of the poor tribals. Above all, it was charged with neglect of humanitarian concerns in the face of starvation deaths. Thus, the Inquiry Judge concluded his Report by recommending that

officers of proven good records dedicated to public service be placed in the districts with offer of incentive if needed and the collector who shall be made accountable for all round development should have fixed tenure at least of 4 years or so as to be able to effectively oversee the implementation of projects. [ibid.: 75].

Contrasting the performance of Government with the successful implementation of development programmes by non-governmental organizations, the Report further stated:

The officers of the welfare department should also be activated to work like social organizations to create awareness among the victims to assert their rights by legal and constitutional means [ibid.: 72].

The Mishra Commission's suggestion that the people of Kalahandi needed to be made aware of their constitutional rights and entitlements showed great perspicacity, even if it was unwarrantedly optimistic regarding the possible source of the putative conscientization, namely public officials. The people of Kalahandi did not mobilize themselves to protest against acute hunger. This was in marked contrast to the drought in Athmallik subdivision of Dhenkanal district where the farmers launched an agitation in early 1988 for better implementation of anti-drought measures. This agitation, under the banner of the Orissa Krushak Mahasangh, launched a 'jail *bharo*' programme, in which 2600 men and women were jailed. It threatened to develop into a mass movement led by the Janata and Communist parties. J. B. Patnaik, also in contrast to his response to the Kalahandi drought, immediately succumbed to the pressure of local Congressmen in negotiating with the agitators. Only a month after capitulating to the demands of these farmers to write off agricultural loans, the ruling party sponsored a state-level farmers' rally, using state resources estimated at Rs 4 crore (*Indian Express*, 20.5.1989). In Kalahandi and Sambalpur, by contrast, farmers resorted to the distress sale of paddy as the crop insurance scheme failed miserably.

An investigation into the 1996 drought yields very similar results, suggesting that in over a decade, and despite vast sums of relief expenditure and development funds, nothing had changed in Kalahandi. In December 1996, at the request of Chaturanan Mishra, the Union Minister of Agriculture, the National Human Rights Commission (NHRC) decided to send a team to investigate complaints of starvation deaths during the drought that year. The Commission considered this report, and also heard the responses of the Union Government and the state government on the observations of the team. In February 1998, the Commission published its Proceedings, directing both the State and Central governments to comply with its recommendations, which are mostly of an interim nature. Chiefly, these included the continuance of the Emergency Feeding Programme, apart from several other social security provisions; employment generation in agriculture; drinking water and public health. In a departure from earlier investigations, the NHRC recommended a set of mechanisms for the implementation and monitoring of the various programmes in operation, and urged the State government to immediately examine the question of land reforms (National Human Rights Commission, 1998: 16–21). It is not without significance that the major issues identified by the NHRC team are largely those that had been emphasized by other teams five years earlier: the non-availability of water for drinking and other purposes; the dismally understaffed public health system; the failure of schemes for old aged pensioners and others to cover all the persons they are meant to cover; the alarming extent of out-migration; and 'partisanship in the sanctioning of relief' (ibid.: 12). Above all, echoing Amartya Sen's entitlement theory of famine, it argued:

despite all of the efforts and plans, it remained uncertain as to whether the 'bundle of commodities', including food, which Professor Sen considered essential to ensuring that deaths did not occur as a result of starvation, was indeed available to all of the people of the 'KBK districts', especially the most vulnerable [ibid.: 13].

Further, it noted the assertion of its team that

because of the very high level of deprivation existing in the area, along with extensive crop damage, malnourishment, inadequate income levels and insufficient outreach of relief measures, the possibility of deaths having occurred owing to prolonged malnutrition and hunger, compounded by diseases, could not be ruled out. Indeed, out of 21 deaths investigated by the team in the districts of Nuapada, Kalahandi and Bolangir, 17 were attributable to such causes [ibid.: 8].

The conclusions of the NHRC Report are unambiguously endorsed by a report of the Rajya Sabha's Committee on Petitions, presented in March 1998 (Rajya Sabha, 1998: 27). This document highlights the obfuscations of official discourse, and the contradictions in the database for policy making suggested by different state agencies. For example, the Government of Orissa's door-to-door household survey on poverty (1992–3) revealed that 78 per cent of families in the state lived below the poverty line. The Lakdawala Report of the Planning Commission, on the other hand, suggested a much lower figure of 48 per cent. The difference of 11 lakh families between the two estimates is clearly significant, as it has a bearing on programme planning and allocations. For its part, the Committee on Petitions suggests that nearly 90 per cent of the people in the KBK districts live below the poverty line (ibid.: 6).

Its investigations into the efficacy of poverty alleviation programmes also reveal inadequacies in both planning and implementation. The Employment Assurance Scheme, for instance, which was intended and designed to function as a virtual right to work, has not been implemented on account of financial constraints (ibid.: 52). Even the Emergency Feeding Programme reveals a startling degree of administrative incompetence:

The Committee during its visit to KBK areas found that at one point of time the Collector was searching for rice. Even the utensils for cooking were not available. At another Centre, even at 1.30 p.m., no food was available and a search was on for utensils, food items, vegetables, etc. The cook was also not available. Many people in the area were not even aware of locations of feeding centres in their areas. This is an (*sic*) ample proof of tardy implementation of the EFP in the KBK areas and callousness on the part of village, Block and District level authorities who are indifferent to the sufferings of the people of those areas [ibid.: 29].

As a report of the Comptroller and Auditor-General of India had already shown in 1995, misappropriation and diversion of funds for other purposes is a familiar feature of every development and poverty alleviation programme in this region (ibid.: 84, Appendix III). Ten years after it became known that large numbers of medical positions here are lying vacant or that laws on minimum wages are routinely flouted, the report reiterates these facts, indicating the absence of administrative response to them in the intervening period.

Thus, despite the fact that several investigations by different agencies, and over a period of at least six years, have repeatedly emphasized the acute deprivation that makes the people of Kalahandi endure hunger, regardless of whether there is a drought or not, these findings have not brought forth an administrative or policy response capable of even seriously addressing, let alone resolving, the problem.

The Drèze–Sen public action model, which argues that a free press and adversarial politics have an important role to play in combating famine, has been sought to be extended to encompass the judiciary (Currie, 1996, 1997). In this study, I argue that it is not enough to draw the distinction, as Currie does, between endemic hunger (in which these democratic institutions are not particularly effective) and acute seasonal hunger (in which, it is claimed, they are). The validity of the public action hypothesis with regard to Kalahandi is contingent on the category of hunger in which we choose to contextualize it. Was it drought or was it famine? Did deaths occur due to starvation or other causes? The answers to these questions are not unequivocal. They are mediated by the politics of nomenclature, on the one hand, and the politics of information control over demographic statistics, on the other. In Section III of this chapter, I examine both these, along with the relationship between hunger and underdevelopment in Kalahandi.

III. THE POLITICS OF NOMENCLATURE

In this section, I shall focus on the constitution and representation, by the State, of Kalahandi's condition, as this has formed the basis of policy initiatives. The various descriptions of Kalahandi as suffering from drought, or famine, or simply abject poverty and backwardness have different normative and policy implications. The politics of nomenclature are, in turn, inextricably linked to theories of famine causation: together, these determine the nature and substance of state intervention. On occasion, despite some policy understanding of structural backwardness and underdevelopment, this does not find reflection in actual policy initiatives, and some examples of these will also be discussed.

A Drought by Any Other Name?

Has Kalahandi been a victim of prolonged and recurrent drought, caused by repetitive monsoon failure, or has it been experiencing hunger and starvation on a scale that can truthfully be described as famine? Further, is the difference between drought and famine merely one of intensity or social consequences or long-term impact, or are the two qualitatively different?[38] Drought is generally indicated by a physical criterion, namely inadequate precipitation in terms of rainfall (Planning Commission, 1981). Drought is also the most frequent trigger of famine, which stands for an extreme and widespread scarcity of food, i.e. hunger and starvation on a vast scale.

Etymologically, the two terms are so entirely dissimilar in their meanings—drought, from Old English, indicates dryness, aridity and lack of moisture, while famine, from its Old French root, *faim*, means hunger—that it is difficult to linguistically discern any common ground between them. Today, however, the two words are frequently used interchangeably, and this becomes comprehensible only when we recognize that historically the most common trigger of famines has been drought, though famines have also been caused by war, conquest and epidemics (Alamgir, 1980). Drought

---

[38] That these terms have an ineluctable specificity has been imaginatively demonstrated by Alexander de Waal in his study of Darfur, Sudan, in which he shows how famine in Darfur means not merely starvation, but also hunger, destitution and social breakdown. When people are actually dying on this account, it becomes a 'famine that kills' (1989: 76).

does not, of course, necessarily or always develop into famine, and public policy has a significant role to play in precluding this. It is however often the stage preceding a famine, and can easily develop into one in the absence of timely and adequate intervention. When the social and human costs and consequences of drought become unmanageable by a community, however organized, the state has willy-nilly to step in and assume responsibility for providing succour. I noted, at the beginning of this chapter, the historically critical role played by states in combating hunger, and its relationship to the legitimacy of the state. Here, I attempt to further relate state action, or inaction, to the description of a particular condition of scarcity as drought or famine, through a discussion of the politics of the label.

In Kalahandi, the Government of Orissa has consistently attempted to establish that the district is recurrently drought-affected, and equally resolutely to deny that hunger of famine proportions has occurred. The choice of nomenclature, regardless of its relationship to 'fact', has at least two clearly identifiable political uses. Admitting, indeed establishing, the existence of drought places some demands on the state, in terms of pressing relief mechanisms into service. In India, the dependence of State governments on the Central government for relief assistance enables the former to plead financial constraint, and thereby shift the moral responsibility for its limited practical abilities to the latter.[39] The amount it is able to recover from the Central government depends less on the objective or observable levels of distress, even were it possible to scientifically measure and comparatively assess these, and more on the party complexion of one State government as it competes with other State governments for funds.

Secondly, drought is attributable to divine will or the whimsy of nature, according to personal and political preference. Thus, while the occurrence of drought can be blamed on the vagaries of nature, the onus for its mitigation can almost as easily be shifted to the Central Government (cf. Lok Sabha debate on drought, 10–17 August 1987). If a hostile political formation happens to be in power at this level, the exoneration of the State government is further facilitated. This has the additional and attractive potential of garnering more votes in the next election for a regime projected

[39] Cf. Mathur and Jayal (1993: ch. 3) for a discussion of the administrative and financial procedures relating to relief.

as sympathetic and compassionate but hopelessly and maliciously constrained by higher levels of power in rendering assistance to its citizens.

The official description of the Kalahandi scarcity was, emphatically underscored, drought. Successive White Papers strove hard at being non-eponymous, by avoiding any description of the magnitude, extent, or spread of drought, concentrating instead on the organizational mechanisms and projects devised or resuscitated to meet the situation (cf. White Papers of 1988 and 1993). It is significant, for this argument, that when, in March 1986, the ruling Congress (I) eventually conceded the demand of the Opposition for an enquiry into the widespread allegations of starvation deaths, nomenclature was a contentious issue. The Chief Whip, S. Sahu, declared that the government was willing to constitute a House Committee only to study *conditions of chronic drought-affectedness* in the state as a whole. This was how it came to bear the relatively ambiguous name 'The Committee of the House on Drought and Other Natural Calamities'. The motion adopted by the Orissa Legislative Assembly in constituting the Committee nowhere mentioned either Kalahandi or the starvation deaths, though Kalahandi and Koraput were the districts taken up for investigation.

From Food Availability to Entitlements

In modern times, it is clearly difficult for a state to concede the existence of famine. Generally understood to represent a decline in the availability of food, the occurrence of famine is a sign of inefficient resource management. Till Amartya Sen's enunciation of his Entitlement Theory of Famine in 1981, the Food Availability Decline (FAD) thesis was the received wisdom and orthodoxy of famine causation. The existence of food surpluses and the availability of modern means of communication and transportation mean that even if local productivity declines due to climatic factors, food availability ought not to be affected. As such, Sen's entitlement theory rightly discredited the FAD explanation of famine, by viewing famines not simply as food crises, but as 'economic disasters' affecting a person's ability to command food, as well as other commodities (Sen, 1982: ch. 10). Sen's theory was supplemented by Ghose, who introduced an element of specificity, by taking into account the nature of the economy in question. Thus, while in a de-monetized exchange economy, famine is most likely to be induced by crop failure, in a monetized exchange economy, a sharp rise in food prices—even without a crop failure—could precipitate famine. Further, the social consequences of famine are significantly class-differentiated: historical evidence has shown that while landless labourers and small artisans starved, landowners and rich traders actually prospered in famine periods (Ghose, 1982: 379). By emphasizing the distributional aspects over the productive, Sen and Ghose have substantially demythologized famine and rendered it open to critical political scrutiny. What are the entitlements of persons in a given society? Are these undermined or even violated by legal rights governing property ownership, contracts and exchanges ? What policy prescriptions are entailed by adopting an entitlement view of food scarcity: only the movement of food to address immediate needs or a more enduring generation of food entitlements? Issues of economic and political organization cannot thus be entirely divorced from these questions.

Though passé in the groves of academe, however, the doctrine of Food Availability Decline continues to enjoy favour in the corridors of power. In its emphasis on crop loss due to failure of rainfall, the Government of Orissa has implicitly subscribed to the FAD theory, which entails a smaller responsibility, and is politically safe and non-threatening. To acknowledge the validity of an entitlements perspective, on the other hand, would be to endorse a far more complex understanding of the malaise that afflicts Kalahandi. This understanding would necessarily have to encompass a whole range of neglected, structural factors, and call for a reformulation of the entire problematic of development in south-western Orissa. While delivering the poor from the servitude of the drought-centred discourse of the state, this could not but be an exercise subversive of the status quo, undermining the interests concerned to maintain it. Interventionist initiatives that address inequitous entitlements and recall uncomfortable questions of social justice are therefore best avoided by recourse to a less demanding conception of welfare as charity. If this conception serves an additional ideological purpose by entrenching dependence on state initiatives, that is only another good reason for encouraging it.

In Kalahandi, thus, the State government highlighted the correlation between crop loss and the absence of adequate rainfall, in consonance with the criterion for officially declaring an area drought-affected (i.e. crop loss of 50 per cent or more). Blaming the rains is clearly most convenient for any regime, because it implicates no human agency, and places minimal responsibility. It is however now well-established that starvation has been endemic in Kalahandi even in years where there has been near-normal precipitation. Further, according to one estimate, throughout the period under consideration, Kalahandi has been a food surplus district (Pradhan, 1993: 1085). It has also continued to remain a net exporter of foodgrains, like only four other districts of Orissa. Thus, neither is hunger in Kalahandi critically correlated to rainfall variation, nor has crop loss or failure resulted in unacceptably low productivity levels in the district. Despite the state government's implicit adherence to the FAD theory, the arguments about crop loss are apparently contentious, and certainly insufficient ground for evading the deep-rooted structural causes of the problem.

Kalahandi: Structural Backwardness and the Demography of Hunger

David Arnold has drawn an important distinction between famine as event and famine as structure. The structural causes of famine, and the greater vulnerability of some regions and communities to it, mandates investigation precisely because, regardless of its proximate cause (drought or any other) it 'acts as a revealing commentary upon a society's deeper and more enduring difficulties' (1988: 7).

If the underlying structural causes of the malaise are location and time specific, so are its manifestations. Of the indicators that are commonly employed in famine demography, to ascertain the extent and nature of particular scarcities, statistics regarding births, deaths, and migration, and the age and sex differentia of these, form the core. Historians have also investigated food-related crimes by gathering data on theft, riots, and looting during famine periods. Mounting indebtedness is a further pointer to hardship in a country like India. In the case of Kalahandi, there are additional indicators of some specificity—such as levels of malnourishment, the sale of children and women, and the prevalence of bonded labour. It is unsurprising that information regarding these is zealously guarded, routinely manipulated, and even altogether omitted from official documents like White Papers.

As this narrative of the recent history of hunger in Kalahandi has shown, the government of Orissa has been consistent in its refusal to concede that any starvation deaths occurred, let alone in the numbers alleged by politicians, the press, and non-governmental agencies. Control over figures in periods of demographic turmoil is a crucial weapon of defence for a beleaguered state. Accountability can be significantly diminished if the problem is essentialized in terms of its factual existence, of whether or not it occurred at all. Even the House Committee's report suggests a dissatisfaction with the government's record in this matter, and though it expresses inability to prove that such deaths did not occur, it remains unconvinced of the veracity of the government's claims. It was only in 1991 that the Baidyanath Mishra Commission conclusively established that at least five deaths did occur in Kalahandi in 1989. The figures given by political workers, the press, and voluntary agencies were in the region of 300–500. The Chief Minister would acknowledge only 80 deaths each in 1987 and 1988, attributing these to dysentery and meningitis.

In the light of recent historical work on famine mortality, which suggests the importance of a location-specific approach,[40] an epidemiological study of Kalahandi may show that the dysentery to which the Government of Orissa attributed the alleged starvation deaths was surely, if indirectly, related to starvation. As the Central Study Team's Report (1992) pointed out, the consumption by tribals of infected and fungus-ridden mango stones and tamarind seeds may well have rendered them vulnerable to dysentery and gastroenteritis, but was dictated only by the absence of other forms of food.

The official demography of Kalahandi in the 1980s suggests a consistently rising birth rate, except in 1984 and 1985, when it dips slightly (District Statistical Handbook, 1990: 24). The number of registered deaths reveals a similar rising trend, except for the year 1986. Of particular significance, however, are the statistics relating to causes of death, which are classified as fever, dysentery, diarrhoea, respiratory diseases, wounds/accidents, and a final category designated 'other causes'. This last category shows a

[40] In irrigated areas along the Western Yamuna Canal (in Uttar Pradesh), for instance, the principal cause of famine mortality was not starvation but epidemic malaria that accompanied the eventual arrival of the rains (Whitcombe, 1993: 1178).

dramatic increase, quadrupling between 1981 and 1982, doubling again between 1982 and 1983, and thereafter maintaining a rising trend. Above all, as a percentage of the total number of (registered) deaths in the district, this category represents a steady average of about 80 per cent between 1983 and 1987, for the years for which figures are available. It is important to remember that these statistics would, in all likelihood, exclude at least some unreported deaths occurring in remote and inaccessible areas inhabited by tribal people.

A sample survey of migration in 1991–2 (not the period of most acute scarcity) has also shown a high migration rate of 11.52 per cent, of which 63 per cent was male migration. 85 per cent of these migrants were illiterate, and 44 per cent of them belonged to the Scheduled Castes (B. Mohanty, 1992: 4). Reliable data on migration for the period of intense scarcity (1985–7) is not available, but newspaper accounts suggest a similar migration rate, with 1.5 lakh persons, out of a population of 13.5 lakhs, allegedly migrating. It is notable that the Central Study Team that visited Kalahandi in March 1993 observed that the rate of migration was probably in the region of 20–22 per cent.[41]

The other indicators, not generally regarded by official statisticians, include evidence of widespread malnourishment, the sale of children and young women, bonded labour, indebtedness, and possibly also the incidence of crime. It will be recalled that Chief Minister J. B. Patnaik had, in a notorious interview, claimed that ants and larvae were a type of delicacy for the tribal people, and not food resorted to in desperation. Study Teams sent by the Central government have repeatedly emphasized the widespread malnourishment and under-nourishment in Kalahandi, particularly among children, women, and the aged (Central Study Team, 1992: 5; 1993: 3). One comparative village-level study of health and nutrition in Kalahandi showed a high mortality rate among children in the 0–4 age group, and moderate to severe levels of malnourishment, by I.C.D.S. gradation, among over 80 per cent of pre-school children (Behura and Das, 1991: 116). It also noted,

---

[41] The development strategy is held responsible for the destruction of wage employment in the area, leading to migration. In 1954, the average labourer had 268 days of work available, which has now fallen by over 50 per cent to 128 days per year (Jagdish Pradhan of the Paschim Orissa Krishijeevi Sangh, quoted in Sainath, 1996: 161).

in these children, stunting and slower skeletal growth, which are generally associated with chronic malnutrition over a long period along with high levels of parasitic infestation. Wasting, or reduced fat mass, a disease characteristic of famine, was also seen in over 60 per cent of pre-school children both from drought-affected and unaffected villages of Kalahandi.

The Tour Report of the Central Study Team (1993) also cites the District Collector as confirming the incidence of bonded labour, taken to Andhra Pradesh from Kalahandi. The economic compulsion of poor parents and sometimes their indebtedness accounts for the servitude of their children. The same report cites recent evidence of the sale of children whose parents could not support them; and of the sale of girls to Bombay brothels.[42]

A study of the credit delivery system in Kalahandi has also recorded large-scale dependence on moneylenders and the predictable accumulation of debt (Rajashekhar and Vyasulu, 1990).[43] On the other hand, it has been argued that moneylenders (*sahukars*) are not seen as greedy and exploitative villains, but as demigods who provide help in times of hardship (Currie, 1993: 169). While it is claimed that efforts have been made in the late 1980s to strengthen the rural credit system of banking in Kalahandi, small farmers were in 1989 being served notices by banks and cooperative societies for non-payment of loans. The Mishra Commission Report, in fact, commented on the coercion and harassment resorted to for their recovery. Unable to produce and sell anything for the preceding three years, their lands and properties were being attached and auctioned with eager new buyers in the person of rich farmers, contractors, and traders (*Economic and Political Weekly*, 11.3.1989: 485), some of these from neighbouring Andhra Pradesh.

---

[42] A Government report published in 1941 dwelt upon the sale of children in this area at some length. It produced evidence of 'domestic serfdom', of the sending of children into perpetual bondage in exchange for loans of money (*Report of the Partially Excluded Areas Enquiry Committee, Orissa*, 1940, cited by J. P. Singh Deo, n.d.: 1).

[43] Most often, it is hunger that compels the taking of usurious loans. The interest rates vary from 120 to 380 per cent a year. Further, moneylenders adapt the forms of extortion to local circumstances: in some blocks, they take land; in others, they extract the produce; and in yet others, they command labour free of charge. Formal rural credit has shrunk, increasing the dependence of the peasant on the moneylender (Sainath, 1996: 216–18).

Crime rates can also be indicators of popular response to
scarcity, particularly if disaggregated in terms of looting, theft, and
rioting for food.[44] In the absence of any phenomenon remotely
akin to food riots in Kalahandi, it is difficult to endow crime rates
with special significance. There is however something mysterious
about the markedly declining trend in all crimes (including murder,
dacoity, burglary, robbery, and rioting) except for the category of
'miscellaneous' that increases sharply in 1986 and 1987 (District
Statistical Handbook: 70).[45]

In the backdrop of these suggestive data, it is interesting to
explore the response of some Study Teams sent by the Central
Government to Kalahandi to make an assessment of the situation.
In 1992, a Central Team[46] visited Orissa to examine the impact of
poverty alleviation/nutrition/health programmes operating in the
districts of Koraput and Kalahandi in Orissa to place in perspective
the reasons why the tribals of this region were 'dying'. The Special
Relief Commissioner of the Orissa Government presented a
memorandum to the Central Team which was described, in its
title, as visiting the State to study 'The Reported Distress Conditions'. Barring these four words in the title, the memorandum
makes no mention of drought, or even 'distress', the genteel official
euphemism for widespread hunger. It refers to the poverty and
illiteracy of a vast segment of the population, and its objective as
that of improving the 'poor nutritional status and health condition'

[44] David Arnold (1984: 92) writes that the famine of 1876–8 in Madras
Presidency resulted in the highest recorded level of crime in Madras between
the 1850s and the 1940s. Even the Bihar Famine Report shows that, during
the famine of 1966–7, robberies increased by 51.6 per cent, and there was a
considerable increase in dacoities, burglaries, and thefts, particularly of
foodgrains. The report concluded that the incidence of crime closely approxi-
mates the degree of distress (Government of Bihar, 1978: 410–22).

[45] Bob Currie (1993: 187) records on the basis of interviews, that levels of
theft had increased in the Boden region during the period of food crisis. These
thefts, mostly of paddy and corn, were generally from the smaller farms, as
large farmers were likely to be more influential, and to have fewer compunc-
tions about handing over the thieves to the police.

[46] This was a team from the Department of Agriculture and Cooperation
in the Union Ministry of Agriculture. Its members included a Deputy
Secretary of this department, along with a Deputy Commissioner from the
Union Ministry of Rural Development, and an Under-Secretary from the
Department of Women and Child Development.

of vulnerable groups 'by strengthening the essential elements of social infrastructure like Nutrition Intervention and Health Services'. (Memorandum to Central Team, 1992: 1.) The Memorandum lists the allocations and coverage of rural development programmes such as the Jawahar Rozgar Yojana, the Integrated Rural Development Programme, and feeding programmes, and makes recommendations for further development projects, especially HANDOUT (Health and Nutrition Development of Undeveloped Territories), for which it requests a grant of Rs 36.29 crores from the Prime Minister's Relief Fund.

The memorandum indicates the tribal population as a special focus, e.g. for housing, repairs, rural water supply, but betrays a continued bias towards paddy. Its long-term solution for food security is the setting up of grain banks to stock rice and wheat. Similarly, it seeks central assistance to prevent shifting (*podu*) cultivation practised by the tribal people, and to replace it by schemes for investment-intensive horticulture and coffee plantations. This is justified by the argument that the tribal people are growing 'uneconomic crops' in the highlands which can be more remuneratively used (op. cit.: 4). That these may be the staple foods of their diet is altogether ignored.

The Report of the Central Study Team retains the focus on the tribal population, but comes to grips more directly with the problems of health and nutrition:

The abject poverty of the tribals leaves them with no choice but to depend on 'tamarind seeds' and 'mango stones' (kernel) to which some ragi or maize is added to make a gruel. During June to September (monsoons) these tribals in the interior do not have any means of employment whatsoever and consequently no food other than 'mango stones' and 'tamarind seeds'. The moist weather conditions and poor storage leads to fungus growth, which makes consumption of mango stones and tamarind seeds a health hazard to the already emaciated tribal population. The tribals, therefore, suffer from Bacillary Dysentery, Gastroenteritis, Jaundice, Anaemia, Food Poisoning, etc. Health care is nonexistent as the lack of communication facilities make it impossible to reach any health centre [Report of the Central Study Team on Koraput and Kalahandi, 1992: 2.]

And further:

The tribals of all age groups are seriously under-nourished. Children, females and the old particularly show signs of undernourishment and physical weakness. Though no statistics were readily available about infant mortality, it was apparent from the severe-malnutrition amongst children that mortality rates would be quite high. This is made worse by the non-availability of preventive or curative medical care. [ibid.: 5.]

The Team observed that, though there were 94 sanctioned medical institutions in Kalahandi district, these were poorly equipped and lacking in basic facilities. The budget for medicines was low, and at least one-third of the staff were generally absent from duty. The lack of vehicles and roads further increased their inaccessibility, and frequent epidemics therefore meant a heavy toll of human lives (ibid.: 3). In the medical service, as in the local educational, agricultural and revenue bureaucracy, it found vacancies of the order of one-third, as it was difficult to persuade officials to accept a posting to a district as backward as this (ibid.: 6).

It concluded that at the root of Kalahandi's distress lay abject poverty: while the immediate causes of the deaths may have been food poisoning, gastroenteritis, and meningitis, it was malnutrition, ignorance, and ill-health that rendered the tribal population vulnerable to these. Such was the magnitude of their insecurity that food aid provided by voluntary groups was being saved for times when even mango stones might not be available (ibid.: 6).

Starvation and poverty, the team recommended, could only be overcome by a comprehensive package of land reform, including the restoration of lands alienated from the tribals; the provision of minimum holdings to them; and the development of common property resources such as village wastelands by giving rights of lease to the landless. Other measures for creating a self-sustaining economy and permanent income-generating assets could only complement this. The Team insisted on monthly monitoring and review of the development programmes by Secretaries of the Orissa Government.

In March 1993, another Central Team, this one from the Union Ministry of Rural Development,[47] visited Kalahandi and Bolangir, to study the implementation of the rural development programmes there. It observed many 'symptoms of distress' (Tour Report of Bolangir and Kalahandi Districts, 1993: 2), including heavy outmigration, underemployment, malnourishment, bondedness,

---

[47] This team included a Joint Secretary (Finance), a Deputy Commissioner (Rural Employment), and Deputy Secretary (Rural Marketing and Rural Housing).

the sale of children, the sale of girls, and a high incidence of disease. From December to June, the villagers, mostly landless *sukhavasis*, would migrate to places like Raipur, Bhilai and even distant Ayodhya, in search of employment as rickshaw-pullers or un-skilled labourers, and the outmigration was of the order of 20–2 per cent, according to official statistics. As there is no *rabi* crop in Kalahandi, there are no opportunities for wage labour from December–June; and even government works such as the Jawahar Rozgar Yojana provide work for only 15–20 days in the year. The Team noted that malnourishment and undernourishment were in evidence everywhere. It was told by the District Collector, Ashok Dalwai, that 24 bonded labourers had been recently found in Karimnagar (Andhra Pradesh), freed, and returned to Kalahandi. Likewise, in Bolangir, it found that children belonging to benefi-ciary families of the TRYSEM (Training of Rural Youth for Self-Employment) programme were not being sent to school because they were held in bondage by the local *mahajan*s to whom their parents were in debt. Some children, it found, were sold because of the inability of their parents to feed them. In Komna Block, Kalahandi, the Team found that girls were sold to a person in Bombay for prostitution. On the reported starvation deaths, the Report observed:

During the course of the tour we were informed that the district authorities have been receiving from time to time over the last six months news of reported deaths due to starvation.... In the village of Babupali in Nawapara Sub- Division...six to seven deaths have been reported some time back. On enquiry from the SDO, Nawapara, it was found that the age of the people who died varied from mid-40s to 70s. The village was virtually cut off from the mainstream for almost four to five months during the monsoon and after due to no culverts and access. As a result of this, it was hard to get essential supplies, medical care, etc. which led to distress. In any case, being a remote village there were [sic] no scope for the local employment over there. So it was incumbent on people who either migrated in search of employment or to suffer destitution in the village. [ibid.:4].

It also noted several cases of tuberculosis, polio, scabies, and water-related diseases, as well as the non-availability of health staff, medicines, and rehabilitative services.

The programmes of rural development being implemented in Kalahandi are many and varied: they include the Drought Prone Areas Programme (DPAP), the Jawahar Rozgar Yojana (JRY), ADAPT, the Integrated National Wasteland Development

Programme, Accelerated Rural Water Supply, Integrated Rural Development Programme (IRDP), Training of Rural Youth for Self-Employment (TRYSEM), Development of Women and Children in Rural Areas (DWCRA), Integrated Child Development Services (ICDS), the Million Wells Scheme, and the Indira Awas Yojana, among others. On the water harvesting structures, the team noted that it was not always possible to take a scientific decision about the location of the works, due to local pulls and pressures (ibid.: 5). In Bhawanipatna, it found that a substantial water body which had the potential to develop a fisheries project generating Rs 15–20,000 per annum, was being auctioned to a private contractor for Rs 2000 only (ibid.: 6). District Rural Development Agencies' (DRDA) funds were being used to augment departmental funds, which were used up in paying salaries. This Team, like the earlier one, also blamed the skewed landholding pattern for the widespread impoverishment. In one successful case, in the Dalguma Diversion Weir in Thomalrampur Block, executed through ADAPT funds in 1989–90, it observed that there was less outmigration and greater material gain to be seen in the families below the poverty line who were involved with the project as wage earners and as future *patta* owners of the wastelands being developed (ibid.: 8).

While commending the efforts of the local development bureaucracy, however, the Team emphasized the need for greater state support to expand the networks of these officials, and the need for voluntary action groups in the fields of literacy, health, and social welfare. In a comprehensive list of 25 recommendations, the Team emphasized that 'State intervention was required both for short-term relief and long-term solutions for sustainable employment for people living below poverty line' (ibid.: 21). While the short-term measures would only provide immediate relief, the long-term investments were required to create improvements in irrigation, land and water management, crop diversification, and to enable *rabi* cultivation.

Has Kalahandi then suffered from a shortage of funds? In absolute terms, perhaps; but in relative terms, Kalahandi has been more generously provisioned than most other districts of Orissa. A glance at the JRY allocations for drought-affected districts in 1992–3 makes this evident. It also shows, however, that Kalahandi's percentage utilization of these funds till 1993, was the lowest; substantially lower than that of other districts. The Central Team from the Ministry of Rural Development which visited Kalahandi in March 1993, was told that the funds arrived late, and that an increase in foodgrain prices had caused problems in calculating the quantities to be lifted from the godowns of the Food Corporation of India.

In the matter of employment-generation through major and medium irrigation projects in drought-affected districts, the highest budgetary provision in 1992–3 was for Kalahandi, which again reported the lowest percentage utilization among the 11 districts till January 1993. The expenditure on drought mitigation measures out of the Calamity Relief Fund (1992–3) similarly shows the highest outlay of Rs 132.39 lakhs for Kalahandi. All other districts, apart from Bolangir, at Rs 126.32 lakhs, are below 90 lakhs (see Table).

Expenditure on Drought Mitigation Measures Out of
Calamity Relief Fund, 1992–3

District	CRF Allotment (Rs in lakhs)
Bolangir	126.32
Balasore	0.05
Cuttack	37.10
Dhenkanal	33.30
Gajapati	–
Ganjam	–
Kalahandi	132.39
Keonjhar	89.95
Koraput	66.40
Malkangiri	80.40
Mayurbhanj	69.40
Nowrangpur	3.50
Phulbani	0.25
Puri	–
Rayagada	39.60
Sambalpur	62.87
Sundergarh	81.90
Total	823.13

Source: Government of Orissa, White Paper on Drought Situation in Orissa, 1992–3.

There is no doubt but that state interventionism in this scenario of destitution has taken the form of massive funding for emergency feeding and gratuitous relief. In 1992-3 alone, 'pure relief' expenditure was Rs 1339.65 lakhs, with Rs 806.53 lakhs allotted for drought mitigation. Between 1985-90, the funds allotted for employment-oriented development works were never fully utilized (Mishra Commission Report, 1991: 45, 50-1). The inability of Kalahandi to utilize development funds and its manifest ability to absorb calamity relief expenditure, without visible improvements, is possibly indicative of irregularities in the use of the latter, which are more difficult in the use of regular development funds. The continuing distress of Kalahandi is a pointer to either misguided and unplanned utilization or misutilization per se.

I have discussed above the politics of nomenclature in the description of a food crisis as drought or famine; the politics of selective appeal to theories of famine causation, as they emphasize falling levels of local productivity rather than entitlements; the politics of information control in relation to famine demography; and, finally, the conditions of structural backwardness and underdevelopment that appear to be comprehended by policy-makers, but fail to find reflection in policy initiatives. I turn now, in the final section of this chapter, to an analysis of the ideology and politics of state intervention as it responds philanthropically, rather than in ways designed to reduce the long-term vulnerability of a people to variations in climatic and productive factors, and enhance their capabilities for sustainable development.

IV. THE STATE, DEMOCRACY AND CITIZENSHIP

How do people cope with scarcity and hunger? In general, the sale of productive assets and migration in search of employment are the most common survival strategies (Chen, 1991). For those who have no assets to sell except their labour, wage labour on relief works and free kitchens provided by the state or non-governmental agencies are frequently the only mode of sustenance. In the eighteenth century, as we have seen, hostility to gratuitous relief was part of the ideology of laissez-faire, and non-interventionism an aspect of the minimal state. Today, it may be used to mount a more radical critique, as initiatives in the form of gratuitous relief can also be seen as disabling, rather than enabling; as creating and entrenching dependence rather than empowering people. There is, thus, an ideological dimension to state provisioning that may be appreciated as welfare or deplored as control through charity. In either perspective, the initiative rests squarely with the state, and there is no space for rights-based claims, e.g. for a right to subsistence or a right to development.

What is considerably more difficult to explain is the mystery of why Kalahandi has silently suffered in this age of democratic politics? From 1985 to 1993, an eight year span, there has, on the government's own account, been no appreciable improvement in Kalahandi. Partisan politics have, at every step, jeopardized the prospects of pulling it out of the morass and several Prime Ministerial visits (including one by P. V. Narasimha Rao in April 1993 and another by H. D. Deve Gowda in November 1996) have not been successful in accomplishing a change in state policy or strategy. What has been a haunting constant is the silence and the passivity of the local populace. Gradually, and almost invisibly, a routinization of destitution has taken place, and the helpless acquiescence of the victims of grinding poverty has also caused the issue to disappear from the political agenda into the same oblivion to which Kalahandi has long been consigned.

State intervention, whether in the form of relief expenditure or of development funds, has clearly not reduced the vulnerability of the poor to hunger, or rendered them capable of independent means of survival. If anything, dependence on state charity has probably accentuated their passivity. Sunk in backwardness and abject poverty, without land to till or employment to labour and without education or training, they are deprived even of the means of articulating protest. Resources have flowed into Kalahandi in the past few years, but have generally come in late, misutilized, misadministered, and possibly even misappropriated on their way to those for whom they were intended. The vested interests and middlemen involved in relief as well as in development programmes have contributed further to the existing distortions.

Meanwhile, the demands articulated by politicians have generally centred around big schemes such as irrigation projects. The development of irrigation schemes would obviously benefit only those who have land, rather than the landless. Schemes sanctioned two decades ago continue to be incomplete, and in any case the identifiable beneficiaries of existing irrigation projects include largely the extended family of the former ruler (Pipal Nalla M.I.P.;

Jamuna Sagar M.I.P.; and Devisagar, M.I.P.); Gountia families (Karuna Sagar M.I.P.); and Government agricultural farms (Ashasagar M.I.P.) (Pradhan, 1993: 1087). The legislators of Kalahandi own irrigated lands, though they are not dependent on agriculture for their livelihood. They have preferred to press demands for projects that would benefit industry rather than agriculture in the chronically drought-affected areas.

The structural causes of Kalahandi's poverty and backwardness have thus gone unattended. The reform of an inequitous landowning structure remains unattempted, though Central Government teams have pointed to the high rate of landlessness, and the large number of marginal and small landholdings, lacking access to irrigation and appropriate technology for rainfed agriculture. There is an urgent need for restoring to the tribal people land illegally alienated from them, and for the development of common property resources to give lease rights to the landless. A change in the landholding pattern, biased towards tribal and other landless people, is a necessary first step for the emancipation of Kalahandi. In addition, the incidence of bonded labour and high levels of indebtedness must also be addressed by public policy.

Meanwhile, the state, local and national, would appear to have participated in a possibly wilful misreading of both the objective condition of Kalahandi, as well as of the meaning of welfare. Poverty and endemic, even epidemic, hunger have been attributed exclusively to drought, disregarding the fact that drought has such social consequences precisely when it strikes an already weak and feeble economy like that of Kalahandi. In any event, Kalahandi, as we have seen, reports starvation even when the monsoon is timely and adequately precipitative.

To read this condition as a problem of drought, and to attempt to resolve it through spasmodic measures of relief in the form of food supplies to meet immediate needs, is therefore inadequate. Drought may and has occurred, but it has acted so as to compound and worsen an already debilitated constitution. On the other hand, however, to read this as a problem of welfare, and to attempt to address it through institutionalized charity is also insufficient. This conception of welfare precludes the provision of conditions for development. In the language of Drèze and Sen (1991: 3), it is a protection-oriented, rather than a promotion-oriented, policy. Eventually, even protection is not achieved, though vast sums of money are ostensibly expended on it. It is not an accident that the Baidyanath Mishra Commission in 1991 recommended that social welfare functionaries of the Government should be instrumental in educating people on how to assert their legal and constitutional rights (op. cit.: 72),[48] and that rehabilitation should not begin and end with provision of Government subsidies as largesse (ibid.: 64).

The policies of the state towards Scheduled Castes and Tribes have always been predominantly expressive of a charity perspective. In Kalahandi, the landless and poor, mostly composed of these social groups, are implicitly governed as subjects, rather than as citizens. Welfare as charity deprives them of the rights and entitlements that accompany citizenship. Lacking effective citizenship, they also lack rights. Lacking information, and the means or opportunity to acquire it, they lack also the wherewithal to access democratic institutions and processes through which to articulate their demands. Like terminal patients, the terminally poor of Kalahandi await neighbours to report them sick, visiting consultants to diagnose their ailment, and philanthropists to sustain them. But the rationale of the prescription remains unclear.

In their judgement on the two public interest litigations before the Orissa High Court, the judges made a significant pronouncement:

When such a large segment of population feels oppressed due to various forms of exploitation, to be tortured further by the vagaries of nature, the Government, who in our constitutional set up has to look after the welfare of the down-trodden, has to come out in a big way to save people from starvation deaths, distress sale of children and other forms of gross extinction and violation of the rights conferred on every citizen of India by the Constitution [O.J.C. 3517/88 and O.J.C. 525/89, 1992: 2].

At one level, the story of Kalahandi is a vindication of the resounding success of adversarial representative democracy. The starvation deaths and the sale of babies by hungry relatives was brought to public notice by state legislators and the press. It was in response to this publicity that the hunger of Kalahandi was

[48] Justice Radhacharan Patnaik, a senior judge of the Orissa High Court and Chairman of the State Legal Aid and Advisory Board, addressing a Lok Adalat at Bhawanipatna (Kalahandi's district headquarters), exhorted his audience to 'rise in revolt against injustice', assuring them that the courts were inclined to help such a movement (*The Telegraph*, 5 Jan. 1989).

catapulted out of dark obscurity into the national and even international limelight. It was this, too, that prompted a defensive state to provide for Kalahandi. The generosity of the state's response could be a perfect illustration of the public action model of democracy. Currie (1993), for instance, has seen in this a reassuring confirmation of the Drèze and Sen thesis (1989). But it is important not to lose sight of the fact that none of this pressure was authentically representative, being the voicing of protest on behalf of, rather than by, the affected people.[49] It is clear today that the local population is completely marginal, not only to the democratic process, but also to the admittedly imperfect model of development adopted by the state. Dehumanized and over-exploited into passivity, its existence bears embarassing testimony to the absence of democracy from the lives and experiences of common people.

On the other hand, even the argument about the success of adversarial democracy, bringing to national light the terrible condition of Kalahandi, is contestable. Thus, when Baidyanath Mishra sent out notices to elicit information about the socio-economic indicators of Kalahandi, and the development projects in operation there, only three voluntary agencies responded. The inquiry judge gloomily noted:

No report has been received from any private individual, public men, mediamen or any elected representative of the district [1991: 4].

The passivity and absence of articulation, whether of demands or of protest, may only partially be explained by the low levels of literacy that obtain in the district. Any explanation must take into account the fact that the situation that came to light in 1985 was by no means in stark contrast to that which preceded it. If the endemic hunger of Kalahandi had been a sudden and dramatic aberration from a previously existing situation of near-sufficiency

[49] Despite the success of radical political formations such as the People's War Group, or the Chhatisgarh Mukti Morcha in the neighbouring states of Andhra Pradesh and Madhya Pradesh, organizations like the Kalahandi Liberation Front or the Western Orissa Liberation Front (WOLF) have virtually no base among the poor, and are principally supported by students and the middle-classes. Their primary aim, in any case, is separate statehood, rather than the redressal of social inequalities which is clearly secondary (Currie, 1993: 403–4).

and food security, protest could have been expected. Historical examples suggest that food riots generally occur when scarcity oocurs in a situation previously characterized by food availability and sufficiency. When high prices and/or hoarding affect entitlements and/or availability, violent protest may indeed occur. In Kalahandi, however, availability was at no time in question. The per capita availability of cereals, pulses, and oilseeds has been calculated as standing at 210 kg, 110 kg, and 40 kg respectively in 1990–1, taking only local production into account. With state control over the public distribution system and state-regulated prices, hoarding and sharp price rises are ruled out. Clearly, it is entitlements, in the sense of means of employment, income generation, and consequently purchasing power, that are lacking, resulting in destitution which, in its extreme form, transmutes into starvation and eventually cessation of being.

Thus, if the money poured into Kalahandi is interpreted as a sign of the dramatic success of democratic politics, its other face is the manifest dependence of Indian democracy on mediatory forces. Too poor, ignorant, and powerless to understand or remedy the structural causes of their misery, the people are silent sufferers, fighting only for survival, too severely handicapped to participate. They have been placed on the agenda by others, constituted by others, and remain completely dependent on assistance initiated by others, through ostensibly democratic means. They lack not only rights, but also the agency by which to claim them.

The democracy enlisted on behalf of these citizens of India is actually exclusionary, underlining their threefold exclusion: from the economy, as landless and sometimes bonded labour; from society, as mostly Scheduled Castes and Tribes; and from the polity, as participation even in the minimal political act of voting without knowledge and information is meaningless. These, then, are the doubly, if not trebly, disadvantaged citizens of Kalahandi. The overlap between particular social groups (namely, the *dalits* and tribals), and the category of landless agricultural labour, is too striking to escape notice. Together, the Scheduled Castes and Tribes account for 84 per cent of the agricultural labour force of Kalahandi district. Viewing the abysmally low literacy rates of these groups (15.58 per cent of the Scheduled Castes and 10.10 per cent of the Scheduled Tribes) in conjunction with this occupational profile, it hardly needs underscoring that the conditions for effective citizenship are absent.

In any assessment of the role of the state, a necessary preliminary is the disaggregation of at least three organizational levels: the local state, the national state, and a crucial intermediary level, that of the regional state.[50] The local state, as we have seen, has been indifferent and apathetic, often making common cause with local élites, rich farmers, moneylenders and contractors. Influential politicians are also often large landowners, having links with *gountia* families, concerned to promote large projects that are likely to benefit the already prosperous. The examples cited of engineers intentionally holding up building works, and of the contentious nature of deciding the location of water-harvesting structures, are aspects of this. Local complaints have also been recorded of bank officials who appropriate a large portion of the loans they grant; of the profiteering by middlemen in the administration of the JRY; of the intimidation of the poor by family planning officials; of the bribery and corruption rampant even in the Welfare Extension Office; and of the illegal 'sale' and transfer of vast amounts of tribal land.

The other face of this supremely exploitable backwardness is its unattractiveness to government officials who regard it as a punishment posting which they actively work to avoid. Thus, about one-third of the total official positions, including in the medical departments, remain unfilled. The lack of staffing, combined with the malfunctioning of existing staff, has been noted by Central teams in 1992 and 1993, and is hardly conducive to the efficient implementation of development policy.

Finally, the local state has been galvanized into activity only when questions have been raised in the Legislative Assembly. Thus, the House Committee

observed with regret that not a single case of death allegation was enquired into by the District Administration in time. All such enquiries were made only after adjournment motions, calling attention notices and starred questions, were put in the House. The District Administration became aware of the

[50] In an interesting historical throwback, Sheila Zurbrigg has argued that relief in the Madras famine of 1876–7 was grossly ineffective 'due in no small part to conflicting policies between the two levels of government', resulting in the death of three million people despite a relief expenditure of Rs 80 million (1996: 4).

gravity of the situation only after the concerned Ministers paid their visits to different districts and the matter was discussed repeatedly on the floor of the Assembly [1987: 14].

The intermediate level of the state government is crucial to our analysis. In relation to the national government, it plays a basically mendicant role, seeking funds and relief assistance. With the Centre too it shares the subsidized rice and cheap saris conception of relief. It is, however, the whipping boy of adversarial politics, which puts it on the defensive, and renders it accountable for the hardship. The Orissa Government has responded to democratic pressures by, on the one hand, firmly denying the occurrence of starvation deaths and, on the other, petitioning the Centre for money, thereby fostering an attitude of abdication of responsibility.

Finally, the national state has been involved primarily in its role as fund-giver. Once the money is given to the state government, the Central government loses interest in it and surrenders control over it.[51] Far from attempting to monitor the expenditure, the Government of India does not even maintain data regarding the district-wise or sectoral allocations made by the State government. Clearly, then, the Centre in turn chooses to abdicate responsibility once it has provisioned the State government.

The more visible, though less meaningful, aspect of the Centre's involvement is in the political visits made by Prime Ministers to the worst-hit areas. These tokens of concern belong to the realm of modern political ritualism and are exercises expected to fructify in terms of enhanced legitimacy as well as votes. The visits of a charismatic leader like Rajiv Gandhi were in keeping with the philosophy of welfare as charity that I have posited. In this case, the charity was initially personalized rather than institutionalized, with Operation Salvage and ADAPT being announced by the Prime Minister himself. The glory of this generosity was expected to redound not only to the long-term credit of the Congress party, but also to add to the aura of his personal lustre. He came as healer, deliverer, and messiah, briefly engaged with his subjects, and left suffused in a glow of personal philanthropic virtue. The visit further underscored the abjectness of a category of citizens,

---

[51] Author's interviews with officials in the Ministry of Rural Development, as well as in the Natural Disaster Management Division of the Ministry of Agriculture, Government of India.

completely lacking in even an awareness of their rights and the requirements of justice, let alone any conception of equality. The 'socialistic' welfare state of independent India responded thus to situations of extreme want.

At each of these levels, the state manifests an uneven relationship with society: combative towards some forces and collusive with others. This is an important pointer to the heterogeneity of society, and a warning against treating it as a unified, undifferentiated category in relation to the state. The national state, at farthest remove from local society, assumes a supererogatory role of paternalistic benevolence, with its attendant negation of the rights of citizenship. A philosophy of welfare divorced from a commitment to, or even recognition of, rights, converts citizens into subjects, albeit enfranchised ones. Enfranchisement confined to a public sphere created by formal democratic institutions is intrinsically less challenging than the articulation of rights-claims by an aware, even if unenfranchised, citizenry. The experience of the movement for independence would appear to endorse this. The Indian state's welfare creed is an effective instrument of governance and of winning legitimacy, even as it simultaneously undermines the participative capabilities of citizens. Institutions of formal democracy enable crises to be reduced to manageable proportions, and prevent them from developing into more threatening forms of extra-institutional protest.

At the intermediate level, a similar relationship prevails, except that the welfarist element is diluted, and a greater vulnerability to dominant local interests is exemplified. The political barometer being geographically closer to the area of its dominion, it is naturally more sensitive to the interests of those who are locally important. In the choice and sanctioning of projects and development schemes, as well as in the selection of intermediaries, these interests play a crucial role. If they happen also to be directly engaged in political activity, their efforts enjoy greater legitimacy as being representative of the popular will.

At the local level, the relationship between state and society becomes less paternalistic, and more directly exploitative, as state functionaries browbeat the illiterate poor into submission, and routinely extract a price, or commission, for every welfare activity of which they happen to be the implementors. This exploitative relationship is accentuated by the overlap between the interests of politicians, rich farmers, contractors, and traders who corner the benefits of development activity, to augment their personal fortunes, while backwardness is further entrenched. Ironically, however, the exploitative practices of moneylenders are perceived as benevolent and charitable.

The relationship between state and society is thus marked by superordination and subordination, for the most part replicating the social relations obtaining within local society. The democratic process is unable to alter this or even mediate it, for the greater the proximity of the state to the sphere of its action, the more pronounced the evanescence of democracy. The local state, as we have seen, manifests the least receptivity to, and participativeness in, the local predicament. The regional and national states are more attentive to legislative and media opinion, but are also thereby released from assuming greater responsibility than the minimum required by formal democratic institutions.

Paradoxically, these structures of democracy actually reduce accountability, instead of enhancing it, and endow with legitimacy policies and practices that deserve to be interrogated. What appears to be the strength of representative democracy is demonstrably a mask of success, disguising failure. As scholars and others celebrate procedural democracy, the search for substantive participatory democracy is altogether abandoned, and with it the struggle for rights and justice.

3

The Secular State

The Indian nation-state at independence was confronted with the task of creating a unified national and political society out of a formidable diversity of regional, religious, linguistic, and caste identities. In large measure, such an exercise of welding together was necessitated by the contrariness of modern institutions and the procedures of political decision-making that invested these divisions with a greater political salience than they had ever before enjoyed. The significant lines of division had been long in the making, and the colonial state had undoubtedly contributed to their crystallization.[1] Indeed, the recognition by the demitting imperial power of the legitimacy of religion underwriting claims to political self-determination, bequeathed to the young republic a legacy that continues to haunt it to the present, with claims to self-determination—in the form of demands for greater autonomy and sometimes even secession—being grounded in a variety of social cleavages.

The most overtly conflictual aspects of Indian politics have, in recent years, been those directly related to ascriptive identities (variously, Punjab, Assam, Kashmir, Ayodhya, Mandal). Class-based conflict has remained on the fringes except where class issues have overlapped with the former type, such as riots related to

[1] Cf. Gyanendra Pandey (1990: ch. 2) on the role of the colonial state in the very construction of communalism through, for instance, the colonial narrative of the communal riot. Sandria Frietag (1990: 5–6) has also explored how communities have been redefined under pressure of an expanding interventionist state, though this is differently expressed in local communities in different parts of the country. On Africa, see David Laitin (1985) on how the colonial state apparatus in the Yorubaland province of Nigeria structured the hierarchy of sociocultural cleavages and shaped long-term political cleavages in society.

job-reservations or violence against *dalits*. On to this map of society, already inscribed with complex and inter-cutting lines of division, the state has, albeit fitfully and inconsistently, attempted to superscribe an alternate pattern, in accordance with a pre-ordained design, the origins and precise content of which however remain obscure.[2]

As the state in 1947 positioned itself above society, it did so not only in consonance with the basic premises of its adopted ideology of liberal neutrality, but chose also to extend this principle to its relationship with a culturally plural society. The extension was altogether too neat to be effective. It rested upon a mistaken equivalence between interest and pressure groups, on the one hand, and cultural and religious communities, on the other, and offered an identical liberal pluralist solution for both. It also ignored the possibility—surprising, given the backdrop of Partition—that these lines of division might be exploited, through cynical ideological gerrymandering to gain easy access to political power.

In no sphere was the imagery of the state standing above society given the lie as effectively as at the point of its intersection with religion. The conception of secularism adopted by the Indian state conveyed an implicit denial of the state's embeddedness in society, suggesting a state benignly disposed towards, but equidistant from, all religions.[3] There are few areas in which this embeddedness is so vividly illustrated as in the case of the reform of religious personal law. This is a complex and multifaceted issue that reveals the tensions between two distinct aspects of the modernizing

---

[2] Subrata Mitra (1991) considers it paradoxical that Indian democracy does not have the institutional means to articulate demands regarding religious policy, even though religion is a political force capable of moving millions of people. What he fails to mention, of course, is the fact that religious appeal is routinely exploited to garner votes, so that electoral politics express the religious impulse, even if state institutions do not. This disjuncture between state discourse and electoral politics may call for a greater emphasis on religion as private faith, rather than for a desecularization of the state, as Mitra suggests.

[3] It has been argued that two very different understandings of secularism— the Nehruvian and the Gandhian—have been competing since Independence for ideological dominance. While Nehru's idea of *dharma nirpekshata* was based on the separation of religion and politics, Gandhi's concept of *sarva dharma sambhava* was based on the principle of equal respect for all religions (Cossman and Kapur, 1996: 2621).

agenda of the Indian state: the first, its promise of providing a secular public sphere and a secular state, and the second, its self-arrogated role as social reformer, seeking to effect gender equality. In this chapter, I focus on the reform of the Muslim Personal Law on maintenance for divorcees, an issue that became a cause célébre in 1985–6 when the Supreme Court delivered a landmark judgement in the case of *Shah Bano* vs. *Mohammed Ahmed Khan* (Criminal Appeal No. 103 of 1981) in April 1985. The scale of mobilization against the judgement was more than matched by the subsequent mobilization of opinion against the Muslim Women (Protection of Rights on Divorce) Bill, introduced by the Rajiv Gandhi government in February 1986, to nullify the effect of the controversial judgement. The Bill received legislative endorsement and presidential assent on 19 May 1986, and so entered the statute books. Most chroniclers of contemporary history are agreed upon the fact that the Shah Bano case constitutes a watershed and is, along with the conflict over the Babri Masjid, one of the two most important landmarks in the recent history of the Indian followers of Islam.[4] The renewed feminist debate on a Uniform Civil Code may also be traced to this case which demonstrated conclusively that claims to gender justice or women's rights had poor prospects when pitted against claims to rights of religious community.

By way of background, it is proposed here to first draw a comparison between the process leading up to the enactment of the various legislations that sought to reform Hindu personal law in the 1950s, and the career of the Muslim personal law till the Shah Bano judgement. As reforms targeted at the personal law of the majority and minority communities respectively, these are almost exactly mirror opposites of each other: in terms of the way in which opinion was ranged; the arguments adduced in support of, and opposition to, them, and, above all, in the role of the state, almost appearing as if no time had elapsed between the two events. While it is reasonable to suppose that the Indian state of the 1950s

[4] Rudolph and Rudolph (1987: 45) describe the judgement as having had 'a national impact on Muslim consciousness', arousing a common concern in a community otherwise divided by region, language, and urban–rural differences. Embree considers the Shah Bano case to be linked to the Babri Masjid issue insofar as 'the report of the opening of the mosque for Hindu worship added to the uneasiness and fears that had been created already by the Shah Bano decision' (1992: 89).

was a substantially different creature from that of 1986, three decades later, a hypothetical elision of time reveals its character (in this respect) as fundamentally unchanged.[5]

The efforts of the state as social reformer thus reveal a state in retreat, in contrast to the officially projected state in the ascendant, firmly and masterfully directing the process of social transformation. In addition to demonstrating the embeddedness of the state in society, and its inability to override or subjugate traditional sources of authority (of whatever religious complexion), this chapter will also seek to highlight the internal divisions in the structure of the state, especially the contradictory pulls of a reformist Supreme Court and a politically cautious Government-in-Parliament. This case study will thus highlight the limits of an otherwise strongly interventionist state, constrained by factors both external (namely religious authority) and internal (divisions among the important agencies of state structure).

I. THE STATE IN RETREAT

In relation to social reform, and religious personal law in particular, the Indian state—including for the most part its colonial ancestor—has vacillated between policies of rigorous non-interference, on the one hand, and cautious intervention, on the other. In this section, I will briefly review the attitude of the colonial and post-colonial state towards personal law reform of both the Hindu and the Muslim communities. The distinction between personal and public law was drawn by the Company state in the mid-nineteenth century, and the state's efforts with regard to laws regulating the right to property in land were, as Washbrook has argued, constantly undermined by its position on personal law. While the one sought to accomplish the freeing of the individual to serve the needs of a market economy, the other sought to entrench 'ascriptive...status as the basis of individual right' (Washbrook, 1981: 654). This entrenchment was effected by the 'saving' of Hindu and Muslim personal laws, identifying a domain—that of laws pertaining to marriage, inheritance, caste rules, religious practices, and institutions—in which the writ of personal

---

[5] This reinforces the argument, in Chapter 1, that the character of the state is neither firmly fixed nor constantly changing, but that similarities and dissimilarities occur across both time and space.

law would continue to run, while other civil disputes and all criminal matters were brought within the ambit of the British law, to be decided in accordance with the canons of 'Justice, Equity and Good Conscience' (Galanter, 1989: 18).

In their administration of Hindu and Muslim personal law, the employees of the East India Company, euphemistically described as judges, were routinely assisted by a Muslim qazi and a Hindu pandit to interpret the law.[6] The policy of non-interference with the personal law of Hindus and Muslims was reinforced when the recommendation of the First Law Commission (appointed in 1834) to codify Hindu and Muslim personal law was overturned by the Second Law Commission on the grounds that a legislature that did not have the power to make religion, did not have the competence to enact religious laws (Government of India, 1958: 13). Further, in 1864, the Government of India did away with the services of *shastris*, by its 'assumption' of the Hindu law. This meant that the interpretation of personal law was immutably fixed, as the state now assumed its knowledge of Hindu law to be adequate (Derrett, 1968: 296). Not surprisingly, this tended to conserve and fossilize, rather than improve, religious law by modification or interpretation.[7]

It was not until the inter-war years that the British Government of India decided to withdraw the ban on social and religious interference. By this time, the colonial state was more openly receptive to the agrarian élite which had also by now become influential in the legislatures. These powerful, landowning members of rural society supported the rescission of the self-imposed

[6] Similar restraint was not however exercised when it came to the personal law of other communities such as the Parsis or Jews.

[7] Despite the economic imperatives of the colonial state, the law continued to support and second the conservative social order of agrarian society. The example of over a score of Gains of Learning Bills being sent from Madras Presidency, and returned unapproved, is a striking illustration of state reluctance to disturb tradition. The Bills sought to allow educated professionals to retain their earnings as their individual private property, but the customary pooling of such income with ancestral property was upheld. Nevertheless, British legal conceptions of rights, justice, and equity did find their way into the administration of even religious laws, quietly transforming them in a variety of ways, including some modifications made, willy-nilly, by the introduction of rules of procedure and evidence (Parashar, 1992: 72–3).

ban on religious interference, as a result of which some legislation was enacted granting women rights in property, and committees were set up to examine the possible reform of Hindu law. It has been suggested that in initiating such legislation, the colonial state was motivated not by any special concern for women's rights or the organization of social relations, but rather by the need to coopt the wielders of rural power (Washbrook, 1981: 698).

While Hindu law reform was being cautiously initiated in the inter-war years,[8] the field of Muslim personal law saw the greater entrenchment of religious authority through the enactment of the Muslim Personal Law (Shariat) Application Act, 1937. This legislation was defended as an attempt to improve the status of Muslim women, through ensuring the uniform applicability, across the country, of shariat law, replacing the customary law under which women enjoyed fewer rights. Even as the bill was justified by reference to its protection of women's rights of succession, however, it remained inapplicable to agricultural land which then constituted 99.5 per cent of all property in India (Parashar, 1992: 148). This was followed by the somewhat more progressive Dissolution of Muslim Marriage Act, 1939, which sought to reform the law pertaining to divorce. The reform was prompted by the fact that, under the prevalent Hanafi law, a marriage could not be dissolved at the instance of the woman. Muslim women seeking release from bad marriages were therefore forced to apostatize and convert to another religion, a matter which could not but be of concern to the clerics.

At independence, then, the Indian state inherited a situation of no inconsiderable ambiguity with regard to personal laws. By colonial tradition, these were within the purview of the state's legal system but at the same time the extent of its power to legislate on religious laws remained undefined and nebulous. Having assumed the mantle of restructuring society, and launching it on the path of modernity, the state could not but address the question of reforming personal law to bring about social change, especially as a major component of its agenda of modernization—an improvement in the status of women—was tied to this.

[8] Some important legislations of this period include the Hindu Inheritance (Removal of Disabilities) Act, 1928; the Child Marriage Restraint Act, 1929; the Hindu Gains of Learning Act, 1930; and the Hindu Women's Right to Property Act, 1937.

The first authoritative cue was provided by the Constituent Assembly, which had already defined the official policy on secularism, and inscribed it into the Constitution. While the Constitution sought to guarantee and protect the individual's right to freedom of conscience and religion, the issue of interpreting the limits of the freedom to profess and practice religion was a controversial one. Rajkumari Amrit Kaur, for instance, was opposed to the free 'practice' of religion on the grounds that it might legitimize abhorrent institutions such as *devadasis*, purdah and sati. A. K. Ayyar, her fellow member on the Rights Sub-Committee, supported this objection to the wide interpretation of 'practice', recalling that even the British, when enacting the Government of India Act of 1935, had been careful not to put in any provision that might close the door to social reform. Consequently, the Advisory Committee laid down that the right to freedom of religious practice should not prevent the state from legislating in the interest of social welfare and reform (Austin, 1976: 64). This caveat was reflected in the constitutional provisions (Article 25) which envisage the limitation of this right, where necessitated by considerations of public order, morality, and health.

Independence had, as it happened, supervened on an ongoing process of legislative deliberation on Hindu personal law reform. A comprehensive Hindu Code Bill—dealing with marriage and divorce, intestate succession, minority and guardianship, maintenance and adoption, and the *mitakshara* joint family—had been introduced in the Federal Legislative Assembly only a few months earlier, on 11 April 1947. A revised draft was debated by the Provisional Parliament, the dissolution of which in 1951 also signalled the lapse of the Bill. In 1948, it was introduced in the Constituent Assembly by the Law Minister, Dr B. R. Ambedkar. The very same legislators who had just written the principle of gender equality into the Constitution now rose as one to oppose the Hindu Code Bill. They included conservatives both within and without the Congress who objected to the provisions enforcing monogamy for Hindus; sanctioning divorce and alimony; and, above all, giving women equal rights to property.[9] Among others,

[9] As even Hindu fundamentalists within the Congress opposed the Bill, the opposition of the Hindu Mahasabha and its women's wing was predictably vociferous. The Mahasabha leaders opposed the Bill, ostensibly because it was

important nationalist leaders such as Sardar Patel, J. B. Kripalani, and Rajendra Prasad expressed their opposition to it. Prasad, as President, even threatened that he might reserve presidential assent were the Bill to go through the legislature.[10]

It is worth remarking that, even as the government justified its intervention in religious personal laws with reference to its right to modernize the nation, it simultaneously sought to establish that the reforms were in conformity with the *dharmashastras*. Much of the debate, prior to 1952, between the supporters and the opponents of the reform legislation was conducted with reference to the 'correct' interpretation of traditional law. Few, if any, sought to ground their arguments in non-ecclesiastical principles. Three decades later, the debate on the Muslim Women's Bill showed that the terms of the debate had not substantially altered.

After the elections, the Nehru government reintroduced the various components of the Hindu Code Bill as separate acts of legislation, and the Hindu Marriage Act (May 1955), the Hindu Succession Act (May 1956), the Hindu Adoption and Maintenance Act (December 1956), and the Dowry Prohibition Act (July 1961) entered the statute book. The new laws embodied some significant compromises, including the retention of the joint family; limited but unequal property rights for women in their paternal property; the possibility of disinheriting or reducing the share of female heirs; and, above all, the exclusion of agricultural land from the ambit of legislation relating to succession. Thus, while the laws relating to marriage and divorce were improved, property continued to

---

a communal (i.e. not universally applicable) measure, but were willing to endorse it if it were made into a uniform civil code applicable to all communities (Som, 1992: 5).

[10] Nehru, in reply, asserted that 'the President has no power or authority to go against the will of Parliament in regard to a Bill that has been well considered by it and passed' (Munshi, 1967: 583). He soon realized, however, that his optimism that the Bill would go through was misplaced, and he therefore decided to split it into separate parts, initially introducing only a Bill dealing with marriage and divorce. Meanwhile, in September 1951, the Bill came up for discussion, but was dropped after only four clauses had been passed. An ailing Ambedkar resigned from the Cabinet shortly thereafter, accusing the Prime Minister of a lack of 'earnestness and determination' (Som, 1992: 35).

remain largely a male preserve, and entirely so in the case of agricultural landholdings.

However, these laws did establish the principle of the legitimacy of state intervention in the field of personal law, hitherto regulated primarily by custom or religious sanction, and always in deference to these. But the outer limits of any such intervention had already been established by the inclusion of Article 44 in the non-justiciable Directive Principles of State Policy of the Constitution, pronouncing that the Uniform Civil Code was an aspiration to be achieved only in the long run. Thus, the national state, which ostensibly broke with colonial practice to assume a progressive interventionist stance in relation to religious personal law, continued to be vulnerable to the power of confessional politics. It also became evident that constraints on legislation to improve the position of women in society stemmed not so much from male conservatism per se, as from an overriding patriarchal concern for the protection of property, on the one hand, and fear of electoral strictures, on the other. Naturally, the impetus for reform was much weaker than compulsions to power and, much as conservative objections to the emancipation of women were garbed in the language of religious orthodoxy, the state also invoked religious sensibilities to justify the emasculation of its reformist will and the sudden truncation of its universalistic secular aspirations. No replacement of religious by secular political authority was either attempted or accomplished. Consequently, if over time, any loosening of the hold of tradition did ensue, it was as much due to the changing nature of economy and society, as to legislative interventions by the state.

The twin constraints imposed by the electoral and political salience of religious divisions, on the one hand, and the economic dependence of women within the structure of the family and the household, on the other, emerge again as the premier obstacles to change in the case of Muslim personal law reform, a full three decades after the efforts to reform Hindu personal law. The precursor to the 1986 Act was the apparently innocuous legislative amendment to Section 125 of the Criminal Procedure Code, enacted by the Congress government of Indira Gandhi in August 1973.[11] This amendment was part of a comprehensive legislative

[11] Ten years earlier, in 1963, the Government of India had sought to appoint a Committee to study legal changes in Muslim countries, in order to

exercise initiated by the government to replace the colonial Criminal Procedure Code of 1898 with a new one. Section 125 enacted in 1973 was precisely the clause that the appellant had sought to attract in the Shah Bano case, as also the clause invoked by the Supreme Court in its sympathetic judgement on her maintenance.

As part of the provisions in criminal law against vagrancy and destitution, the amendment to this clause sought to bring divorced wives within the purview of the term 'wife', to disable husbands from taking advantage of extra-judicial divorce, and the courts from denying maintenance on the grounds that the term wife did not include divorced wives. Lok Sabha members of the Muslim League argued that this amendment constituted an interference with Muslim personal law, and that Muslims should therefore be excluded from its purview (Lok Sabha debates, 30.8.1973: 236). Law Minister Ram Niwas Mirdha, however, denied that this amendment had any bearing on personal law, claiming that its sole motivation was 'humanitarian' concern for destitute women, regardless of their religious affiliations (ibid.: 245).

The provision on maintenance was adopted by the Lok Sabha on 30 August 1973, but the government came under pressure to postpone consideration of the Criminal Procedure Bill.[12] When the Bill came up for the Lok Sabha's consideration again in December 1973, the decision taken in August was rescinded by the Government and the clause, along with all its proposed amendments, was once more reopened for discussion.[13] The renewed debate, includ-

---

reform Muslim personal law in India, but the project was quickly abandoned in the face of vocal opposition.

[12] Prime Minister Indira Gandhi was petitioned by several religious leaders, including the head of the Jamaat-i-Islami, Maulana Mohammed Yusuf Amir, and the president of the Muslim Majlis Mushawarat, Maulana Mufti Ateeqir Rehman. A delegation of prominent Muslims led by Sheikh Abdullah also sought to persuade her to the same effect (cf. Mody, 1987: 939).

[13] Sections 125 and 127 were adopted on 30 August 1973, though the clause-by-clause consideration of the new Criminal Procedure Code could not be concluded during the session. In the context of the 1986 Act, parliamentarian Madhu Limaye published a first-person account of the opposition to these clauses, and the politics of the events leading to their reopening: 'The government surrendered to this clamour. This was an opportunist move undoing the good work of the JPC. It was largely designed to preserve

ing arguments for and against the provision, was marked by attempts to establish the consistency of the clause on maintenance with the dictates of religious texts. A change in the government's stand followed in the form of an amendment to Section 127 which now stated that if, under the personal law of certain communities, certain sums were payable to divorced women (e.g. *mehr* or dower, agreed upon at the time of marriage), then its payment and her maintenance for the period of *iddat*,[14] released her husband from further obligations of maintenance.

Thus, the Government which had in August 1973 blandly denied any bearing of this Bill on Muslim Personal Law, barely five months later succumbed to pressure to avow that some women could be excluded from the 'humanitarian' provisions against destitution on grounds of non-interference with religious personal law. As matters stood, Sections 125 and 127 of the Criminal Procedure Code remained permissively open to interpretation, enabling Shah Bano's husband to appeal to the Supreme Court in 1985, using precisely the opening left by the government's rescission in 1973. The Shah Bano case was not, however, a flash in the pan. Several other cases of maintenance for divorced Muslim women had also been filed and adjudicated in the interim period. Of this probably vast corpus of case law, two cases are notable, in both of which the judgements granted maintenance to divorced Muslim women. The cases in question were *Bai Tahira* v. *Ali Hussain Fidaali Chothia*, 1979(2) (A.I.R. 75 S.C.) and *Fazlun Bi* v. *Khader Vali* 1980(3), (A.I.R. 1730 S.C.).[15] In both cases, the Supreme Court held that Section 125 was applicable to Muslims, and Justice

---

Mrs Gandhi's social alliance of Brahmins, Muslims, Harijans, Adivasis, and other backward classes. The government wanted to reopen Section 127 which was barred by the rules. There was opposition to the reopening of this clause. But the ruling party was determined to use its huge majority' (*The Telegraph*, 26 Feb. 1986).

[14] *Iddat* refers to the period of three menstrual courses after the date of divorce (or three lunar months if the woman is not subject to menstruation). If she is pregnant at the time of the divorce, *iddat* extends to the date of delivery of her child or the termination of the pregnancy, whichever is earlier (Engineer, 1987: 85).

[15] Apart from these cases decided by the Supreme Court, the Bombay High Court also had, in a series of cases between 1975 and 1977—including *Ahmedalli Muhammed Hanif Makander* v. *Rabiya* (1977 BLR 238) and *Khurshid*

V. K. Krishna Iyer (who was on the bench in both cases) ruled in the latter case as follows:

We must first remember that Section 125-7 is a secular code deliberately designed to protect destitute women who are victims of neglect during marriage and after divorce. It is rooted in the State's responsibility for the welfare of the weaker sections of women and children and is not confined to members of one religion or region, but the whole community of womanhood [A.I.R. 1730 S.C.].

II. THE STATE DIVIDED

On the face of it, the story of Shah Bano was not the stuff of which great historical events are made. It was an ordinary story which has, within the walls of domesticity, probably been enacted a countless number of times before and since, and will doubtless continue to be re-enacted in the future. But the circumstances that brought it to the centre-stage of national politics imparted to it a singularity not shared by the countless other such stories lived out by as many other women. These circumstances gave Shah Bano a pivotal role in redefining Muslim religious identity; indeed, in the foregrounding of this identity and the consequent submergence of gender identity, as also in raising the question of cultural community rights vis-à-vis the political rights equally guaranteed to all citizens of the Indian state. Shah Bano's eventual retraction from the Supreme Court judgement in her favour could not, however, undo what had been done, as the forces unleashed by this case soon acquired a life of their own.

Shah Bano was seventy-three years old when the momentous Supreme Court judgement was delivered in April 1985. She had been married to Mohammed Ahmed Khan, her first cousin, since 1932. Ahmed Khan married again in 1946, and his second wife, Halima Begum too was his first cousin, as also Shah Bano's. Ahmed Khan had three sons and two daughters by Shah Bano, and one son and six daughters by Halima Begum. While Shah Bano's sons were, in 1986, working in a textile mill, a transport company, and a bank respectively, Ahmed Khan's son by his second marriage assisted his father in his legal practice in Indore, in the state of

---

Khan (1978 BLR 240) and *Mehbubabi* (1978 BLR 258)—applied Section 125 to Muslim wives and ex-wives.

Madhya Pradesh. Behind the family's *haveli* in Indore, and virtually attached to it, were a set of two- to three-roomed apartments, and it was to one of these that Shah Bano and her children moved out from the *haveli* in 1975, on account of domestic and property-related conflicts between the two wives. In 1978, encouraged by her sons, she filed a maintenance suit against her husband as well as several suits relating to the ownership of properties.

Shah Bano's maintenance petition, filed in the Judicial Magistrate's Court at Indore; appealed to Section 125 of the Criminal Procedure Code, and pleaded for Rs 500 as monthly maintenance. Wishing to avoid attracting the provisions of this section, Ahmad Khan divorced Shah Bano by irrevocable triple *talaq* on 6 November 1978. Since she was no longer his wife, he argued, he was under no obligation to pay Shah Bano maintenance, particularly since he had already paid her about Rs 200 a month for two years, and had deposited a sum of Rs 3000 in the Court in settlement of the obligatory *mehr* (dower). In August 1979, the local magistrate ordered that Ahmed Khan pay Rs 25 per month to Shah Bano, and she appealed to the High Court for a higher maintenance allowance, claiming that her husband earned Rs 5000 a month. The Madhya Pradesh High Court revised the monthly maintenance allowance to Rs 179.20.

Ahmed Khan now moved the Supreme Court as an appellant, arguing that since Shah Bano was no longer his wife, and since he had paid her maintenance for the *iddat* period, under Islamic personal law he was bound to do no more. Section 125, he asserted, conflicted with his rights under religious personal law. Since, moreover, he had fulfilled the obligation of paying the *mehr* in accordance with Section 127 (3)(s), Islamic personal law placed no further maintenance liability upon him.

The Supreme Court was thus implicitly asked to pronounce on the relationship between these sections of the Criminal Procedure Code of 1973 and religious personal law. This was, as already noted, not the first time that such an appeal had come up before the courts. When the Shah Bano case came up before the Supreme Court, Justices Murtaza Fazal Ali and A. Varadarajan referred it to a larger bench. The Reference Order of 3 February 1981 stated that the two earlier judgements of the Supreme Court called for reconsideration because they contradicted the provisions of Section 127 (3) (b) of the Criminal Procedure Code, 1973. This provision, it stated, was meant to protect and apply Muslim personal law rather than override it, in cases where *mehr* had been paid and the obligations during *iddat* fulfilled. The decisions in *Bai Tahira* and *Fazlun Bi*, further, did not take due account of the Muslim Personal Law (Shariat) Application Act, 1937. But the Supreme Court bench, headed by Chief Justice Y.V. Chandrachud, on 23 April 1985 dismissed the appeal and confirmed the judgement of the Madhya Pradesh High Court, leaving it open to the respondent, Shah Bano, to apply for an enhancement of the maintenance allowance. The judgement stated that Section 125, as a part of the criminal rather than the civil law of the country, overrides all personal law and is uniformly applicable to all women, including Muslim women.

> The religion professed by a spouse or by the spouses has no place in the scheme of these provisions. Whether the spouses are Hindus or Muslims, Christians or Parsis, pagans or heathens, is wholly irrelevant in the application of these provisions. The reason for this is axiomatic, in the sense that Section 125 is a part of the Code of Criminal Procedure, not of the civil laws which define and govern the rights and obligations of the parties belonging to particular religions, like the Hindu Adoption and Maintenance Act, the Shariat, or the Parsi Matrimonial Act...Section 125 is truly secular in character [A.I.R. 1985 SC 945].

This assertion was supported by detailed citations from, and interpretations of, the relevant *aiyat*s and *sura*s of the Koran, to show that Muslim husbands were obliged to provide for their divorced wives, if the wife was unable to provide for herself, till her remarriage or death. On Section 127 (3) (b), the Court held that Muslims are not exempt from the purview of Section 125, since *mehr* is not an amount payable on divorce, and does not fall within the meaning of that provision.[16]

The judgement also—somewhat gratuitously, it was subsequently alleged—raised the question of a uniform civil code,

---

[16] The Muslim Personal Law Board (which had been an intervener supporting the appellant in this case) had made a written submission to the Supreme Court, arguing that the system of *mehr* had been devised to meet the requirements of women. If in straitened or indigent circumstances, the Board held, they must look to their natal families for support. But, said the Bench, an amount payable 'as a mark of respect for the wife' could not be converted into an amount payable on divorce.

arguing that piecemeal attempts by courts to bridge the gap between personal laws could not take the place of a common civil code, so that if the Constitution was to have any meaning, the aspiration contained in Article 44 must be concretized.

A common civil code will help the cause of national integration by removing disparate loyalties to laws which have conflicting ideologies. No community is likely to bell the cat by making gratuitous concessions on this issue. It is the state which is charged with the duty of securing a uniform civil code for the citizens of the country and, unquestionably, it has the legislative competence to do so.... Inevitably, the role of the reformer has to be assumed by the courts because it is beyond the endurance of sensitive minds to allow injustice to be suffered when it is so palpable   [ibid].

Barely six weeks before the judgement was delivered, G. M. Banatwala (Member of Parliament and General Secretary of the Indian Union Muslim League) had introduced a Private Members' Bill in the Lok Sabha, seeking to undo the effects of the earlier two judgements and to expressly exempt Muslims from the purview of Section 125. The two ministries (Law and Home Affairs) to which the Bill was referred, prepared the Government's response to it in the shadow of the judgement in the Shah Bano case. In a note dated 25 May 1985, the Legal Adviser endorsed the Supreme Court's interpretation of the law, and stated that the Court had interpreted these provisions without any interference with Muslim Personal Law. The Secretary in the Ministry of Law, B. S. Sekho also recommended opposing the Bill on the same grounds: namely that Sections 125 and 127 of the Criminal Procedure Code could not be said to constitute an encroachment on Muslim Personal Law. This view was endorsed, first by the Minister of State for Law, H. R. Bharadwaj on 1 June 1985, and the following day by the Union Law Minister, Asoke Sen (Parashar, 1992: 176). On July 24, the Ministry of Home Affairs also prepared a comprehensive note opposing the Banatwala Bill. Thus far, there appeared to be perfect unanimity between the judiciary and both the relevant departments of the executive.

In the Lok Sabha debate on the Banatwala Bill (the Code of Criminal Procedure (Amendment) Bill), the Minister of State for Home Affairs, Arif Mohammed Khan opposed the Bill, and endorsed the Supreme Court's judgement in the Shah Bano case, while carefully distancing the government from the recommendation for a Uniform Civil Code. The provisions of the Criminal

Procedure Code, he said, had been invoked by a destitute divorced woman in her appeal to the court.

If under that provision the court considered that she had a right, the court might grant justice to her, and if the court considered that she had no right, the court might not grant that, and if the Court considered that she was not covered by that provision, the court could give its opinion accordingly. However, the Supreme Court went a step further and gave its opinion about a uniform civil code also. But since the Supreme Court has no power to frame a uniform civil code, it simply gave its opinion. After the judgement of the Supreme Court, when the Prime Minister made a statement clarifying the position on behalf of Government, I think that meant that we had rejected that opinion   [Lok Sabha Debates, 23.8.1985: 419–20].

In his lengthy and erudite speech, the Minister sought to demonstrate the high status accorded to women in Islam, and quoted chapter and verse from religious texts to substantiate the argument in favour of maintenance for divorced women. But, in a subtle comment on the political uses of religion, he asked Banatwala if he would support a restriction on banks whereby they were prevented from paying interest to Muslim depositors on grounds that the Shariat required it. This speech by Arif Mohammed Khan was widely appreciated by his party colleagues, and earned him congratulatory messages from Prime Minister Rajiv Gandhi and Deputy Chairperson of the Rajya Sabha, Najma Heptullah. However, it soon became clear that this position might cost the Congress some Muslim support. Khan was attacked by the Urdu press, and stoned at Hyderabad airport, in the course of the agitation against the judgement. Thus it came about that, between the monsoon and winter sessions of Parliament, the Prime Minister decided that the damage done by the 'secular' speech had to be controlled and if possible rectified. Arif Mohammed Khan was sacrificed at the altar of political necessity,[17] much as Ambedkar had been thirty years previously, and the Government's new choice of spokesman on the issue was Z. R. Ansari, then Minister of State for the Environment. Ansari argued in Parliament that the judges had erred in granting maintenance, and was vitriolic in his condemnation of the Chief Justice's assumption of a reformist role, describing him sarcastically as 'a grand Mufti, a grand Mujtahid'

[17] A. M. Khan resigned from the Government, though not from the party, and declared himself ready to contest a re-election on this issue (Sunday Observer, 2.3.1986).

on whose account the authentic ulemas and muftis should close
down their offices (*Lok Sabha Debates*, 20.12.1985: 415).

As it proceeded, the debate on the Banatwala Bill brought
together most of the arguments that were current, especially
regarding the sanctity of personal law. Frequent reference was also
made to the adversarial relationship between the legislature and the
judiciary, with legislative intent being thwarted by judicial activism. Thus, two kinds of arguments reinforced the plea for the
sanctity of personal law. The first, weaker, argument appealed to
the doctrine of parliamentary sovereignty and posited a contradiction between an elected body of legislators and a nominated body
of arbitrators. Thus, it was argued, the Supreme Court had
thwarted the intention of Parliament as expressed in 1973 (*Lok
Sabha Debates*, 23.8.1985: 406) and ventured beyond its terms of
reference in assuming the role of social reformer.

They are not concerned with social reform. We are the people's representatives.... There will be a day when we shall have to prove that Parliament is
supreme because we are the law makers. They have only to interpret
law. [Saifuddin Soz, *Lok Sabha Debates*, 22.11.1985: 370].

The second argument made a stronger assertion by denying both
the legislature and the judiciary the right to enact laws in a sphere
deemed to be sacrosanct. Thus, Abdulwahed Owaisi argued that
neither the Supreme Court nor Parliament had the right to
pronounce on such matters:

This issue pertains to a religion and only a Muslim judge should decide such
cases because in such cases only a Muslim has got the right to do *iztihad*, i.e.
right to give opinion where there is a conflict between the order of the law
and that of the Prophet.... Neither the Supreme Court nor the Parliament has
got this right. No power on earth has got the right to enact such a law which
may cause mental agony. I would like to say that this august House should
postpone consideration of the Bill [*Lok Sabha Debates*, 23.8.1985: 399].

This assertion was implicitly grounded in the claim to rights of
cultural community. Such claims deny the coterminality of cultural and political communities, and conceptualize cultural communities as self-defining, self-determining entities possessed of
agency. Only those who belong to the community in question are
entitled to speak on its behalf. It has long been a problematical
aspect of communitarian arguments that they fail to take account
of the possibility of dissent within the community, and construct
a definition of community such that its supposed homogeneity and

uniformity has alarming consequences. Thus, the question of whether this unified response of indignation to the judgement was representative also of Muslim women in similarly vulnerable situations was never raised. While there cannot be definitive evidence of the response of Muslim women, there are a few suggestive indications, some of which actually predate the events under consideration. The first of these is a survey conducted for the Committee on the Status of Women, 1974, which sought to assess the extent to which Muslim women were constrained by personal law, and the direction of their desire for change.[18] The survey showed that while the achieved status of Muslim women varied greatly depending on their socio–economic background, their 'ascribed' status was inferior to that of other Indian women. Another survey of Muslim women in the city of Mirzapur in Uttar Pradesh, undertaken in 1988, to explore the questions of marriage, inheritance, divorce, and maintenance, found a widespread absence of awareness about these issues. However, once acquainted with the facts of the Shah Bano case, close to 30 per cent approved the judgement (Khan, 1993).[19]

[18] This survey covered nine states (Jammu & Kashmir, Gujarat, Maharashtra, Uttar Pradesh, Delhi, West Bengal, Tamil Nadu, Andhra Pradesh, and Kerala), and the areas covered by the sample accounted for 73.5 per cent of the urban female population at the time. A stratified sampling technique was used, with the strata based on fields of activity, e.g. college students, housewives and working women from slum areas, middle-class housewives, and professional career women. The survey showed that a significant percentage of these women were not aware of their entitlement to inherit property from their fathers or husbands, and in eight out of nine states surveyed, 50 to 90 per cent did not know how to secure their inheritance rights (Lateef, 1983: 180–1; Government of India, 1974, App. II).

[19] The study used purposive sampling techniques to investigate a sample of 200 women, 100 of whom were upper caste and the remainder lower caste, with 51.5 per cent of the total being illiterate. Among them, there were 18 divorced or separated women in the lower caste group and 7 in the upper caste group. The researcher found that only 6 per cent of her respondents were aware of the Shah Bano case. After being apprised of the facts of the case, 29 per cent said that Shah Bano was right to have gone to court, and approved the Supreme Court's judgement, while 21 per cent disapproved of both Shah Bano and the Court for departing from the shariat. The latter category of women were from families where the husbands were literate, but not the wives. On the other hand, it was illiterate lower caste women with a history of divorce and separation in their families who approved of the judgement

A chronology of the events following the judgement suggests that the issue generated a collective emotional response of staggering proportions. The movement was launched, cautiously at first, by the Muslim Personal Law Board, with a call to protest issued on the last Friday of the holy month of Ramadan. The positive response to the call encouraged the Board to decide on an intensification of the agitation. Soon, other elements of the Muslim leadership also entered the fray, and succeeded in organizing hugely attended rallies, meetings, marches, and conferences, to protest against the judgement. The important milestones in this long catalogue of events (Engineer, 1987: 237–40) from September 1985 to January 1986 include a conference attended by 35,000 women in Malegaon, Maharashtra; a complete strike in Bengal; a conference of 600 Islamic scholars from all over India in Delhi; a conference joined by 400,000 Muslims in Siwan, Bihar; a march by 500,000 Muslims to the Mantralaya in Bombay; a procession of 300,000 Muslims in Dhanbad, and another by many lakhs of people to the collectorate in Gaya, Bihar. Occasionally, violent eruptions and encounters with the police also occurred in which the people were subject to lathi-charge or the firing of a few rounds to disperse them. In all, the movement acquired an all-India character, spreading also to smaller towns like Bhiwandi, Indore, Muzaffarpur, Lucknow, Akola, Varanasi, Darbhanga, and elsewhere. As the central issue in the agitation was the sanctity of the personal law (and the incompetence of any human agency to reform what was essentially divine law), it is not surprising that this issue brought together, on a common platform, major sections of the religious leadership which had otherwise been long divided on doctrinal matters. These included the Jamaat-i-Islami, the Jamiat-al-Ulema (bearing allegiance to the Deoband School), and the All India Muslim Personal Law Board.

Countering the mobilization of opinion against the judgement was some mobilization of forces supporting it.[20] The reasons for

---

(Khan, 1993: 83–4). An earlier survey of mostly illiterate and working class Muslim women in Delhi had also demonstrated that they had a 'modern' secular approach to social questions. (Haniff, 1983.)

[20] The role of the press in giving greater currency to the various opinions has also been analysed to show that the Urdu press was almost unanimous in its condemnation of the judgement, with the sole exception of *Urdu Blitz*. The stand taken by the English language press was diametrically opposed to this, which only sharpened the polarization (Mody, 1987: 939).

this support varied widely, and the judgement became temporarily a common platform for the most diverse, and otherwise contradictory, interests. They included, broadly, organizations championing the cause of women's rights, 'progressive' Muslims who considered the reform of the personal law desirable, and even Hindu communal organizations and political parties who, for altogether different reasons, endorsed the move for a uniform civil code.[21] The liberal secular mobilization received a greater fillip when, in February 1986, the Rajiv Gandhi government introduced the Muslim Women (Protection of Rights on Divorce) Bill in Parliament.

Meanwhile, in a dramatic turnabout, Shah Bano, apparently under ecclesiastical pressure, publicly retracted. Addressing her 'Brethren-in-Faith' through an Open Letter, dated 2 November 1985, to which she affixed her thumb impression, she said

Maulana Mohammad Habib Yar Khan, Haji Abdul Ghaffar Saheb and other respectable gentlemen of Indore came to me and explained to me the Commands concerning *nikah*, divorce, dower and maintenance in the light of the Quran and *hadith*....

Since women were getting maintenance through the law courts, I also filed a suit for the same in a court of law and was successful. It may be noted that till then I had no idea that it would amount to going against the *shariat* and no person had informed me about the *shariat*'s view in this regard [Reproduced in Engineer, 1987: 211].

Moreover, she said, though the Supreme Court had given a judgement 'apparently in my favour', since this judgement was contrary to the Quran and the *hadith*, and an open interference with Muslim personal law,

I, Shah Bano, being a Muslim, reject it and dissociate myself from every judgement which is contrary to the Islamic *shariat* [ibid.: 211]

[21] Some Muslim women's groups in Delhi, Bombay, Bengal, and Kerala supported the judgement and opposed the AIMPLB's call for a *bandh* on 'Shariat Day' in October 1985. On the Banatwala Bill, 200 Muslim women wrote to the Prime Minister protesting the move to exempt Muslims from the purview of Section 125. The Bharatiya Janata Party resolved to 'help' Muslim women in their struggle for justice, and observe 1986 as Common Civil Code Year. Meanwhile, the Hindu Mahasabha filed a case in the Supreme Court challenging Muslim Personal Law, and the Hindu Jagran Manch held a rally in Bombay, also in support of a Uniform Civil Code.

On 15 November she issued another statement clarifying that her retraction was not the result of any pressure and, in March 1986, she went to court again, demanding a *mehr* of 3000 silver coins from her former husband. She also stated that it was now impossible for her to live in Indore as 'the whole of my community is against me', and sought the Government's assistance to start a new life in Delhi (*The Statesman*, 10 March 1986). But the retraction could not slip back into the hat the rabbit that had already been pulled out by political sleight of hand. The question of guaranteeing and safeguarding personal law remained obstinately intransigent.

The Government had to act to pacify the apprehensions of the Muslim religious leadership, as also to counteract the effects of the Supreme Court judgement, and it had to do this before the All India Muslim Personal Board launched the all-India agitation planned for 21 February. A series of events contributed to this decision, central to which were the results of the Assam elections of December 1985, and the by-elections in the parliamentary constituencies of Bijnor, Kishanganj, Bolpur, Kedrappa, and Sayajiganj. In Assam, the United Minorities Front won 18 Assembly seats, most of them by a Muslim majority. The UMF campaign all over Assam centred around a two-point manifesto: one, the threat to immigrant Muslims from the Assam accord, which sought to seal the Assam–Bangladesh border; and two, the threat to the identity of Indian Muslims from the Shah Bano judgement. The Congress Party's defeat in the Sayajiganj (Gujarat) assembly constituency, as also the unusually high margins of defeat in Kendrapara (Orissa) and Bolpur (West Bengal), were attributed to the loss of the Muslim vote on account of the Shah Bano judgement. In Bijnor, the Congress candidate Meira Kumar just managed to scrape through without the Muslim vote of 1.6 lakhs, most of which was estimated to have gone to the Lok Dal.

The most significant verdict was that of the Kishanganj by-election where the Janata Party leader, Syed Shahabuddin[22] won a landslide victory by a margin of 73,718 votes against the Congress (I) candidate, Isarul Haque, General Secretary of the Jamiat-ul-Ulema-i-Hind and a prominent theologian of the Deoband

---

[22] Syed Shahabuddin is the editor of the monthly magazine *Muslim India*, and was at this time a member of the Muslim Personal Law Board.

school. Kishanganj is located at the trijunction of India, Bangladesh, and Nepal, and the question of Bangladeshi immigrants was also an issue there. Even as Shahabuddin claimed that his 'absolutely secular platform' highlighted only economic issues and refrained from even mentioning the Shah Bano case, the Congress interpreted its defeat as a warning signal.

III. THE STATE IN RETREAT AGAIN

The Muslim Women's Bill in Parliament

It was clear to the party of government that a policy initiative was needed if Congress wished to retain or regain the sympathy of its Muslim constituents. This was to take the form of a legislation that was drafted in haste and hurriedly pushed through Parliament. Prime Minister Rajiv Gandhi met a wide variety of delegations, including members of the Opposition, which he assured would be consulted to ascertain all possible views on the subject. He also promised the Opposition a background paper on the complex issues involved.[23] The Opposition, however, stood divided on the proposed Bill. While some favoured a boycott, others argued that a negative response might prove politically counter-productive.[24]

The Muslim Women (Protection of Rights on Divorce) Bill was moved in the Lok Sabha on 25 February 1986, though it was not

[23] Press accounts suggest that the Prime Minister depended largely on six important advisers. They were Syed Abdul Hasan Ali Nadwi, Chairman of the Muslim Personal Law Board; Minnatwala Rehmani, Secretary of the Board; G. M. Banatwala and Sulaiman Sait of the Muslim League; and, occasionally, Syed Shahabuddin. None of the prominent Congress M.P.s, such as Z. R. Ansari, Najma Heptullah, Abdul Ghafoor, or Abida Ahmed, were consulted. As for Arif Mohammed Khan, he was summoned and told that party discipline demanded that he cooperate with the Government when the Bill was introduced in Parliament.

[24] The Janata Party, for instance, was internally divided with Syed Shahabuddin and Chandra Shekhar supporting the Bill and Morarji Desai opposing it. The Mahila Janata Party had earlier welcomed the Supreme Court's judgement, describing it as a landmark in India's judicial history and favouring the enactment of a Uniform Civil Code (*Muslim India*, Nov. 1985: 488). This was naturally strongly denounced by Shahabuddin and five other self-styled 'Muslim Workers' of the Party. Likewise, the 11-member AIADMK first pleaded with the Prime Minister to withdraw the Bill, but just before it was introduced, announced that the party would vote for it.

mentioned in the list of business or even in the supplementary list circulated an hour before the House was convened. In the House, the Government was reminded that it had not honoured its promise of consulting the Opposition in the formulation of the Bill, and was advised against haste. The Bill contained in its title a deep irony, as the substance of the legislation sought to abrogate altogether the very minimal and limited right to maintenance enjoyed by the Muslim woman divorcee under Section 125 of the Criminal Procedure Code. The Statement of Objects and Reasons of the Bill located it unequivocally in the context of the controversy around the Supreme Court judgement in the Shah Bano case:

Opportunity has, therefore, been taken to specify the rights which a Muslim divorced woman is entitled to at the time of divorce and to protect her interests   [Engineer, 1987: 87].

The Act provides that a divorced Muslim woman is entitled to, (a) 'a reasonable and fair provision of maintenance' within the period of *iddat*; (ii) two years' maintenance for her children; and (iii) *mehr/*dower and all the properties given to her by her relatives, friends, husband, and husband's relatives. If these are not given to her at the time of divorce, she may apply to the Magistrate for an order directing her husband to do so. In cases where the woman is unable to maintain herself after the *iddat* period, the Magistrate can order such of her relatives to maintain her as are entitled to inherit her property, and in proportion to which they would so inherit it in accordance with Islamic law. If the woman has no such relatives, or they do not possess the means to maintain her, or default in doing so, the Magistrate would ask the State Wakf Board to pay the maintenance.

An amendment to the Act also provided that if the woman and her husband so decided, they could apply to be governed by the provisions of Sections 125–8 of the Criminal Procedure Code, which had till this time been available to all women—including Muslim women—regardless of their husbands' consent. As many critics were to point out, it was not a little ludicrous to expect that a couple, recently estranged and divorced, would in such conditions work together amicably to ensure a fair maintenance allowance for the ex-wife. Thus, even as divorced Muslim women were removed from the purview of Section 125, it was supposedly made possible for them to appeal to it, but only acting in concert with their former husbands. Introducing the requirement of male consent was, in a sense, even more retrograde than disallowing women recourse to a clause in criminal law against destitution. The second peculiar consequence of this amendment was that while upholding the sanctity of religious personal law was the ostensible purpose of the enactment, voluntary exemption from its purview, and thereby an appeal to Section 125, was made permissible, implying that the sacrosanctity of religious law could, in some special cases, be overridden and compromised.

A new campaign was initiated, bringing together several women's organizations, as also some fora that came into being for the specific purpose of countering this legislation. A few hundred women from fifteen women's organizations in Delhi held a rally at the Boat Club; several *morchas* were organized in Bombay, Pune, and Lucknow through March and April 1986. Social worker Baba Amte and politician Raj Narain joined the protest. Rajiv Gandhi was regularly petitioned with letters and memoranda, not least from eminent Muslims of the intelligentsia and many Muslim and other lawyers. As the day of the debate drew closer, the campaign intensified and on 5 May over a hundred women courted arrest outside Parliament House, while shouting slogans against the Bill.

The Lok Sabha debate on 5 May lasted for over twelve hours, concluding only at 2:48 a.m. on 6 May. Two days later, the Rajya Sabha also saw a prolonged debate with the Bill being passed in the early hours of 8 May.[25] Together, these debates span almost seven hundred columns of the debates as published. It is possible to disaggregate and identify at least three major strands of argument in the parliamentary debate that have a bearing on the central concerns of this study. These pertain to the following issues:

- religion and politics in a secular state;
- representative democracy and majoritarian discourse;
- patriarchy and the claims of gender justice.

[25] In the Lok Sabha, the Bill was passed by a resounding majority of 372 Ayes to 54 Noes, with every move of the Opposition to have the Bill sent to a Select Committee having been defeated. The Congress party whip had issued a three line whip to members, but there were nevertheless 44 absentees from the ruling party. H. K. L. Bhagat, Minister for Parliamentary Affairs, denied of course that this absence signalled wilful defiance. By contrast, the Janata Party gave its members freedom of conscience on this Bill (*Lok Sabha Debates*, 5.5.1985: 354).

Religion and Politics in a Secular State

The entire debate was conducted in the shadow of constitutionally ordained state secularism, commonly interpreted as the absence of the state's identification with any particular faith, and its equal distance from all. The demographic disproportionality between the Hindu majority and those professing other faiths has, however, repeatedly highlighted the fragility of the principle of equidistance. The Government, in this debate, constantly projects itself as the protector of Muslim minority rights, and appears to implicitly identify itself with the majority community. There is a strong underlying strain of argument in the 'us' and 'them' mode, 'they' being seen as in need of protection, guarantees and safeguards provided by 'us'. This finds an echo in the speech of K. C. Pant, Minister of Steel:

Gandhiji, Panditji and all the others, have repeatedly emphasized that every minority has a guarantee that it could conduct its own affairs; it could have its own way of life; preserve its own cultural identity; have full freedom to practice its religion and so on. We are familiar with this and have taught tolerance to the majority. After all, the majority has a certain duty in this matter. The majority if it is not sensitive to the needs of the minority can steamroller sometimes the view of the minority....

...I think we have to be sensitive to the fact that since *they* are in a minority *we* have all to be very careful that this House does not steamroller.... [*Lok Sabha Debates*, 5.5.1986: 389–90; emphasis added].

The sudden switch from the majority identified as an impersonal 'it' in the first paragraph, to the more personal 'we' in the second, is notable, as is the corresponding shift in the description of the minority from the neutral 'it' to 'they'. This legislation was thus defended on the grounds that 'they' felt threatened by the Supreme Court judgement, which they feared imperilled their basic right to profess and practise religion (N. K. P. Salve, *Rajya Sabha Debates*, 8.5.86: 338).

On the other hand, members opposing the Bill in both Houses described it as a surrender to communal and fundamentalist forces. Some even argued that the Bill inflicted lasting damage on the Muslim community by giving the impression of a special favour even as basic Muslim grievances remained unredressed (ibid.: 233–4). Others argued the unconstitutionality of the Bill insofar as it made 'religion the basis of law-making' (ibid.: 245). Yet others asked, rhetorically, whether the Government would as sympathetically consider the question of the revival of 'sati' if a section of the Hindu community wanted it (ibid.: 291, 321).

The charge of unconstitutionality was a dominant strain in the debate, as the Bill was described as contravening several Articles guaranteeing fundamental rights, especially Articles 13(2), 14, 15, 16, as also Articles 38 and 44 in the Directive Principles of State Policy. The Bill, it was claimed, discriminated between women and women on the basis of religion, contravened the duty of the state (Article 38) to provide for social justice and welfare, and above all violated the preamble of the Constitution which describes India as a secular state.

The Government's case, however, rested on the need to provide 'protection' for minority identity, defined in religious or cultural terms. It argued the undesirability of imposing a single pattern in society, and as such provided an argument in favour of differentiated criteria of citizenship as against universalistic criteria. This argument was supported by Syed Shahabuddin who said:

This Bill, whatever it might contain, today has become a symbol; it is a symbol of the continuing struggle in our country between the forces of coexistence and national integration on the one side and the forces of assimilation and absorption on the other. It has become a symbol of the struggle between the principle of unity in diversity on one side and the principle of homogenization on the other; it has become a symbol of the urge of the Muslim community to establish and retain its religious identity on the one side and the pressures that come both from aesthetic sources and the communal sources to destroy or erode that identity. [Lok Sabha Debates, 5.5.86: 501–2].

The Government also asserted that the impetus for change, if any, must come from within the Muslim community, and be initiated by it. Thus, it implicitly voted for a conception of community rights that gave priority to the community's self-defining and self-determining character. As some argued, what was important was not the right or wrong of an issue, but rather the perception of that issue in the eyes of the community (Raoof Valiullah, Rajya Sabha Debates, 8.5.86: 435). Some of this was justified by appealing to the historic promise of the Congress (from independence to the present) to the minorities. But for the most part, it was defended in terms of its faithfulness to religious law.

Government has done the right thing in putting together in this law the formulation which is by the Islamic religious leaders and by the jurists who know the Islamic law. In fact, this Bill is but a statement of the law as contained in the Islamic law, that is, Mullah's authoritative statement of law that has been incorporated in this Bill   [Eduardo Faleiro, *Lok Sabha Debates*, 5.5.86: 348].

The conception of secularism at the heart of this debate is, thus, one that presupposes that the majority is doing the legislating while the minority is in a position of being legislated for or even perhaps against. There is, indeed, running through this debate, a varied and complex majoritarian discourse as also a minoritarian one. Central to both these is the theory of representative democracy.

Representative Democracy and Majoritarian Discourse

It is possible to identify, in this debate, five strands of argument about representative majoritarian democracy, the first two of which pertain exclusively to majoritarianism as a procedural principle.

(1) The first strand fuels the argument of parliamentary competence to legislate so as to counter the effect of the court's judgement. This seeks to privilege the legislature over the judiciary by pointing out that while judges are merely nominated/appointed, members of parliament are elected and therefore better placed to express the will of the people whom they represent. A sort of carte blanche mandate is here implied and asserted, with the theory of democratic representation serving to legitimate parliamentary action. There is also an implicit claim that the government-in-parliament has the exclusive power to enact law and make policy, while the judiciary is confined to the tasks of enforcement. Underlying this claim, of course, is the idea of the state as the embodiment of common interest. Regardless of the substance of the legislation, or of the extent to which it upholds the principles of rights or equality or justice, on this interpretation of democracy, it is the representativeness of the legislature that is the sole determinant of the legitimacy of its actions.

Thus, Syed Shahabuddin argued that the Court's judgement had triggered off a hostile reaction because it contained unworthy remarks against Islam; made a gratuitous observation about the desirability of a common civil code; interpreted the relationship between Sections 125 and 127 (3) (b) of the Criminal Procedure Code in a manner that contradicted the intent of Parliament as expressed in 1973; and took it upon itself to interpret the holy scriptures. He supported the Bill, he said, because

the Bill places beyond challenge the legitimacy, the legal supremacy, the constitutional supremacy of Parliament of India to legislate on matters of concern to the Muslim community as a religious community beyond all doubt [*Lok Sabha Debates*, 5.5.1986: 503].

(2) The argument of parliamentary sovereignty was reinforced by the assertion of a second (and arguably vulgar) type of majoritarian argument, invoking the notion of majority as a procedural rule for decision-making within the legislature. This most common, though usually unstated, usage of the majority principle is evident in the following statement by the Lok Sabha Speaker:

this is a democracy. It is a question of whose will prevail [sic] and the will of the majority will prevail, and the will of those who get the backing will prevail [ibid.: 308].

(3) The third type of majoritarian argument draws upon the identification between the state and the majority community (as discussed in the previous section), and prescribes legislative restraint in the matter of the personal law of the minorities. The sanctity of the Muslim personal law is established by reference to historical precedent, namely the debate in the Constituent Assembly and the promises made by the Congress party under Indira and Rajiv Gandhi, as well as by reference to the insecurity and alienation of the minority community, and its perception of a threat to its religious and cultural identity. Thus, Law Minister A.K. Sen in his concluding speech in the Rajya Sabha said:

so long as our Constitution will last, so long as our democracy will survive, so long as our Government will be run by great people who have inherited great traditions, the interests of the minorities will be safe and their personal laws will not be affected. Let that assurance not merely enliven the minorities but also strengthen our democratic fabric [*Rajya Sabha Debates*, 8.5.86: 578].

(4) The fourth argument, apparently considered most persuasive by the advocates of the Bill, centred around the wishes of the minority community. It is perhaps ironical that various Congress speakers, including several ministers, repeatedly sought to establish the legitimacy of the Bill by citing the percentage of Muslims who,

in their estimation, supported it. This majority of the minority was held up as the acid test of the Bill's acceptability. A derivative argument was that the so-called progressive and liberal members of the Muslim intelligentsia who had petitioned the Prime Minister against the Bill, were a mere minority in the Muslim community; the exception rather than the rule. Thus, while members of the Opposition asked the Government whether it had consulted all Muslims, the Government's spokesmen clung to the Prime Minister's statement, that 90 per cent of the Muslims were supporting the Bill. Some Congressmen even upped this figure to 99 per cent, leading the Opposition benches to demand a referendum of Muslim women on this issue (Saifuddin Chowdhary, *Lok Sabha Debates*, 5.5.86: 363). Members tried to establish numerical support for the Bill by resorting to a variety of indicators: Tariq Anwar said that had the Bill been supported by only 10 per cent of Muslims, it would not have been introduced, and the fact that it had showed that 90 per cent of Muslims were in favour of it (ibid.: 467); and Santosh Mohan Deo, who had recently won the election in Silchar, Assam, claimed that as 80 per cent of the Muslim voters in his constituency voted for him and the Congress in an election where the Bill was an issue, they clearly supported it (ibid.: 483); Indrajit Gupta asked the Government if it had corresponding figures for Muslim sentiments on the Babri Masjid, and if 99 per cent of them were exercised about that issue, why did the Government not bother to act upon it? (ibid.: 605).

In the Rajya Sabha, P. V. Narasimha Rao, then Minister of Home Affairs, put the Government's case as baldly and preposterously as possible:

We happen to be in charge of the Government. We happen to be the body which has to make an assessment of the situation. We have made it. You have every right to differ. You may say 90 per cent of the Muslims don't want this Bill, but only 5 per cent want it. Whether it is 95 per cent or 5 per cent it is up to you.

...We stick to our assessments. There is no question of your arithmetic changing ours. Only time will show. Maybe a time will come when it will be possible for us to verify in a more verifiable manner what the Muslim opinion in this country thinks about this Bill, but at the moment, we are convinced, this party is convinced, this Government is convinced that an overwhelming [sic] of Muslims are for this Bill [*Rajya Sabha Debates*, 8.5.86: 420–1].

(5) The opinion of those who would be directly affected by the legislation is barely mentioned, except by the Opposition. Clearly, if the government was at all seized of the question of minority rights, it was concerned exclusively to protect male minority rights. Muslim women, divorced or otherwise, are clearly a minority within a minority, and as such too miniscule a minority in the polity as a whole to be entitled to a solicitation of its opinion by the Government. One sympathizer of the Bill expressed this starkly in the Rajya Sabha when he said that the press and public figures had become so 'obsessed' with this issue

that one would think that India's population consists mainly of Muslim women...that too divorced women and that India had no greater problem to solve than this. Sir, as a matter of fact, the Muslim population is 12 per cent. Of them, children and adolescents form 6 per cent. Then males are 3 per cent and females another 3 per cent. Among them married women will be 1 per cent and the divorced will be .001 per cent, a miniscule minority within the minority...there are far more serious social problems involving millions and millions of Indian women, both Muslim as well as non-Muslim [*Rajya Sabha Debates*, 8.5.86: 329].

While the Opposition asked why the Government chose to disregard the views of 'those educated Muslim women who demonstrated in the streets of various capitals' (P. Upendra, ibid.: 379), the Government remained firm in its resolve, with C. K. Jaffer Sharief exhorting his fellow-members to not look merely to the Muslim women, but to the Muslim minority as a whole 'which needs your moral support today' (*Lok Sabha Debates*, 5.5.86: 373–4).

These five versions of the majoritarian principle serve to underwrite its validity both as a procedural rule for decision-making and as a normative principle, at times justifying the overriding of minorities if they are numerically insignificant or powerless, and at other times justifying their 'protection'. At the same time, many of the statements in the debate convey a tacit admission of the idea that if the satisfaction of minority opinion can be useful in securing ballot paper endorsements at the hustings, then it is perfectly legitimate to do so. Here, there is an almost subterranean switch in the projected role of the legislation: success in elections is taken to signify its popularity and wide acceptability, while actually it is the promise of the legislation, situated in a certain political rhetoric, that is expected to yield electoral support.

The minoritarian argument is much less layered and complex than the majoritarian one. The first strand in this is the familiar one that sees minority identity as endangered. Unsurprisingly, this argument was also enthusiastically advanced by Hindu Congressmen, who emphasized the need to provide 'protection' for minority identity, defined in religious or cultural terms. The Government saw its role as one of providing conditions for the safeguarding of culture, religion, and tradition, asserting that the impetus for change, if any, must come from within the Muslim community, and be initiated by it.

The second important strand in the minoritarian discourse is the idea, frequently expressed, of the authenticity of the representative voice. Several members belonging to the Muslim community argued that shariat law is sacred, and not everyone is competent to speak, much less to legislate, on it. The Government also on occasion adopted this discourse, as when the Law Minister A. K. Sen, introducing the Bill, said:

When we hear all the representatives of the Muslim community on the floor of the House... [*Lok Sabha Debates*, 5.5.86: 318].

and was swiftly countered by Saifuddin Chowdhary:

How can he say this? Nobody is a Hindu representative or a Muslim representative in this House.... He is communalizing the whole country [ibid.].

It is not a little ironical that those who expressed minoritarian views of this nature were also expressly supporting the Bill, even as its chief initiators and defenders in the Congress party used a complex majoritarian discourse to ensure its passage. Thus, the theory of representative democracy provides (a) the grounds from which the legislative competence of parliament and its priority over judicial interpretation are established; (b) the grounds on which the procedural correctness of the legislation—as supported by a majority of members in both chambers, as well as by an alleged majority of Muslims outside—is established; and (c) the ground from which questions are raised about the authenticity of representatives, and of who is entitled to speak on the issue. At one level, all these arguments belong with the Ayes on the Bill. But, at another level, they signify a deep contradiction within the ranks of the Ayes: between the Congress politicians who would endorse (a) and (b), but much less (c); and conservative Muslim leaders who would support (c), remain ambivalent on (b), and reject (a). Thus, the same theory of representative democracy ordains and justifies the enactment of the Muslim Women's Bill from a majoritarian perspective, and subverts the notion of undifferentiated representation from a minoritarian perspective.

The minoritarian argument in the public (as distinct from parliamentary) debate on the Bill also addresses itself to the vexed question of representation. We find here a much greater acceptance of the principle of liberal representation among Muslim leaders than Shaikh's account of colonial India (1991) suggests.[26] The writings of Syed Shahabuddin provide an influential, even if not strictly representative, view of this kind. In 1985–6, Shahabuddin made extensive editorial comment on the judgement and the Bill, arguing that the Supreme Court had transgressed permissible limits and interfered with Muslim personal law. In doing so, it had set itself up as a 'super legislature, or a third chamber of the legislature' (*Muslim India*, May 1985). Its constitutional mandate, however, is to interpret the Constitution and not the Holy Quran. It is for the Muslim community to reform itself on the question of maintenance, and such reform is consonant with religious texts. For this task, Muslim Indians need a leadership, distinct from the national leadership, which they can trust on matters pertaining to their interests as Muslims.

Addressing himself to the Burkean[27] question of whom the Muslim legislator represents—the people of his constituency, the

[26] The Islamic critique of principles of liberal representation, based on majority rule and shifting political loyalties, has been documented in Shaikh's study (1991) of the construction of a case for Pakistan on the ideological divide between Muslims and non-Muslims in colonial India. This critique, which provided the rationale for the claim to separate electorates towards the end of the nineteenth century, is explained by reference to the alienness, to the normative framework of Islam, of the Western liberal notion of individual political autonomy.

[27] Historically, in the liberal tradition, the role of the elected political representative has been conceptualized in two ways: first, in accordance with the Whig theory of representation, the idea of the elected representative as an independent maker of national policies, obliged to consult only his own judgement and not, on every issue, the wishes of his constituents. This position was most famously defended in Edmund Burke's (1774) Speech to the Electors

people of his religious community, or the nation as a whole—Shahabuddin argues

> a Muslim legislator also represents the Muslim community. He acts as a channel of communication between the community and the system .... When he promises to carry the legitimate and felt grievances to the powers-that-be, he builds up the confidence that justice will be done. The Muslim Legislator is thus both an advocate of the community and a pillar of the system. With his presence in the corridors of power, he is the agent of History for bridging the psychological gap that still exists between the community and the administration [*Muslim India*, July 1985].

Writing on the eve of a National Convention of Muslim Legislators, he also suggests ways of institutionalizing these ideas:

> Time has come to institutionalize such democratic processes in order to discover what a social group wants, to moderate its demands, to balance its perceptions, to determine what is feasible and then to engage the system to implement what is feasible. It would be a glorious day if in every legislature, by convention, if not by regulation, the Muslim legislators—cutting across party lines—would meet in order to render advice on a matter of interest or on a problem the community faces [ibid].

These arguments have two significant implications: first, that the question of representing community interests cannot be left to the undifferentiated representative institutions of democracy, namely political parties and legislatures; and, secondly, that the community is defined as an internally coherent monolith, presumed to be devoid of differences of opinion, much less differences of interest such as those generated by gender inequalities.

The opponents of the Bill use the theory of representation differently. They point to the unrepresentativeness of Government opinion, arguing that it is undemocratic insofar as it disregards the wishes of most or many or some of the Muslims who do not approve of the Bill, and takes into account only the approval of the conservative or affluent and male sections of Muslim society. They also suggest a referendum of those affected, again implying that electoral procedures of representation are insufficient and

---

of Bristol. The second conception, expressed in the ideas of the Levellers, is underpinned by a radical notion of popular sovereignty, and sees the political representative as an agent sent to Parliament by his electors to give or withhold *their* consent to measures of taxation and legislation proposed by the executive.

unreliable guarantors of democracy. They point to the forthcoming elections in Kerala, West Bengal and Jammu & Kashmir, all three states with sizeable Muslim populations, as keys to understanding the haste in which this legislation was passed. The by-elections in Bihar, Assam, and elsewhere had already established the electoral efficacy of the Bill in no uncertain terms.

Patriarchy and the Claims of Gender Justice

The terms of discourse of the legislative debate obscured to a large extent the central issue at stake, namely the question of gender justice. Both the Opposition and the Government strove to establish their sympathy for the cause of divorced Muslim women, though from slightly different premises: the Opposition invoked ideas of social welfare and women's rights, while the Government adopted the discourse of patriarchy. Members of the Opposition argued that this legislation subserved male interests, and was interested only in benefiting Muslim men[28] (*Rajya Sabha Debates*, 8.5.86: 238, 244; *Lok Sabha Debates*, 5.5.86: 466, 608). This viewpoint found an unexpected, and surely unintended, echo in the excited concluding speech of the Law Minister:

> *the Muslim women are not unhappy*, their brothers and husbands are not unhappy. *Their menfolk are very happy* [emphasis added; *Rajya Sabha Debates*, 8.5.86: 578].

Some Opposition M.P.s even argued that the bill benefited only the affluent sections of Muslim society, for the poorer Muslims from the rural areas had not come to the Boat Club to raise the cry of personal law in danger (ibid.: 457). Saifuddin Ahmed said that in the villages *mehr* is generally a very small amount—as little as Rs 3.50 along with some plastic or chemical ornaments—and that Section 3(1)(b) and (c) which deals with the return of the woman's *mehr*, properties, and assets was incorporated in the Bill only with an eye on the well-off people of the community.

---

[28] Some members sarcastically suggested that the Bill could be more appropriately entitled the 'Muslim Men Protection of Rights on Divorce Bill' (*Lok Sabha Debates*, 5.5.86: 608) or the 'Muslim Women Katal Bill' (ibid.: 424), while others claimed that the Bill 'legalizes vagrancy and destitution for Muslim women' (ibid.: 608) and would only encourage men to divorce their wives by oral *talaq*.

Thus, the only and rather precarious security offered to divorced Muslim women was that of Wakf Boards which, it is widely known, have been caught in a morass of mismanagement, corruption, and unaudited accounts.[29] For their part, the Wakfs in Uttar Pradesh and Bihar appeared seriously worried about this additional burden, for many of them were already in financial crisis and unable to afford even the bare necessities for their orphanages (*The Statesman*, 8.3.86). Other Boards, including those in West Bengal, claimed that they had no provisions for maintenance (*The Times of India*, 2.8.88).

The apprehensions of members in the debate on the Muslim Women's Bill were confirmed when, ten months later, in March 1987, the Minister for Social Welfare, Rajendra Kumari Bajpai, told Arif Mohammed Khan in a written reply that not a single divorced woman in India had been granted maintenance by Wakf Boards in 1986. While many boards had not made any financial provision for this purpose, others had provided for it in their budgets but the amounts remained unutilized. In another Lok Sabha reply (in answer to Syed Shahabuddin), the Government stated that 19 State and Union Territory Wakf Boards had reported that they had received no applications for a maintenance grant by divorced Muslim women during 1986–7. Only one Board , that in Rajasthan, had actually given a sum of Rs 250 each to 21 indigent Muslim women, who also happened to be divorcees (*Muslim India*, 3/88: 114).

The Government was however steadfast in its claim that it had not denied, but extended, the rights and security available to Muslim women. The Law Minister offered this reassurance:

We are sympathetic to the fairer sex. We love [*sic*] either as mothers or as sisters or as wives or as lovers…they are all part of us and we are part of them.

[29] Wakfs are trusts created under, and governed by, Muslim law. These are permanent dedications of movable or immovable properties for purposes recognized by Muslim law as religious or charitable. The Wakf Act of 1954, with a few amendments introduced in 1984, is the governing legislation in most states, except Jammu & Kashmir, Uttar Pradesh, West Bengal, and parts of Gujarat and Maharashtra. The Central Wakf Council receives an annual grant-in-aid from the Government of India, as well as 1 per cent of the income of the state Wakf Boards, in addition to income from dividends. The state Wakf Boards ensure that Wakfs are properly maintained and administered, and by a decision of the Supreme Court in 1993, they have been directed to pay salaries to the Imams.

Therefore, it is wrong to say that we are throwing women into the winds or throwing them into the dens of wolves and lions. [*Rajya Sabha Debates*, 8.5.86: 491–2].

The other face of such patriarchal sentiments was the argument of self-respect advanced by Congress member Begum Abida Ahmed:

why women should [*sic*] beg maintenance from a person who has become a stranger to her. The woman has her own self-respect and dignity.... The judgement delivered in favour of the women is actually to look down upon the women and to insult them. No self-respecting woman will prefer to give up her high status given in Shariat to become a beggar and beg maintenance from a person [*sic*] stranger to her.... The object of this Bill is to maintain the self-respect of the woman and it enhances it... [*Lok Sabha Debates*, 5.5.86: 418].

Here, the appeal was clearly to the principle of marriage as contract in Islam, as opposed to marriage as sacrosanct in Hinduism. But the effect of such arguments is to unite the claims of patriarchy with those of property to the manifest disadvantage of women. Women in penury, without the wherewithal for basic sustenance, are unlikely to be reassured by any argument of self-respect and individuality. Indeed, this ostensible rejection of patriarchy, namely the husband as stranger after divorce, does not emancipate the woman from her status of economic vulnerability and dependence. Responsibility for her condition is transferred and scattered in a manner that permits each of the agencies to take cover behind some excuse or other. In liberating the ex-husband from the financial liability of his former wife, it serves his interests both in terms of property and patriarchy.

That the interests of patriarchy and of property frequently work in tandem has also been demonstrated in the willingness of the Muslim community leadership in India to adopt a flexible position in some matters, but not in others. Thus, while the theological validity of the oral triple *talaq* has remained a contentious issue,[30]

---

[30] When the Jamait Ahle Haditha, an apex body of Islamic scholars, pronounced in May 1993 that the oral triple *talaq* at one sitting was invalid, the fatwa was hailed by some, but hotly contested by the Jamait Ulema-i-Hind, which defended the practice as valid in accordance with the Quran and Hadith, even as it confirmed that it was a condemnable act. Subsequently, in a judgement of the Lucknow bench of the Allahabad High Court of 15 April 1994, Justice H. N. Tilhari held that the recitation of *talaq* thrice at one sitting,

55 leading theologians of different schools collectively decided in 1992 that the grave damage caused by communal riots warranted a reinterpretation and modification of the shariat, such that Muslims could be permitted to insure their persons and property. Four years earlier, the process of *ijtehad* (interpretation of the shariat) was revived on the grounds that shariat law lacked the dynamism essential for any jurisprudence. The recognition of the importance of modern science, and the consequent legalization of organ transplants as well as the recognition of earnings in the form of *pagri* followed.[31]

Given the largely patriarchal tenor of the debate, it is not surprising that there was little assertion of maintenance as a woman's right, and more frequent references to it as compensation for destitution. There was no attempt to argue that women's rights are non-negotiable, regardless of faith. Feminists have also deplored the perspective implicit in the Criminal Procedure Code which sees destitute women as potential vagrants and, as such, threats to

---

or during one *tuhar* (menstrual period), without substantial ground, was not operative either under the Constitution or the Shariat Application Act. This controversial judgement was delivered in the course of a hearing on a land ceiling case, in which the husband was issued a notice in respect of excess land, but claimed that the land belonged to his divorced wife. Both Rahmatullah and Khatoon Nisa repeatedly appealed against the order about surplus land; both repeatedly confirmed the fact of their divorce, and despite repeated trials to determine whether the divorce was merely a pretext to save the land from ceiling, the authorities reconfirmed the order. The *talaqnama*, including the evidence of others, were not held to be proof of divorce. The judgement has the curious effect of denying Khatoon Nisa the right to her own land (by clubbing it with that of her ex-husband) and, at the same time, through the provisions of the Muslim Women's Act, denying her maintenance, even though she is divorced under the Shariat Act of 1937 (Agnes, 1994). The judgement also briefly sparked off a campaign for the abolition of the triple *talaq*.

[31] Indian feminists frequently cite the reform of marriage and divorce laws (as in Tunisia) or the legalization of birth control (as in Indonesia) as exemplars. Indeed, a conference of Muslim women from nine countries, held at Lahore in 1986, passed a resolution condemning the Muslim Women's Bill. However, the Indian state has constantly justified its reluctance to reform personal law by reference to the fact that those are countries where Muslims are in a majority, while in India they are a minority community.

public order and morality. Ironically, Section 125 offers them access to a public space through legal action only when they put the public place in danger (Das, 1997: 311). Indeed, the discourses of 'protection' for women and for minorities often converge:

An alliance is formed between protector and protected against a common opponent from whom danger is perceived and protection offered or sought, and this alliance tends to efface the will to power exercised by the protector. Thus, the term conceals the opposition between protector and protected, a hierarchical opposition that assigns higher value to the first term: strong/weak, man/woman, majority/minority, state/individual   [Pathak and Sunder Rajan, 1989: 566].

IV. DIVORCE AND THE JUDICIARY AFTER SHAH BANO

Till the Act became law, women continued to file cases under Section 125. One compilation showed that 144 such cases were pending in Indore alone and, ironically, in four of these, Shah Bano's stepson was the lawyer. From October 1985, there were 147 such cases filed by Muslim women, pending in three courts in Madras, and 80 in nine courts in Hyderabad. Between April 1985 and February 1986, a survey of three courts in Muslim-dominated areas of Bombay showed that 95 such cases were pending, 50 of them filed by Muslims, of which 10 were filed in 1986. In July 1986, in response to several cases filed in the public interest by women's organizations and individuals,[32] the Supreme Court directed the courts not to dismiss pending petitions of divorced Muslim women until further orders.

---

[32] The new Act had been quickly challenged in the Supreme Court by several groups, the first being Husain Dalwai's Anjuman-i-Taraqqi Pasand Muslimeen on 22 May 1986. Other cases challenging the validity of the Act were also filed in the Supreme Court: *Danial Latifi and Sona Khan* v. *Union of India; Susheela Gopalan and others* v. *Union of India; Tara Ali Baig, Anupam Mehta, Lotika Sarkar and Upendra Baxi* v. *Union of India; Abdul Kader Alibhai Sheth* v. *Union of India; Shanaz Sheikh, Kamila Tyabji and Anees Sayyad* v. *Union of India; and Rashidaben* v. *Union of India* (Parashar, 1992: 311). Still pending, these cases challenge the constitutionality of the Act, its violation of several articles on fundamental rights, and its discriminatory character vis-à-vis Muslim women.

Several maintenance cases have since been decided by High Courts and the Supreme Court. In many of these, judges have been sympathetic to applications for maintenance, and have sought to locate some space within the legislation to justify their rulings. In the following pages, I will review a few such judgements to reinforce my earlier metaphor of the divided state.

The first such case was that of *Begum Subanu alias Saira Banu (appellant)* v. *A.M. Abdul Ghafoor (respondent)*. Saira Banu had married Abdul Ghafoor in 1980, but only six months after their marriage, she left him and returned home as her father-in-law beat her frequently and disallowed her parents from visiting. Three months later, her daughter Shamim was born. In her application to the First Class Magistrate of Kasargod (North Kerala), she filed a maintenance petition, charging neglect. The magistrate dismissed her petition, saying she had failed to adequately justify living separately, but awarded Rs 50 per month as maintenance for the child. On appeal to the Sessions Court, this was raised to Rs 75. Meanwhile, Ghafoor had remarried, but offered to take her back even after his second marriage, and this generosity moved the Sessions Judge to dismiss her petition. The judgements of the lower courts were upheld by the Kerala High Court at Ernakulam, which nevertheless increased the maintenance to Rs 125. In 1987, in the Supreme Court, Ghafoor argued that he was entitled, under Islamic law, to remarry, and Saira Banu was welcome to join him and his new wife. The bench had two issues to decide: (a) whether Saira Banu was entitled to live separately because her husband had remarried; and (b) whether personal law made any difference to the rights under Section 125. The Court pronounced in Saira Banu's favour, on the grounds of injury to her matrimonial rights, and directed Ghafoor to pay maintenance (including arrears in instalments) for both his wife and child. The judgement was unequivocally located in the Explanation to Section 125 of the Criminal Procedure Code (A.I.R. 1987, S.C. 1103).

Clearly, what made it possible for the Court to take this stand, despite the new Act being in force, was the fact that Saira Banu was not a *divorced wife* and therefore not exempted from the purview of this section. Nevertheless, the Supreme Court did implicitly reaffirm that Section 125 could apply to persons of all faiths, and interpreted it in the light of its purpose of preventing destitution. It however sidestepped the question of the husband's right to remarry (a matter of personal law), interpreting the law from the perspective of injury to the matrimonial rights of the wife.[33]

A completely contrary trend may be seen in another important judgement of 1987, in the case of *Mohammed Yunus* v. *Bibi Phenkani alias Tasrun Nisa* (1987, MLR 214), in which the Patna High Court opined that Section 125 had been 'impliedly repealed' with respect to maintenance for a divorced Muslim woman. Justice A. P. Sinha tried, in fact, to endow the Act with retrospective force:

if a divorced Muslim woman divorced prior to coming into force of the Act, in whose favour order of maintenance has been passed.... become final or is pending in revision or other court being challenged by the husband is allowed to get maintenance, it will be in complete contravention of the intention of the legislature and will amount to frustrate the very object of the Act for which it has been passed   [*Muslim India*, no. 71, 11/1988: 501].

In subsequent years, courts have delivered very diverse decisions on maintenance cases. In January 1988, Rekha Dixit, a *munsif* magistrate in Lucknow, gave two separate judgements in which she awarded, respectively, Rs 30,000 and Rs 85,000 under Clause 3 of the Muslim Women's Act which provides for 'reasonable and fair provision'. The Muslim Personal Law Board welcomed the judgement, though there were divisions within (*The Times of India*, 8.2.88). Likewise, Justice M. B. Shah of the Gujarat High Court, in two cases in 1988, sought to interpret the title of the Act as being indicative of its object. The judgement stated:

While construing a welfare legislation a liberal construction should be placed on the provisions so that the purpose of the legislation may be allowed to be achieved rather than frustrated or stultified   [*Muslim India*, No. 68, 8/1988: 359].

[33] This equating of a second wife with a mistress in terms of matrimonial injury did, however, come under attack. The Urdu daily *Mashriqi Awaz* called it 'another fatal attack' on Muslim personal law. Meanwhile, in a strange denouement, a journalist visiting Kasargod found that the judges had given a ruling on a case that had ceased to exist. He met Saira Banu in her father's home and discovered that she knew nothing about the judgement, and had in fact been remarried for over two years to Abdul Salam by whom she had a six month old daughter (Saeed Naqvi in the *Hindustan Times*, 19.4.1987).

Further,

it would be reasonable to conclude that the Parliament in passing the Muslim Women Act did not intend to interfere with or abrogate any rights of the divorced wife.... As such there is no inconsistency or repugnancy in the Muslim Women Act and the law laid down by the Supreme Court [ibid.: 358].

In yet another judgement, the Kerala High Court awarded maintenance to an ex-wife by grounding it in the Shafei school of Muslim law, under which maintenance due to the wife is a debt, and not gratuity as in Hanafi law. The award was justified by the claim that the majority of Muslims in Kerala followed the Shafei school, as did the parties in question (*Abdul Karim M.* v. *P. K. Nabeesa,* A.I.R. 1988, Kerala 258). But, in the same court, a less liberal construction of the Act prevailed in the case of *A. Abdul Gafoor Kunju* v. *Avva Ummal Pathumma Beevi* (Criminal Miscellaneous Case No. 1212 of 1988). In this case, maintenance had been awarded by the Sessions Judge to the wife and daughter before the Act came into force, stating that since there was no express or implied repeal of Sections 125 to 128, the Act 'supplemented, widened or enriched the contents of rights' of the wife. She could therefore legitimately apply for enhancement of maintenance. But, in his verdict of 27 January 1989, Justice Sankaran Nair of the Kerala High Court set aside the lower court's order, citing the provisions of the New Act (A.I.R. 1989 NOC 26, Kerala).

The Guwahati High Court, on the other hand, stated that giving retrospective effect to the Act of 1986 could result in serious complications. In *Idris Ali* v. *Ramesha Khatun*, the judges said that the legislature could never have intended that benefits, such as award of maintenance, already acquired by a divorced Muslim woman under the law, could be cancelled simply because a new Act had come into force (A.I.R. 1989, Guwahati 24). Courts across the country were thus interpreting the new legislation in a variety of ways, some in terms of the intention of the legislature to pronounce compassionate judgements, others adhering strictly to the letter of the law.

The most daring judgement, however, came from a division bench of the Allahabad High Court in Lucknow, upholding a divorced Muslim woman's right to maintenance, without reference to the absence of a retrospective clause. It ruled that Hamidan bibi, a middle-aged woman with two children, would be entitled to maintenance not just for the *iddat* period, but till she remarried. Not surprisingly, the Muslim Personal Law Board construed this as an interference in personal law.

This case was significant also because it provided one example of the fears expressed by many parliamentarians in the debate on the passage of the Act, that this Act would lead to an avalanche of oral *talaqs* from husbands wishing to be free of the liability of maintenance.[34] Hamidan bibi had been thrown out by her husband ten years earlier but without a divorce. It was only when, in 1980, she heard of his having secured a job in the Railways, that she asked him for her *haq* (right), and got a *talaq* instead. The Lucknow Family Court awarded her (and her children) a small maintenance allowance, which the High Court confirmed but reduced. Rafiq contested her application for enhancement on the grounds that he had already divorced Hamidan, and it was amply evident that his decision to formalize the divorce in order to avoid paying maintenance was influenced by the availability of the new Act, to which in fact he now appealed. The High Court ruled that, under Section 127, she was entitled to maintenance till she remarried (*The Pioneer*, 18.2.1993). What is notable about this judgement is the fact that the Bench, which could easily have given the same decision by interpreting this as a case predating the Muslim Women's Act of 1986, chose instead to emphasize the clause in the Criminal Procedure Code pertaining to remarriage.

This illustrative survey of case law shows that the metaphor of the divided state has been echoed in courtrooms across the country in the aftermath of the passage of the Act. In the state's simultaneous commitment to gender equality and minority rights, a

---

[34] In the immediate aftermath of the Act, a significant decline in the number of maintenance cases filed by Muslim divorcees in 1986 and 1987 was reported. The Bombay High Court, for example, had 30 maintenance cases instituted in 1984 and 45 in 1985. In 1986 and 1987, the number had dropped to 3 and 1 respectively. Likewise, in Madhya Pradesh, 26 maintenance cases were filed by Muslim divorcees in 1984 and 28 in 1985. In 1986 and 1987, the number had fallen to 6 and 8 respectively. At the Allahabad High Court alone, the figures for 1986 (31 cases) and 1987 (45 cases) are substantially higher than those for 1984 (21) and 1985 (30). (Lok Sabha Unstarred Question, No. 7334, 21.4.87, asked by S. Shahabuddin.) Press reports also indicate that, among the side-effects of the Act, parents of brides were now beginning to demand larger sums as *mehr* to better secure their daughters in the event of a divorce.

particularly conservative construction of the latter has indefatigably prevailed.

Meanwhile, with the Supreme Court's judgement in the case of *Sarla Mudgal, President, Kalyani and others* v. *Union of India* (Writ Petition (Civil) No. 1079 of 1989) case, the issue of the Uniform Civil Code has now been placed at the heart of the controversy about the conflicting claims of gender justice and community identity.[35] In this case, the judges held that while freedom of religion is inviolable,

religious practices violative of human rights and dignity and sacerdotal suffocation of essentially civil and material freedoms, are not autonomy but oppression [[1995] 3 Supreme Court Cases 635: 652].

V. STATE SECULARISM, DEMOCRACY, COMMUNITY AND GENDER

What, it may be asked, explains the retreat of the state and its manifest reluctance to tread in the sphere of religious personal law, even though it possesses a readymade constitutional mandate to do so ? In an avowedly non-theocratic, secular state, though some have argued it practices a multi-theocratic secularism, religion may continue to be an important social force. It possesses an ideological power that is sometimes sought to be actualized through the political process. Communities of citizens, defining themselves in religio–political terms, as separate from the rest of the political community seek to do this, as also do states, political parties, and classes as they construct identities as a vehicle for their essentially secular political purposes. As such, the common-sense explanation of the state's relationship with confessional politics has always centred on the importance of so-called 'vote banks' in the electoral

[35] The right-wing Bharatiya Janata Party's call for a Uniform Civil Code has become a source of political discomfort for feminist groups championing the cause of gender justice. These groups have sought to distance themselves from such politics, and many have been engaged in drafting a common civil code that incorporates the best elements of all personal laws. The contradiction, of course, remains insofar as 'when women claim rights as women, they have often to do so in such a way that markers of class, caste and community become invisible.... Shahbano could claim maintenance as woman, but in the very granting of her petition she stood revealed as Muslim (Anveshi Law Committee, 1997: 456).

process. Thus, it has been argued that the decision to introduce the Bill was (for the Congress) 'a desperate bid to regain the Muslim constituency' (Hasan, 1989: 48).[36]

There are two kinds of problems at issue here: the first pertains to the adequacy of democratic institutions for the expression and recognition of claims of particularistic identity within the context of a secular state. The second is the difficulty that attends societies in which the claims of community identity sometimes conflict with claims to other kinds of identity (e.g. gender), raising important questions about the adequacy of representative institutions as a guarantee of not merely procedural but also substantive democracy, as well as about the state's avowed commitment to secular political practices and discourses.

Majoritarian democracy, almost everywhere, has shown itself to be less than capable of handling the problems of multicultural heterogeneous societies. Institutions of representative democracy, which were arguably designed for more or less homogeneous societies, have therefore been modified to allow for special provisions of a protective nature for minorities, as well as efforts to rule out what Dworkin has called 'double counting'.[37] In practice, however, these institutions remain open to the charge that they

[36] One analysis of the electoral significance of minorities for the Congress party classifies 207 constituencies with a Muslim population of 10 per cent or more into three categories: Muslim I (constituencies with 10–20 per cent Muslims); Muslim II (20–50 per cent); and Muslim III (over 50 per cent). There are only 10 constituencies in the last category, 64 in Muslim II, and the bulk in Muslim I. It is concluded that where Muslims are a small minority (Muslim I), they tend to vote for centrist parties like the Congress or Janata, but when they are a plurality or a majority (Muslim II or III), they are more likely to vote for class parties like the CPI(M) or confessional parties like the Muslim League, especially in Kerala (Rudolph and Rudolph, 1987: 193–7). If we look also at Muslim membership in Parliament, it has never approximated the 13.2 per cent figure that it stood at in the Constituent Assembly, elected on the basis of separate electorates. Since then, the percentage has varied between 4.74 and 7.60 per cent, going up to 8.50 per cent only once, in 1980.

[37] The idea of double counting is premised upon the distinction between personal preferences (for one's own enjoyment of some goods and opportunities) and external preferences (for the assignment of goods and opportunities to others). Given that external preferences, political or moral, are generally not independent of personal preferences, but grafted on to the personal preferences they reinforce, counting them as if they were independent has grave consequences for equality, e.g. racism (Dworkin, 1977: 235–6).

function in ways that give majorities greater purchase in the polity, and also undermine the constitutional guarantees of equal citizenship enjoyed by individuals belonging to minority social groups, however defined. Consequently, the charge of majoritarianism as an institutional bias is manifestly not mitigated by the state's formal adoption of secularism as a goal.

The second issue problematizes the question of democratic citizenship in situations in which it is possible to construct more than one identity on behalf of the same 'community'. In our case, the religious and gender identities of the Muslim woman citizen were counterposed to each other. But the choice of which identity should be politically privileged as the critical criterion of collective self-definition is not an easy one. The search for a substantive conception of democracy must necessarily encompass a search for ways of rendering compatible conflicting identities, without the effacement of either.

To explicate these issues in a manner that goes beyond the minority rights *vs.* majoritarian democracy formulation, it may be useful to recast the controversy around the judgement in terms of the tension between the claim of rights for cultural communities *vs.* the claim of women's rights of equal citizenship. This formulation recalls an important theoretical debate in political theory, namely the conflict between liberal–individualist and communitarian claims to political voice. The assertion of community rights refutes the liberal conception of individual citizens as the sole legitimate subject of rights, and advances instead the claim that collective entities, such as culturally homogeneous communities are entitled to rights, too. It subverts the simple bipolarity of the statist model which vests autonomy, agency and legal personality in either individuals or states, but in no third entity, and interpellates the community between the individual and the state.

As community rights are asserted, the sources of community are identified as determined by birth. Filiative identity is underscored, while affiliative and affinitive identities suffer being ignored. Filiative identities, however, are not identical in the kinds of values they invoke (about, for instance, rights, justice and citizenship) or in the claims they make upon the state (of assimilation, isolation or compensatory provisions). At a basic minimum, however, they all represent the claims of cultural community against an hegemonic and hegemonizing political community. Political community as customarily defined is seen as insufficiently sensitive to the special requirements of cultural community. The political community is not in itself a cultural community, neither can it claim to exhaust community as such. The projection of the Muslim demand for an inviolate and inviolable personal law, as constitutive of its cultural identity, places it within this category.

It is however a well-worn dilemma of communitarian arguments that romanticizing the community can undermine the sovereignty of its individual constituents as self-defining and self-determining subjects, possessing consciousness and agency, resurrecting in its place the autonomy of collective entities based on common descent or other cultural attributes of an heritable nature. The present case is a telling example of this dilemma, with the community leadership asserting its rights against the state, but not permitting its individual members to interrogate the norms of the community, much less its leadership. The community is not merely hegemonically, but also oppressively and patriarchally, defined in a manner that is imitative of the state.[38]

Viewing the Shah Bano case and its aftermath as an issue of community claims can yield both a conservative and a non-conservative argument. The conservative position was argued by the religious leadership of the Muslim community at the time of the drafting of the Bill. A non-conservative position that may follow from the assertion of community may mandate giving a 'participatory negotiating voice to the different communal interests' (Bilgrami, 1994: 1755). While this latter view has a certain eclectic attractiveness, it is problematical because it does not address three related issues:

- the institutional problem of representation, namely the way in which the authentic voice of the community may be discovered;
- the problem of the hegemony of a community's leadership, the possibility of such leadership not allowing dissent to be voiced within the community or community norms to be interrogated; as also the possibility of oppressive and, in this case, patriarchal, social practices internal to the community;
- the problem of women's rights which could, hypothetically, be disapproved of by the community as violative of its norms.

---

[38] Engineer (1995) has castigated the Muslim leadership for not being sincerely committed to the welfare of Muslims, instead pursuing opportunistic policies to further their personal political ambitions.

On the other hand, viewing the Shah Bano issue as one of gender justice implies approaching it from an essentially liberal–individualist perspective. The consequences of this view—asserting claims expressed in terms of women's rights—for secularism are that religious affiliation and minority status are deemed to be irrelevant to certain fundamental rights, in this case, the claims of gender justice and the equal rights of citizenship. This perspective also entails some contradictions, chiefly an institutional problem of representation, of how to discover what Muslim women really want? If many Muslim women believed that the protection of minority identity was indeed more important than maintenance, could advocates of women's rights legitimately force them to accept maintenance and give up on minority identity?

While the second (liberal–individualist) perspective is self-evidently a rights-based one, even the first (communitarian) view does not altogether eschew rights-claims. Indeed, it may be seen to be arguing for a recognition of communities, rather than individuals, as the proper agents or bearers of rights. That this category of rights-claims may be detrimental to or diminishing of certain categories of individual rights is an unavoidable consequence of this position.[39] Where the rights of minorities as cultural communities are to be weighed in the balance against the rights of women belonging to that minority, the problem is rendered more complex. There are difficulties in upholding the right of a community to practise certain rituals or forms of worship that impinge on the rights of others, or are seriously repugnant or offensive to them. The difficulties are however manifestly greater in situations where the conflict remains internal to the community, insofar as the community leadership's claim to certain cultural rights may adversely affect, rather than advance, the interests of some of its own members.

[39] It is, of course, not necessary that a recognition of the rights of individuals and those of communities should be mutually exclusive or disjoined. Religion is a clear example of such a right: it can simultaneously encompass an individual's right to practise her/his religion and the right of collectivities to undertake religious activities such as the building of places of worship, and the setting up of publishing houses to propagate their faith (Makinson, 1988: 72). Indeed, in some cases, minority rights may be seen as a prerequisite for the effective implementation of the fundamental human rights of individuals.

The recognition of the community as a cultural monolith has obvious political uses. In the present case, such community claims deny not only the factual heterogeneity of the Muslim community,[40] but also deny the chasm of interests that separates the male and female members of the community. The rights of cultural community that are asserted against the state are manifestly at the expense of the rights of women within the community. In emphasizing their filiative identity as Muslims, their affiliative identity as women is refused any space whatever. The spokesmen of the community enlist the assistance of the state in (1) facilitating its continuing control over its individual members, in this case, women; (2) paradoxically legitimizing the rule of the shariat through the agency of the authority of the state; and (3) subverting the rights of citizenship, constitutionally guaranteed to Muslim women, by restricting the sphere of operation of their citizenship rights to a narrow space that they are, in any case, effectively prevented from entering.

Thus, as the Muslim woman's community identity is privileged over her identity as a citizen, there is a filter of community control through which alone she has access to the state, and that access is further restricted by the state's self-limiting assumption of the role of a mere arbiter in determining who shall be responsible, and in what measure, for the care of a divorced Muslim woman. The span of the state's interest in her is shortened to the minimum possible as, in the name of efficiency, she has recourse to a magistrate who will quickly apportion and allocate the liability that she represents, first to her natal relatives, and then to the charity of the Wakf Boards of the community. In the absence of a reformed divorce law, women are unequal vis-à-vis men and vulnerable to unilateral divorce; they are also now rendered unequal vis-à-vis other women who at least have recourse to the law in regard to maintenance.

Through this legislation, the primacy of the rights to cultural community over the political rights of citizenship is unambiguously endorsed, and the state willingly circumscribes its own domain by editing even its criminal legislation so as to exclude some citizens from rights uniformly available to others. It permits religious personal law to invade the sphere of criminal law, hitherto

[40] The heterogeneity of the Muslim community has been underscored by Imtiaz Ahmad (1983), but disputed by Khalidi (1993).

considered non-negotiable and uniformly applicable to all citizens, admitting of no exceptions. It abets the community leadership in confining Shah Bano's sisters to a life narrowly circumscribed within the community, and dependent upon the provisions that the community can or will make for their welfare and sustenance. It thus conspires to efface a whole section of citizens from its purview, thus denying them even their minimal constitutional entitlement. It withdraws its telluric laws to make way for those of ecclesiastical origin, in a gesture that is portentuous as it provides dangerous precedents liable to misuse by the majority community.

The state is thus in retreat in more ways than one. Not only does it abrogate its constitutional promises of social justice, but also admits its own incompetence to legislate for all citizens. By an unsaintly act of renunciation, it voluntarily abridges the sphere of its command, and opens the doors, maybe even floodgates, to future abridgements that may undercut its own existence. That such risks are taken ostensibly in the name of pluralist democracy, but actually from fear of 'democratic', i.e. electoral, censure, is an irony of no mean importance. The discourse of democracy is remarkably malleable. It can be used to service a wide variety of political initiatives, including some that dispense with consider-ations of equality and justice.[41] Here, the liberal discourse of representative, majoritarian democracy may be seen to have been manipulated to serve distinctly inegalitarian, unjust, rights-violat-ing, and illiberal ends.

The secular project, clearly, cannot be merely a negative project of state abstinence, or even simply a positive project of prosely-tizing toleration in society. It must also necessarily be a project of democratic citizenship. Multiple identities are, as caricatured in Benjamin Barber's 'portrait in pieces', of the man whose 'life is splintered into quarters and fifths' (1984: 208), a fact of modern societies, and such identities (including those of class, sex and race) frequently overlap instead of conflicting with one another. Thus, the oppression of a female black worker in an advanced capitalist society stems from different, but mutually reinforcing social structures of patriarchy, race, and class. Here, on the other hand,

---

[41] As C.B. Macpherson, wrote (1996: 1–2), 'the word democracy has changed its meaning more than once, and in more than one direction', and has come to have different meanings for different peoples.

we have a case where identities conflict with one another in certain critical respects. The Muslim female citizen is doubly disadvantaged: both as a member of a minority community and as a woman. The sources of her oppression, material as well as ideological, may also on occasion be mutually reinforcing, as when the state and patriarchy act in tandem. But there is a third dimension yet to her oppression. Her membership of a religious minority renders her simultaneously vulnerable as a Muslim (vis-à-vis a predominantly Hindu society as well as the state) and as a woman (vis-à-vis the state and Muslim men). Ironically, it is the realization of the community's project of obtaining recognition for its cultural rights and securing legal safeguards for these, that compounds her vulnerability. But must her emancipation as a woman be necessarily contingent upon her disengagement from her religious community affiliations ? What implications does this have for the theory of democratic citizenship?

A secular society may be difficult to achieve unless it is underwritten by two requirements of democratic citizenship: (a) the requirement of uniform conditions of citizenship, i.e. the necessity of generating a procedural consensus, including a consensus on principles of representation; and (b) the requirement of equal rights of citizenship, requiring that community voices be rendered receptive to the goal of gender equality (and any other kind of equality necessary for the equal rights of citizenship to be effectuated) or else that gender questions be removed from all community agendas. The problem is how to arrive at a conception of democratic citizenship that provides sufficient space for the articulation of both (gender and religious, in this case) kinds of identities without securing one at the expense of the other; and ensures that the expression and recognition of neither identity is subversive of the principles of equality and justice.

4

The Developmental State[1]

Development was an integral and even non-negotiable part of the modernizing agenda of the Indian state at Independence. It was comprehensively defined to encompass not only an industrial economy, but also simultaneously a programme of social transformation and political democratization. Underlying this aspiration was a belief that progress, as represented by the historical trajectory of development in the West, could at once be telescoped and replicated. What we recognize today as the failed aspects of the developmental agenda are, to some degree, attributable to the thoughtlessly derivative nature of its conception. At its core lay an unreflective faithfulness to the developmental dogma, interpreting it purely in terms of quantifiable measures of economic growth. The limitations of this definition were manifest on the ground even before it came to be widely challenged and discredited within the international development community itself. In the course of the last decade, the opposition to the Narmada Valley Projects has unambiguously placed the development debate on the public agenda, and become a potent symbol of its interrogation and critique.

[1] The term 'developmental state' is being used here in a manner that is distinct from another current usage of it. This latter usage sees the developmental state as a subtype of state in the modern world, to be found in East Asia and Africa. In this characterization, 'developmental states are dominated by nationalistic and determined developmental élites. Combining varying degrees of repression and legitimacy, where civil society is weak or weakened, these states concentrate considerable power, authority, autonomy, and competence in the central political and especially bureaucratic institutions of the state, notably their economic bureaucracies...to achieve their developmental objectives'. Further, 'their political purposes and institutional structures have been politically driven' (Leftwich, 1995: 289–90). For a discussion of these issues, and especially of the relationship between development and democracy, see Jayal (1997).

In the debate on the Narmada Valley Projects, there have appeared two powerful, though contrasting, images of the Narmada river. Since the 1940s, planners have been inspired by the vision of harnessing this bountiful source of water for irrigation and hydroelectric power by damming India's oldest and fifth longest river, which originates in the Amarkantak mountain range and, unmindful of humanly demarcated political boundaries, flows westwards through the states of Madhya Pradesh, Maharashtra, and Gujarat to eventually empty itself, at the Gulf of Cambay, into the Arabian Sea. Neither the initial lack of agreement between the three riparian states on the sharing of this natural wealth, nor the vigorous and sustained movement against the dam, have diminished the enthusiasm of the planners. If anything, the project has been energetically propagated, through what is surely the most elaborate, expensive, and politicized publicity campaign for any development project in India.

The works collectively described as the Narmada Valley Projects, including 30 major, 130 medium, and over 3000 minor dams, have been justified by, on the one hand, the requirements of development interpreted as economic growth, and, on the other, by the socially useful purpose of providing drinking water to chronically drought-affected regions. The justificatory principle, in this first image of the Narmada, is thus developmental, while its informing vision is technocratic. In more innocent times, developmental efforts encouraged an illusion of benevolent neutrality, but such commitments are manifestly political choices with profound social and political consequences.

The second compelling imagery of the Narmada may be described as cultural-conservationist, and early opposition to the project frequently invoked elements of this. The rejection of the dominant model of development fired images of the Narmada as a powerful cultural symbol, invoking the religious sanctity associated with the river—apparently superior in Hinduism to that of the Ganga—and the sacred and liberating ritual of the *parikrama* (circumambulation) around it. It also recalled the civilizational significance of the Narmada as a vast cultural repository of myths and legends; of the archaeological remains of prehistoric and proto-historic civilizations in the valley; of a diversity of cultures nurtured within it, from simple tribal communities to more complex forms of social organization; of important temples of antiquity; and of the valuable diversity of plant and animal life that has flourished in the forests of the Narmada basin.

Both these images, the developmental–technocratic as well as the cultural–conservationist, carry important political messages. The primary inspiration of the first is the technological and engineering achievement involved in accomplishing the biggest dam project the world has yet seen, and of generating an impressive potential for irrigation and hydroelectric power for agricultural and industrial development. Its belief that the key to development lies in such projects, regardless of their sustainability or social consequences, comes to acquire the status of a self-perpetuating dogma, to which, with time and practise, a constellation of political and commercial interests get linked.

The second image questions not merely the validity of the model of development that inspires such projects, but also the viability of the project itself. It points to the unacceptable social consequences of the project in terms of the displacement of a vast tribal population from its traditional habitat and unique way of life, as well as the environmental destruction that is necessarily entailed. The conservationist impulse in this perspective thus embraces both community life as well as nature, sometimes drawing uncomfortably close to a romanticized view of tribal life; of a golden irrecoverable past in which man and nature subsisted in harmony.

Underlying these contrasting visions of the river—the technocratic and the cultural—are political purposes, arguments, and imperatives to action that make the Narmada Valley Projects, and the movement in opposition to them, symbolic of an important dimension of political practice in contemporary India. This political practice encompasses a wide range of issues: development, environment, democracy, minority cultures, human rights and social justice; and implicates a variety of institutions, especially the state. Above all, it points to the restrictive notion of democracy that currently enjoys purchase in our polity; and seeks a more broad-based conception of democracy to include self-determination and meaningful political participation in decisions that directly affect the lives of communities.

I. THE NARMADA VALLEY PROJECTS

The ancestry of the Narmada Valley Projects (henceforth NVP) is generally traced back to 1946, when, in response to a suggestion by Sardar Vallabhbhai Patel, the Central Waterways, Irrigation, and Navigation Commission was asked by the Governments of Bombay and the Central Provinces and Berar, to investigate the development of the Narmada basin for purposes of irrigation, power, flood control, and navigation. The idea of harnessing the waters of the Narmada for irrigation was not a new one, having been mooted as early as 1863 by a certain Mr Balston who suggested the formation of a Joint Stock Company for the construction of a dam across the river to reserve water and sell it at a profit to farmers. At the turn of the century, the *malguzars* of the Central Provinces were enthusiastically supportive of any plan for the construction of canals and dams, but it was the First Irrigation Report of 1901 that pronounced decisively against such schemes, on the grounds that irrigation was unsuitable, unprofitable, and even harmful for the black cotton soil of the Narmada basin.[2] This example from the colonial period is, of course, in striking, and even ironical, contrast to more recent history, which has witnessed marked collusion between a nationalist state and commercial interests.

In 1948, the work of the reconnaissance and detailed investigation of seven different sites was referred to the three-member A. N. Khosla Committee, on the basis of which the Central Water and Power Commission submitted its first project proposal in 1959. When, in 1960, Bombay was bifurcated into the two new States of Maharashtra and Gujarat, the planning and works were transferred to Gujarat, where the project was inaugurated by the high priest of India's secular temples, Jawaharlal Nehru, in April 1961. The earliest acquisitions, and the attendant displacements, took place at this time, with lands from six villages being acquired for the construction of the Kevadia Colony, the headquarters of what later became the Sardar Sarovar Dam.

Meanwhile, disagreements arose about the sharing of the costs and benefits of the project between Gujarat and Madhya Pradesh, and were again referred to a committee headed by Dr Khosla. In

---

[2] Commenting on the regional disparities effected by irrigation systems in western India, Parita Mukta argues that the expansion of capitalist agriculture in north-western and southern Gujarat was based on cotton and sugarcane cultivation, made possible by these canal systems. She suggests that this history provides the backdrop for the contemporary conflicts over the building of the dam and the continuity of interests that support it (Mukta, 1995: 100).

its report of September 1965, this committee recommended the allocation of the waters to Rajasthan, and also pronounced in favour of raising the height of the Navagam dam. The report was welcomed by the Government of Gujarat, which insisted that a higher dam was its only insurance against drought, but rejected by the Governments of Maharashtra and Madhya Pradesh, which were equally insistent on a lower height, to save potential sites for hydroelectric power within their States.

To resolve the disagreements between the three riparian states, the Government of India, moved by the Gujarat government, constituted the Narmada Waters Dispute Tribunal, on 6 October 1969. The deliberations of the Tribunal were temporarily stayed when an interim judgement directing the exclusion of Rajasthan from a share in the waters was contested in the Supreme Court by the Governments of Rajasthan and Madhya Pradesh in 1972. The career of the Tribunal provides a revealing micro-example of the politics of planning, of the way in which technical and political considerations are weighted and traded in planning exercises. Even today, the Supreme Court is engaged with the problem of determining the extent of its sanctity, and the constitutionality of reviewing its award.

In July 1972, the four states of Gujarat, Rajasthan, Madhya Pradesh and Maharashtra decided to refer the disputed matter to the Prime Minister Indira Gandhi, asking her to allocate the water between the States, and fix the height of the Navagam dam, (Narmada Water Disputes Tribunal Report, vol. iii, 1978: 48). This decision naturally led to the adjournment of the proceedings of the Tribunal. Two years later, in July 1974, the States arrived at a preliminary agreement on the terms of reference of the Tribunal. These were narrowed down—notably, by political consensus between the affected States, and not by its appointing authority— to the allocation of 27.25 MAF of water between Gujarat and Madhya Pradesh; the height of the Navagam (now Sardar Sarovar) dam; and the level of the canal taking off from this dam. Consequent upon this agreement, M.P. and Rajasthan withdrew their petitions from the Supreme Court. It was in this context that the Tribunal once again commenced work, a full two years later, in August 1974, began hearing arguments, and delivered its Award in August 1978.

Some significance has been attached to the fact that, at the time of the Award's publication, there was a coalition government at the Centre, headed by the veteran Gujarat politician Morarji Desai. Gujarat, too, was at this time governed by a Janata Party coalition ministry, as indeed was Madhya Pradesh. Arjun Singh, the then leader of the Congress opposition in the Madhya Pradesh Assembly, launched the Nimar Bachao Andolan, agitating to save this fertile and prosperous area from submergence by the Narmada Sagar Dam, which had the active support of the party of government. The agitation died unlamented when, in 1980, the Congress returned to office at the Centre and in the State, with Arjun Singh himself as chief minister.

There is little doubt that the agenda of the Tribunal was politically constrained. The Chief Ministers' agreement in 1972 asking the Prime Minister to decide the height of the dam, as well as the allocation of water, implicitly suggested that technical matters could be politically decided. The Tribunal was asked to work within a non-negotiable estimate of the amount of water available. Despite its own calculation of the run-off yield (at 75 per cent dependability of rainfall, i.e. rainfall in every three out of four years) which put water availability at 22.60 MAF, it had to go along with the Chief Ministers' agreement on the figure of 28 MAF. Thus, even the most important issue of how much water existed to be shared was placed beyond the competence of the Tribunal.[3] Rajasthan's eventual inclusion among the beneficiaries was also an act of political will, in direct contravention of the Tribunal's judgement of 1971. The functioning of the Tribunal as an independent, arbitrating mechanism was, thus, unconscionably constrained by bargains struck between the four Chief Ministers and the Central Government. It is hardly surprising, then, that the Tribunal's final orders contained an implicit acknowledgment of its helplessness:

Nothing contained in this Order shall prevent the alteration, amendment or modification of all or any of the foregoing clauses by agreement between all the states concerned   [Report of the N.W.D.T., vol. ii, Clause xiv(16): 135].

On its considerably truncated agenda, the main contentious issue remaining related to the apportionment of water between Gujarat and Madhya Pradesh. The Tribunal interpreted the

[3] The extent of water availability continues to be disputed and controversial, with detractors of the dam insisting that it is approximately 22 MAF, and its supporters standing by the original estimates.

principle of equitable apportionment to mean equality of consideration and equality of opportunity, rather than equal division, and the criteria applied included the cultivable area, the net sown area, the population dependent on agriculture, the drought-prone area, and the population affected by drought in these two States. On this basis, the Award decreed that the 28 MAF of available water would be shared in a ratio of 65:32:2:1 between Madhya Pradesh, Gujarat, Rajasthan, and Maharashtra. Thus, M.P. would get 18.25 MAF, Gujarat 9 MAF, Rajasthan 0.5 MAF, and Maharashtra 0.25 MAF. Any excess or shortage would be shared in the same proportion.

Regarding the height and gradient of the Navagam Canal, Gujarat and Rajasthan proposed higher gradients, while Madhya Pradesh and Maharashtra bemoaned the loss of potential hydel power due to the height of the canal. The NWDT ruled that the additional areas commanded by a higher canal in Gujarat and Rajasthan made this trade-off necessary. On the question of the height of the Sardar Sarovar dam, the higher the dam (as proposed by Gujarat), the greater would be the area of submergence in Madhya Pradesh. The Tribunal fixed the height of the dam at 460 ft., and today the question of lowering it is one of the most important options being considered by the Supreme Court.

In the allocation of the benefits of hydroelectric power, M.P. would, the Tribunal ruled, get 57 per cent of the power generated from Sardar Sarovar. The Government of Gujarat was also directed to share a part (17.8 per cent) of the cost of the irrigation component of the Narmada Sagar Dam in Madhya Pradesh, on the principle that the downstream beneficiary State must compensate the upstream one because 17.8 per cent of the irrigation benefits of the SSP would be due to regulated releases from the Narmada Sagar dam.

The most significant aspect of the NWDT Award was its provisions relating to rehabilitation. Despite several lacunae, this has been considered the most liberal rehabilitation policy devised for any such project in India, even if, as is sometimes argued, the liberality of the policy was extracted as the price of agreement on a higher Sardar Sarovar dam by Madhya Pradesh and Maharashtra. The Tribunal directed the Government of Gujarat to bear the cost of land acquisition and rehabilitation of displaced persons from Maharashtra and Madhya Pradesh, regardless of whether they chose to settle in their home state or in Gujarat. Any family which stood to lose more than 25 per cent of its holdings would be entitled to a minimum of 5 acres of irrigation land in the command area. Further, every major son would be treated as a separate family for this purpose. The Tribunal neglected, however, to take into account the landless labourers in the areas to be submerged. Even more striking was its failure to provide for the vast tribal population with its forest-based economy. Living by common resources in nature, completely outside the modern individualistic system of property rights, and lacking legal title to land, these tribal communities have proved to be among the major casualties of the projects. In legal euphemism, however, they were 'encroachers' and, as such, could claim no entitlement to substitute land, much less to living conditions even remotely comparable to those they currently enjoyed.

Some of these lacunae were sought to be addressed by the World Bank, which had its own detailed policy on involuntary resettlement,[4] requiring the borrower country to prepare a resettlement plan, simultaneously with the plans on the engineering and technical aspects of the project. This would enable the project proposal to be appraised as a whole, based on which recommendations for or against approval would be made to the Executive Board of the Bank. The governing principle of the resettlement plan was that the relocated people at least recover their present living standards, and hence the plans should show how many people are to be displaced, what their current standards of living are, how and where they will be resettled, and what provisions will be made to ensure that their standards of living do not fall as a result of their relocation. In the case of the SSP, India prepared no resettlement plan, and therefore no appraisal of this project was carried out, either by the Bank's missions for the pre-appraisal of the project, nor by the two missions for project appraisal during 1982–3, all of which limited themselves to an examination of the technical and economic aspects, completely ignoring the social, cultural, and human consequences of the projects.

In 1983, the World Bank engaged as consultant a well-known development anthropologist, Professor Thayer Scudder, whose mission to India met with opposition from the India Country

---

[4] Operational Manual Statement, No. 2.33, Feb. 1980, since superseded by Operational Directive 4.30, June 1990.

Department of the Bank, and with ill-concealed defensiveness by the Government of India.[5] The Scudder mission concluded that the NWDT's provisions, though a major advance for India, did not meet the World Bank's guidelines on involuntary resettlement, especially on the important question of landless people and forest cultivators. It also stated that the concerned State governments did not appear to have serious intentions, let alone the means and skills needed for honouring the Tribunal's Award, and indeed that past experience clearly showed that India had neither a national policy on rehabilitation, nor the necessary institutional framework in any of the three States for a sensitive and skilful approach to the social and community aspects of displacement and resettlement. The Land Acquisition Act of 1894 was, it argued finally, an inappropriate legal instrument for land acquisition and compensation.

Despite Scudder's unambiguous conclusion that the environment for the resettlement of Sardar Sarovar oustees was likely to be 'very unfavourable', primarily on account of a lack of information, the World Bank continued to negotiate the loan, and extended its deadline for the submission of the Resettlement and Rehabilitation (henceforth R & R) plan, even modifying its requirements to a plan for Stage One oustees only. Though the Loan Agreements of 1985 included, as a separate component, a loan for the rehabilitation programme (also making provisions for the landless and 'encroacher' oustees), the fact that they were finalized, the *Independent Review* said, 'on so slender a basis reveals its readiness to accept whatever India offered, and to disregard the World Bank's own requirements and expertise' (1992: 47). The Bank's approach to the Sardar Sarovar project, henceforth, gave priority to project approval over compliance with its own policies. Despite lobbying by Professor Scudder and Anil Patel (of a non-governmental organization, ARCH-Vahini), the Bank chose to rely exclusively on the Tribunal's Award, with all its avowed shortcomings, as the legal and practical foundation of resettlement policy in all the three States. The Bank's wilful neglect of the fulfilment of R & R

[5] An under-secretary in the Ministry of Finance wrote to the Acting Chief of the Agriculture Division of the Bank's Delhi office that India was taking steps to formulate a rehabilitation plan, and a Bank mission need not be organized specifically for this purpose (*Independent Review*, 1992: 43). Two missions led by Scudder found that there was inadequate information on the extent and implications of displacement.

requirements in this project was again commented upon by Michael Cernea, the Bank expert on this subject, in a report in 1986, but pressure from consultants and Bank staff, even as late as 1986 and 1989, to suspend aid till R&R conditions were met, had no effect.

The World Bank had also laid down the need for an environmental impact assessment. In 1986, the Ministry of Environment and Forests, established only the previous year, expressed its disapproval of the Sardar Sarovar Dam, and more so the Narmada Sagar Dam, on grounds of their likely environmental impact. Proper Environmental Impact Assessments, the Ministry argued, would take another two to three years, and it made a case for reducing the height of the dam, with the objective of reducing the area of submergence and, therefore, the number of people likely to be displaced. Similar views were already being echoed by environmentalists, as also by university departments that had been commissioned to undertake studies.

In response to this, the Ministry of Water Resources brought out a note emphasizing the urgency of a decision for the Governments of Gujarat and Madhya Pradesh. It argued that since substantial expenditure had already been incurred on these projects, they should be sanctioned conditionally, till the studies on environmental impact were complete. The NSP and SSP should, moreover, be approved simultaneously, as they were linked to each other. In the end, hectic lobbying led to a meeting of the Prime Minister with the three Chief Ministers, and the projects were cleared on 13 April 1987. In the words of a former civil servant:

The Prime Minister was pressurized to give environmental clearance within six hours to a project which had been hanging fire for more than two decades. The fortunate induction of the former Chief Minister of Gujarat as Minister for Planning in the Central Cabinet has resulted in Planning clearance also being given for this project [Buch, 1991: 50].

It is not without significance that, at the time of clearance, both Gujarat and Madhya Pradesh were ruled by Congress ministries, and were manifestly impatient to proceed with the projects. In the Assembly elections of 1987, the Congress had suffered reverses in West Bengal, as also in the only southern state in its control, Kerala. The Rajiv Gandhi Government at the Centre, too, had by 1987, lost some of the euphoria that attended the early days of its tenure, and beleaguered by crises—Bofors, Assam, Punjab—had begun to take recourse to populist measures. The decision to clear the NSP and the SSP may be seen in this context, as an effort to prevent electoral setbacks in Gujarat and Madhya Pradesh, and to placate the local political leaderships of these two states, comprising in the main powerful landed élites. In June 1987, the Ministry of Environment followed the Prime Minister's cue and granted conditional sanction, and in October, it also conditionally cleared the release of forest land for submergence, consequent upon the project. The World Bank's requirement of an environmental work plan, which was to have been met by December 1985 remained, despite an extension of the deadline to 1989, unavailable till the time the Independent Review completed its report.

II. CHRONICLES OF PROTEST

II. 1 *Resistance*

The earliest opposition to the projects was articulated, not in the form of direct action, but through publicizing the findings of grassroots organizations that had been engaged in welfare and development work in the areas to be affected by submergence. Among the first of such reports was that by a group of university students in Delhi, who argued in favour of complete Environmental Impact Assessments, a comprehensive scheme for rehabilitation, a thorough cost–benefit analysis, and an exploration of possible alternatives for achieving these objectives. They asked, in fact, that the projects be scrutinized for the river valley as a whole, rather than in terms of the SSP and NSP alone (Kothari and Bhartari, 1984).

In another series of studies published between May 1986 and August 1988, the Delhi-based Multiple Action Research Group showed that, despite the Tribunal's injunction that the affected people be informed at least a year prior to submergence, and resettled at least six months earlier, people in the Jhabua, Dhar, and Khargone districts of Madhya Pradesh were largely ignorant about the project, much less apprised about the resettlement choices available to them, and their entitlements to compensation under the Award. People came to hear about the proposed dam from curious sources: sometimes from itinerant sadhus, and at other times by inference from the stone markers being put up to demarcate the area of submergence. The MARG team pointed to the need for raising popular awareness about the extent and nature of compensation available, to better equip the people to assert their rights.[6] It was not however overly optimistic about the potential for mobilizing the people in struggle. In Alirajpur *tehsil* of Jhabua district, for instance, they concluded that the Bhils were so terrified of government officials that they could hardly look them in the eye, much less protest. By contrast, in Barwani *tehsil* of Khargone district, the people had been active in anti-dam agitations since 1978, with one village *patel* even having spent two days in jail as punishment.

Another survey in and around Harsud, falling within the area of maximal submergence in Madhya Pradesh, conducted by the World Wildlife Fund India, showed widespread opposition to the dam, frequently cutting across class boundaries. It also highlighted the poignant fact that time had come to a standstill in the areas anticipating submergence. Three decades of uncertainty about the future had inhibited both private investment as well as public banking: as a result, most economic activity, including the construction of infrastructure like roads and school buildings, had also stopped (World Wildlife Fund, 1986: 109).

The first oppositional initiatives came from non-governmental organizations such as the Society for Social Education and Action, SETU, the Gandhi Peace Foundation and the Narmada Dharangrastha Samiti. In July 1988, eighty environmentalists and activists met at the ashram of Baba Amte at Anandwan, to assert their 'collective will' against big dams, and decided that Amte would flag off a *Bharat Jodo* marathon in November to mobilize activists against large dams. In August, environmental and civil liberties groups—including the Narmada Dharangrastha Samiti, the Narmada Asargrast Samiti, and the Lok Adhikar Sangh—submitted memoranda to the three State governments, expressing their concern about displacement and rehabilitation. They also, perhaps for the first time, drew attention to the continued destitution of the 15,000 tribals who had been displaced when lands from six villages in Kevadia were acquired in 1961 to build the project

[6] The question of consulting the affected communities was not, at any time, considered by the Government, though this is required by World Bank guidelines, which insist on popular consultation at every stage. Indeed, when Bank-aided projects succeed, as in the Arenal Hydroelectric Power Project in Costa Rica, Bank officials often attribute such successes to people's participation (*Independent Review*, 1992: 58).

headquarters. By the end of August, Medha Patkar (a social researcher turned grass-roots worker), Girish Patel (a Supreme Court advocate), and others were beginning to threaten a mass agitation with *dharnas*, rallies and public meetings, especially asserting a right to information on all aspects of the project.

Up to this point, it appears clear that the attention of the oppositional groups had been focused on the question of rehabilitation. When environmental issues came to be highlighted—eventually culminating in the expression of an anti-dam, alternative development strategy—there occurred a parting of ways between, on the one hand, the ARCH-Vahini and SETU (led by Anil Patel and Achyut Yagnik respectively) and, on the other, the Narmada Dharangrastha Samiti and its affiliate groups which eventually joined forces under the umbrella of the Narmada Bachao Andolan. The NBA thus started life as a loose federative body of affiliated groups, most notably the Narmada Dharangrastha Samiti, an organization of tribals from Maharashtra that came into being in 1985; the Narmada Ghati Navnirman Samiti from the Nimar region of Madhya Pradesh; and the Narmada Asargrastha Sangharsh Samiti of Gujarat which came into being in 1987–8. The social heterogeneity of the oustees has resulted in a fairly broad-based movement, encompassing small farmers and tribals, as well as middle peasants and wealthy landowners, from different caste, religious, and ethnic groups. The leadership of the movement has mostly rested with educated social workers from urban backgrounds, who became activists involved in the collection and dissemination of information, the articulation of dissent, and the formulation of strategies of protest.

Till 1989, thus, when direct action was undertaken for the first time, protest largely took the form of petitions to the government from experts and intellectuals; a strategy that had yielded dividends in the case of the Silent Valley project six years earlier. Why did pressure from the intelligentsia not carry weight on this issue, as it had in the case of the Silent Valley project (D'Monte, 1985), particularly since environmental awareness by this time was more widespread than before? Medha Patkar has said that Mrs Gandhi's professed environment consciousness had much to do with it, (Interview, 1992). It is also likely that, among other factors, the vigorous campaign in support of the project, launched and since sustained by the Government of Gujarat, marks this out from other projects. Movements of protest are not unknown in relation to development projects, but such a powerful phalanx of political support is relatively rare.

Official discourse, describing the Narmada river as 'liquid gold', not only highlighted its potential for energy and irrigation, but also projected the dam as intrinsic to the very cultural identity of Gujarat.[7] Thus, Mrinalini Sarabhai and P. G. Mavalankar, a former Member of Parliament, who signed a memorandum to the Prime Minister urging a reappraisal of the project, were angrily and publicly denounced as 'enemies of Gujarat' by Chief Minister Amarsinh Chaudhary, the Leader of the Opposition Chimanbhai Patel, two former Chief Ministers, members of political parties as diverse as the BJP, the CPI and the Congress (I), and even the Governor. Sarabhai was unceremoniously removed from the chairmanship of the Gujarat Handloom and Handicrafts Development Corporation. The politicization of this issue resulted in the withdrawal of their signatures. In another episode, the investment clearance for the project from the Planning Commission is believed to have been facilitated by the fact that the then Union Minister for Planning and Implementation was Madhavsinh Solanki, formerly the Chief Minister of Gujarat. Though at political odds with Amarsinh Chaudhary, he was compelled by the chauvinist campaign around the project, to oblige his political rival and successor.

Another major source of support was the World Bank. Its mission of November 1987 had noted the non-compliance of the Gujarat Government with the provision of a 2 ha. minimum entitlement by way of compensation. In response, the state government issued a Resolution committing itself to this minimum entitlement, but in April the following year, another Bank mission found that organizations representing the oustees were agitated about administrative prevarication and footdragging on the implementation of this policy. In 1988, Gujarat satisfied the Bank by

[7] It has been argued that neither the Kutch region, water scarcity in which has been propagated as the rationale for the project, nor the eastern tribal region of the State which is its major casualty, are in any real sense part of Gujarat State. Culturally and historically, they are quite distinct from Gujarat, which is therefore quite willing to cynically exploit these regions, even as the real Gujarat prospers and benefits at their cost (Jashbhai Patel, 1994: 1957–8).

further broadening its policies, and the ARCH-Vahini decided to cooperate with the government in its rehabilitation efforts.[8]

Not everyone, however, was as sanguine as the World Bank, and among those who expressed reservations were senior government officials and state agencies. In July 1988, the Ministry of Environment advised that the Narmada Valley Projects be deferred to the following year, by which time more data would become available. Its environmental costs were already estimated at Rs 8190 crores, in addition to the large-scale displacement of people from three states. Dr M. S. Swaminathan, chairman of a Planning Commission steering group, charged with incorporating environmental principles into every sector of the Eighth Five Year Plan, also expressed grave doubts about the project. The Union Secretary for Social Welfare, S. S. Varma, pointed out at a meeting of the Narmada Control Authority[9] that land for relocating the oustees was simply not available. This was endorsed by the Union Secretary for the Environment, S. Geethakrishnan, who categorically stated that forest land would not be released for this

[8] Anil Patel of the ARCH-Vahini sees (1997: 77–8) the 1987 policy announced by the Government of Gujarat as a major victory, made possible by combined pressure of the tribals under the Vahini's leadership, international NGOs, and the World Bank. Soon enough, the policy stances of different agencies came to be implicated in the rivalry between the two major strands of the movement: the one represented by ARCH-Vahini and the other by the NBA. Thus, the Ministry of Environment's reluctance to release forest land in Taloda in 1990 was supported by the NBA, but perceived by the Vahini as violative of the Tribunal's directives as well as the Loan Agreement. On the other hand, the NBA's mounting criticism of the World Bank implicitly pointed a finger at the Vahini for its cooperation with the rehabilitation efforts (ibid.: 82–3).

[9] The Narmada Control Authority, headquartered at Indore in Madhya Pradesh, reports to the Union Ministry of Water Resources, and is the central body responsible for the entire Narmada Valley Projects. Its Chairman is also the Chairman of the Central Water Commission, and generally the Union Secretary for Water Resources, too. The Prime Minister, the Union Ministers for Water Resources, Environment and Forests, and Social Welfare, as well as the Chief Ministers of Gujarat, Maharashtra, Madhya Pradesh, and Rajasthan constitute the Review Committee of the NCA, to which all major decisions are referred. The NCA also has three sub-groups on technical matters, environment, and rehabilitation, and the latter two generally include a representative from a non-governmental organization.

purpose.[10] Less than a year later, many former civil servants also spoke out against the project, questioning the wisdom of large dams, defending the rights of the tribals to be displaced, and so on.[11] Even the Bombay Natural History Society, which conducted an ecological appraisal of the submergence area of the SSP in Gujarat, at the request of the Narmada Valley Development Authority,[12] announced its refusal to be party to 'a fraud on the people' (*Indian Express*, 6.9.1989).

In response to the growing opposition to the project, the Government of Gujarat, in October 1988, imposed the Official Secrets Act on twelve villages in the vicinity of the dam site at Navagam. In January, eighteen persons who demonstrated against this at Kevadia were arrested on charges of spying, and various provisions of the Act began to be invoked to arrest activists, or to summon and interrogate them. It was in September 1989 that the Narmada Bachao Andolan, in its first spectacular show of strength, organized a large rally at the submergence area of Harsud in Madhya Pradesh. Estimates of attendance at the rally varied from 25,000 to 60,000. The NGOs gathered there from India and abroad pledged to oppose destructive development projects— irrigation, power, nuclear—that cause displacement and submergence; facilitate exploitation and repression; and destroy natural resources and distinct cultures. The Harsud rally expressed, perhaps for the first time at the popular level, a critique of development as conventionally understood, and underscored the importance of environmental issues and of an alternative strategy for sustainable development. Above all, Harsud represents the first

---

[10] In February 1988, the Chairman of the Narmada Valley Development Authority, S. C. Varma resigned his position, ostensibly to lead an agitation to safeguard the interests of the displaced tribals. Not long after, however, Varma joined the Lok Sabha as a BJP member, confirming the allegations of activists that his action had been opportunistic (Patkar, Interview, 1992).

[11] These included M. N. Buch, a former Chief Secretary and Forests Secretary of Madhya Pradesh, B. B. Vohra, a former Union Secretary for Petroleum, and N. D. Jayal, a former Union Secretary for Environment.

[12] The Narmada Valley Development Authority, based in Bhopal in Madhya Pradesh, is the body responsible for the Narmada Sagar (now Indira Sagar) Project, the second major project that was planned simultaneously with the SSP, but received no clearances or financing. The NSP is of course based upstream in the Madhya Pradesh region.

attempt by the anti-dam activists to carve out a political space outside the arena of institutionalized democratic politics, while at the same time making it impossible for the mainstream political parties to ignore the issue. Even as they threatened a boycott of the forthcoming parliamentary elections in November, they sought to compel politicians contesting these elections to take a stand on the projects. A Harsud Narmada Sagar Struggle Committee, dating back to 1977, with all its office-bearers belonging to the ruling Congress (I), declared that the residents of the 254 villages in Khandwa and Khargone districts, scheduled to be submerged, would boycott the elections.[13]

The rally also asserted the right of people to influence government policy, and in the campaign for the Lok Sabha elections in November, V. P. Singh promised to review the scheme if the Janata Dal was voted to power. However, when his attention was drawn to the fact that such promises could jeopardize his party's prospects in the Gujarat elections, he quickly recanted. The National Front Government, headed by him, had been in power for barely two months when the contradictions between public policy and electoral compulsions began to surface, leading to a shift in the official position on the projects. Not only were policy reviews promised, and then quickly retracted for fear of electoral reverses, but the projects also became useful as a political lever for discrediting individual politicians.[14] During the subsequent campaign for the state Assembly elections in February 1990, Prime

[13] In Khandwa parliamentary constituency (within which Harsud falls), a senior Congress politician, Shiv Narain Singh, rebelled against his party and contested the election as an Independent candidate. Laxmi Narain Khandelwal resigned his membership of the BJP to lead the non-partisan Narmada Sagar Sangharsh Samiti.

[14] One of these contradictions became apparent when, in January 1991, the West German Minister for Economic Affairs Hans Repnik visited India and met Maneka Gandhi, Minister for Environment in the new government. Gandhi had also attended the Harsud rally, and the Congress opposition lost no time in asking for her resignation on grounds that she had appealed to a foreign government, which was among the donors of the project, against her own government's policy on a matter of national importance. Gandhi was forced to call and reassure Chimanbhai Patel that the allegations were false. She subsequently maintained a diplomatic silence on both the Narmada and Tehri dams for some time.

Minister Singh gave unequivocal assurances on the project in all his election meetings in Gujarat.

Meanwhile, even the Narmada Control Authority, in its Status Report of May 1989, had declared itself dissatisfied on several counts, including inadequate rehabilitation plans, incomplete surveys, and the absence of proper action plans from the State governments. The Narmada Sagar Project still awaited clearance from the Planning Commission and the World Bank. The Bank, meanwhile, was reported to be having serious differences with the Indian government, even threatening to stop further disbursements on account of poor performance on rehabilitation. This threat, in addition to implementation problems such as cost and time overruns, provoked the Government of Gujarat to moot the idea of raising additional money from Non-Resident Indians, especially Gujaratis in the UK, USA, Africa, and West Asia who, it claimed, had conveyed their willingness to invest in debentures for the prosperity of their homeland. In 1990, Chimanbhai Patel and his Irrigation Minister visited the UK and the USA to attract investment and to counter the adverse publicity given to the project (Sheth, 1991: 37–8). Within Gujarat, the campaign launched by the Sardar Sarovar Nigam Limited[15] was becoming increasingly aggressive, with its Chairman Sanat Mehta stating unabashedly that no political party in Gujarat could survive even for a day, if its commitment to the project was suspect (*Times of India*, 15.9.1989).

Cultural chauvinism has been a key ingredient in the image-making exercises undertaken by the project authorities. In September 1989, the Gujarat Minister for Water Resources Development, Mahant Vijaydas, moved a resolution in the Legislative Assembly, supported by the Leader of the Opposition, Chimanbhai Patel, as well as by BJP and Congress (I) members, attacking anti-dam activists for being 'air-conditioned critics' and anti-national agents of foreign interests. The people of Gujarat, he affirmed, would fight

[15] The Sardar Sarovar Narmada Nigam Limited (SSNNL) was established in April 1988, with its headquarters in Gandhinagar, Gujarat. It is an autonomous corporation responsible for the implementation of the Sardar Sarovar Project, and was set up because it was believed that a corporation would be better equipped for this task than an executive body like the already existing Narmada Planning Group. Both the SSNNL and the Narmada Valley Development Authority report to the Narmada Control Authority which, in turn, reports to the Union Ministry of Water Resources.

to their last breath to save the project. This resolution of the State assembly was subsequently cited by Barber Conable, the World Bank President, to demonstrate to a US Congressional Committee, the extent of popular support for the project. Among the provocations for this resolution was the foreign lobbying undertaken by the NBA against the project. In September 1989, anti-dam activists mobilized protests outside the offices of the World Bank in Washington DC, while the Bank held its annual meeting. They also lobbied senators and, along with over a hundred NGOs from several countries, sent resolutions to the US Congress to pressurize the Bank to withdraw from this and other such projects.[16]

In this first phase of resistance to the Sardar Sarovar and Narmada Sagar projects, thus, we see the beginnings of a movement that was to gather considerable strength in the next few years. The pre-eminence of the ARCH-Vahini, and its attempts to pressurize the State government and the World Bank for a better rehabilitation policy were superseded, by 1988–9, by the Narmada Bachao Andolan. The Vahini's decision to involve itself with the monitoring of the rehabilitation policy and its implementation gradually came to be seen as a conservative position of collusion with official agencies, when compared with the more radical opposition of the Andolan to the environmental and social consequences of the project and the interrrogation of the development strategy it represented. Their respective claims to be the authentic representatives of the tribals in the Narmada Valley continued however to be contentious.

The role of the state calls for disaggregation in terms of the federal and regional levels. The Government of Gujarat had already

[16] Medha Patkar and two others testified before a Congressional Sub-Committee on the project, in which the US Treasury Department, while expressing concern about the loss of forests and the problems of resettlement, highlighted the benefits of the project for the farmers of the drought-prone areas of Gujarat. In his reply to the committee, Barber Conable, President of the Bank, insisted that its original decision to support this project remained sound, and cited the Gujarat Assembly resolution as evidence of this (*Patriot*, 18.11.1989). Meanwhile, in the Indian media, the NBA became the object of harsh, even hysterical, criticism. *The Times of India* commented editorially that 'their effort to instigate international interference in India's affairs has to be deplored. It demonstrates their lack of faith in the sense of the people of India' (1.11.1989).

launched a strident publicity campaign in favour of the project, drawing upon parochial sentiment and cultural chauvinism to whip up support. The more aggressive, flashy, and expensive phase of this campaign was yet to follow. The role of the Union Government in hastily securing clearance for the project, despite reservations from several departments was, as we have seen, dictated by electoral considerations. In the general election that took place in 1989, senior politicians equivocated in their responses to the project, exemplifying the uncertainty and confusion that characterized this phase. Political instability at the Centre continued, through the next phase, to contribute to the changeableness of political positions on the project, internal divisions within political parties, and contradictions between politics at the State and federal levels.

Finally, it is certain that while the NBA enjoyed widespread support from the international NGO community, especially from environmental NGOs, the World Bank's willingness to shut its eyes to some of the unpleasanter realities of resettlement assisted the aggressive posturing of the Government of Gujarat. Under pressure from its own consultants like Thayer Scudder, and from organizations like the ARCH-Vahini, the Bank insisted on and secured some improvements in R&R policy, but engaged in a willing suspension of disbelief when it came to the evidence of governmental failure to implement these.[17]

II.2 *Confrontation*

The second phase in this narrative is characterized by a hardening of positions on the part of the government, on the one hand, and an expansion and strengthening of the movement against the dam, on the other. In the State assembly elections of 1990, the Janata Dal won the elections in Gujarat, and Chimanbhai Patel was sworn in as Chief Minister. In Madhya Pradesh, a BJP government headed by Sunderlal Patwa was voted in by a huge majority. This became the stage of the next phase of the struggle against the Narmada projects, not least because 8 MLAs from constituencies in the submergence areas were elected on the express assurance that they

---

[17] The low credibility of governmental efforts was due, among other things, to the persisting problem of the non-availability of land, the absence of data about the extent of displacement, and disturbing evidence about poor living conditions in the existing resettlement sites (Parasuraman, 1997: 45).

would support the movement against the dam, and nearly 40 MLAs in the new Assembly had pledged their support to the movement.

Only a day into his Chief Ministership, Patwa was faced by a *rasta roko* agitation near Indore, in which a 'human chain' of 15,000 persons blocked traffic for 28 hours and lifted the blockade only after an assurance that the Chief Minister would approach the Centre for a review of the project. S. C. Shukla, the former Chief Minister, and now Leader of the Opposition in the Assembly, again raised the issue of reducing the height of the dam to reduce the area of submergence, a position he had consistently espoused (*Patriot*, 14.4.1990; Interview, 4.3.1992).

It however soon became apparent that though the BJP Government in Madhya Pradesh had committed itself, in its election manifesto, to a review of the NVP, it was internally divided on the issue of the dams, with its official position very gradually crystallizing into one favouring the dam. Even as Patwa agreed to appeal to the Centre for a reappraisal of the project, he decided to go ahead with the work, pending a review, as the Gujarat Government was going ahead in any case. At the heart of his inability to take a strongly pro-dam position was probably the fact that the BJP had won 16 out of the 17 seats in Khandwa and Khargone districts, largely on account of their promise to withdraw support for the dam. MLAs from Barwani, Kasrawad, Nimarkheri, and Harsud had vowed to work against the Narmada Sagar Project. The State government, now inclined to proceed with the dam, attempted to deflect the agitation towards the Central and Gujarat Governments.

Meanwhile, the Narmada Bachao Andolan turned its attention to Delhi, where it held a demonstration of 300 tribals outside Shram Shakti Bhawan, the offices of the Ministry of Labour, as well as a three-day rally at the Boat Club in April 1990. Though they lobbied several Ministers, including two—Madhu Dandavate and Ramakrishna Hegde—who were sympathetic to their cause, the ministerial statements that emanated from these discussions were often contradictory and confusing. Prime Minister V. P. Singh gave an assurance that the Land Acquisition Act would be suitably amended making the takeover of tribal lands difficult. Ram Vilas Paswan, the Minister for Labour, promised adequate compensation in terms of land or money to those affected. Manubhai Kotadia, Minister for Water Resources, said the SSP would be reviewed only if any of the conditions laid down by the NWDT Award were violated, but refused to concede that Canal Affected Persons were also entitled to compensation like the Project Affected Persons. Baba Amte pleaded for a comprehensive reappraisal of the project, threatening *jal samadhi* (suicide by drowning) on a large scale, but the PM agreed only to a limited review by a Committee of Secretaries from the Ministries of Water Resources, Environment, and Social Welfare, while refusing to stop work on the project pending the report of this committee.

Chimanbhai Patel, however, ruled out any review, saying that the Tribunal's Award was binding on the Centre and all the concerned States that were signatories to it. If the Centre was, he said, responsive to rallyists at the Boat Club in Delhi, another rally could easily be organized in support of the projects. His counter-mobilization took the form of the Gujarat Bachao Andolan, a rally of 5000 people representing various political parties, voluntary agencies, farmers, Gandhian social workers, and tribal area organizations brought from Gujarat at enormous cost, estimated at Rs 40 lakhs. The meeting, held in June 1990, was addressed by Patel himself, and many others, including the Leader of the Opposition in the Assembly and President of the Gujarat Congress (I) Natwarlal Shah, and the BJP state unit President, Shankarsinh Waghela. This rally was unusual in that it represented the unanimity of all major parties in the State, and was led by a State Chief Minister against his own party's government at the Centre. A memorandum demanding the speedy completion of the projects was submitted to the Prime Minister under the banner of the Narmada Abhiyan Samiti. Similar rallies were organized in Bombay and in South Gujarat. They were heavily subsidized by the Narmada Foundation Trust, set up by the Gujarat Chamber of Commerce and Industry, which has consistently given moral and material support to the project.

Meanwhile, in May, the environmental status report of the Ministry of Environment on the SSP pointed out that the engineering work on the project was far ahead of the work on the rehabilitation and environmental aspects, which were supposed to be implemented *pari passu*.[18] Plans for rehabilitation and environment protection, which were supposed to have been ready by 1989

---

[18] In September 1990, at a meeting of the Narmada Control Authority, the Government of Gujarat admitted that it had not met several conditions laid down in the clearances given by the Ministry of Environment and the Planning

and implemented simultaneously with the construction work, were still not ready. Indeed, all the concerned States asked for another two to three years' time to even complete the necessary studies and formulate the plans. The Planning Commission also took a serious view of the fact that the environmental clearance given to the project three years earlier had lapsed, and that the Gujarat Government had failed to act on the conditions stipulated in the clearance. The Gujarat Government, however, relied upon its mobilization of popular support to prevent any possible institutional obstacles to the project at the Centre.

The World Bank meanwhile released another instalment of the loan, conveying not only its implicit approval of the project, but also making it possible for Gujarat to make more confident promises about its speedy execution.[19] The one reverse it suffered was when Japan, under pressure from its own environmentalist lobby, decided to suspend aid for the project from its Overseas Development Assistance, which had agreed to finance the power generation equipment for the SSP.

The NBA, meanwhile, planned a long march called the Jan Vikas Sangharsh Yatra, to begin on 25 December 1990. Described as 'the first move in the "final phase" of the anti-Sardar Sarovar

---

Commission, including the requirement of command area development to prevent the problems of waterlogging and salinity which have resulted from large dam projects the world over (Goldsmith and Hildyard, 1984a: 141–63). Rajasthan too repeatedly protested against this, as it was likely to suffer the salinity (*Sunday Observer*, 30.9.1990). Reports from some resettlement sites set up by the Gujarat Government also showed that, contrary to the promised resettlement package, the oustees were living in pitiable conditions in transit camps, with tin shed housing that was hot in summer and not rainproof, without electricity or even adequate water. Frequently, barren or waterlogged land was given instead of the promised 5 acres of fertile land.

[19] At one stage, the Government of Gujarat even contemplated launching a Rs 5 crore advertising campaign in India and abroad, and the SSNNL retained the advertising agency Lintas for this purpose. It was restrained by an interim order of the Gujarat High Court in response to a petition filed by a BJP MLA challenging the Government's action as unconstitutional, and arguing that the Rs 5 crore would be better spent on rehabilitation than on advertising. In the meantime, an NBA campaign of protest telephone calls and letters resulted in a withdrawal by the agency itself, though not without having sparked off an animated debate between media and advertising professionals about the conflict between professionalism and social consciousness.

Project movement' (*Narmada*, 7/8, 1991: 3), the Yatra was intended to physically stop work on the dam, by offering satyagraha at the dam site, hoping thereby to pressurize the government into a comprehensive review of the SSP. As with the Delhi demonstration, the Chief Minister of Gujarat announced plans for a counter-mobilization.

The Sangharsh Yatra, attended by people from Bihar, Madhya Pradesh, and Maharashtra, as well as visitors from Japan and the USA, commenced in the Nimar region of Madhya Pradesh. Camping at various places en route, it made its way to Ferkuwa on the Gujarat–Madhya Pradesh border, where Section 144 was enforced. The counter-rally also approached the border, though from the Gujarat side. Attempts by the NBA rallyists to enter Gujarat were thwarted by the police, leading to some arrests and violence. A week passed, and with entry into Gujarat still barred by the police, the NBA resorted to an indefinite fast by Medha Patkar and six others. In the face of the Gujarat Government's intransigence, the protestors were left with little option except to withdraw on 28 January, the twenty-second day of the fast. Prime Minister Chandra Shekhar intervened only to request the Gujarat administration to allow Baba Amte to cross over to the State and address the pro-dam rallyists. As head of a minority government, dependent for the smallest scrap of political support, he could not be persuaded to commit the government to a review, however partial, of the project, and the Centre's efforts were thus restricted to avoiding violence between the two sides in what was, rather dramatically, described as a 'people vs. people' confrontation. There is little doubt that the Gujarat Government won this skirmish easily, even if at an estimated cost of Rs 3 crores raised by organizations like the Gujarat Chamber of Commerce and Industry. But there is even less doubt that this was, more than Harsud, a dramatic event that not only generated widespread sympathy for the movement, but also brought it to the notice of the nation, and placed it at the very centre of the debate on development and environment in India.

Even as the Ferkuwa agitation was coming to a head, a *dharna* of 400 tribal people in Delhi met the President and the Prime Minister, and represented the central issues of their struggle as the Narmada dam; the right of tribal village society to manage its affairs democratically through its institutions of local self-government; and the rights of tribals to minor forest produce. Asserting their rights over the common property resources of the village—water, forests, lands, and mines—they generated the slogan that the retreating protestors of Ferkuwa carried away with them: *hamara gaon, hamara raj* (*Narmada*, 7/8, 1991: 16–20).

After the Ferkuwa agitation, the Narmada flowed relatively quietly, the construction work on the dam proceeded apace, and few, if any, ripples were created by the occasional dissenting voices from within state agencies and academic institutions.[20] Among these was Dr U. R. Rao, Secretary in the Department of Space, who used remote sensing to show how a reduction in the height of the dam would save 184 villages from submergence. This document, prepared in 1990, was submitted to the Planning Commission, but did not reach the Ministry of Environment. This Ministry, for its part, held that the NCA had not approached it for a fresh environmental approval, while at the Planning Commission, the Deputy Chairman Mohan Dharia was lobbied by Chimanbhai Patel for speedy execution of the project. The commitment of the State governments to proceed at the quickest possible pace was also underlined by the Governors' addresses in the legislative assemblies of both Gujarat and Madhya Pradesh.

As the Lok Sabha elections of 1991 drew closer, the NBA threatened an election boycott as a gesture to demonstrate its lack of trust in the political process and the hollow claims of representative democracy. This threat was foreshadowed by its earlier boycott of the census operations of the Government in the villages of three districts, Khargone, Jhabua and Dhar, which had forced the census authorities to resort to secondary means of enumeration, such as the records of ration cards, schools, hospitals, and voters' lists. In some villages, total non-cooperation or *gaon bandi* (literally, village closure) was effected by barring entrance to officials or not paying agricultural taxes. The boycott of Lok Sabha elections was announced in 33 villages of Dhule district in

---

[20] The Anthropological Survey of India refused to undertake a study of the effects of displacement on tribal communities, being reluctant to provide a politically useful report. Likewise, the Tata Institute of Social Sciences in Bombay, which had been retained as one of the principal monitoring and evaluation agencies for the project, insisted, without success, that its reports, demonstrating the high mortality rates among outstees resettled in Parveta, should be made public, as displaced persons had a right to this information.

Maharashtra in March, and similar discussions in 195 villages of Khargone and Dhar districts were reported to be in progress, with village-level committees expected to announce their decisions. But in mid-April, following a meeting with about a dozen other 'people's movements' in Delhi, Patkar modified this decision, leaving it to individual villages to decide on the boycott. The voters were advised only to ask the candidates who came to campaign whether their manifesto mentioned the right to life of the tribals and farmers of the Narmada Valley and, depending on their response to this question, to decide how to cast their votes. Eventually, 33 villages on the Maharashtra–Gujarat border of the Akrani and Dhadgaon parliamentary constituencies in Maharashtra, announced their decision to boycott the elections, adopting the slogan *Amra gaon, amra raj* (Our village, our rule). The Andolan's overall strategy, however, of boycotting all government operations in the Valley, was neither rescinded nor reviewed. One rather dramatic example of this strategy was the alleged abduction of an official of the Maharashtra government and the interrogation, in a dense forest, of the newly appointed Special Assistant Collector for Rehabilitation, M. S. Gill.[21]

In July 1991, a new Congress government assumed office at the Centre, with P. V. Narasimha Rao as Prime Minister. Among the Congress MPs from Madhya Pradesh, Kamal Nath was appointed Minister of State for Environment and Forests, while V. C. Shukla was given the Water Resources portfolio. Both ministers made statements supporting the Narmada Valley Projects shortly after assuming office.[22] The State governments in Gujarat and Madhya Pradesh remained unchanged for the time being, though in June 1992, a merger was effected between Chimanbhai Patel's Janata Dal (Gujarat) and the Congress (I). Patel led his flock back to the

---

[21] On the NBA's version, when Gill visited the disputed tribal area of Bamni, he was merely surrounded by the local people, who wanted to complain to him about the government's palpable lack of sympathy. Gill himself has claimed that members of his team were abused and violently attacked (Gill, 1995: 242–3).

[22] Kamal Nath declared the dam environmentally safe as Gujarat, he claimed, had fulfilled almost all the environmental conditions, and only Maharashtra was yet to fully comply (*Indian Express*, 23.8.1991). Likewise, Shukla, in a statement in Parliament, cited the opinion of the European Commission that the SSP was deserving of support.

Congress after 18 years, and was unanimously elected leader of the Congress Legislature Party. Significantly, the only member of the State cabinet who was allowed to continue as a minister without aligning himself with the Congress was Babubhai Patel, the Minister for Narmada Development. His Gandhian record, and his association with the project since its inception, obviously meant that he could perform a useful role in countering the arguments of the anti-dam activists. That Chimanbhai Patel did not sacrifice the Narmada minister is an indication of the importance attached to this portfolio in the Gujarat government.

In Gujarat, work on the SSP continued apace, while in Madhya Pradesh, the Patwa government continued to be hostile and repressive towards the anti-dam activists,[23] even as it vacillated on the question of lowering the height of the dam.[24] It also continued to petition the World Bank for assistance for the Narmada Sagar Project, pointing out that the anti-dam agitators were all 'outsiders'

[23] Protest at various locations in Madhya Pradesh continued to be met with repression: arrests, harassment, lathi-charges, and police brutality. Arrest and physical injury were the price paid by agitators organizing roadblocks; preventing work from being carried on at bridges; or protesting, through rallies and marches, against survey work. This last incident involved 238 arrests, including that of Nandini Oza, an associate of Baba Amte.

[24] In addition to S. C. Shukla, Leader of the Congress Party Opposition in the Assembly, who had consistently favoured lowering the height of the dam, another influential politician V. M. Saklecha, also now began to espouse the same cause. The NWDT Award had been given during Saklecha's tenure as Chief Minister of Madhya Pradesh, but it was suggested that his acquiescence to the projects at the time was due to political pressure from the Gujarat Government, and the support it enjoyed of the then Prime Minister Morarji Desai. Now in the BJP, Saklecha demanded a reduction in the height of the dam to reduce submergence in M. P. His party colleague, Vijayraje Scindia went even further, threatening to launch a movement against the projects if the displaced were not properly rehabilitated. BJP President, Murli Manohar Joshi also called for a review of the project at a press conference in Indore, but retracted his statement only a week later in Baroda on the advice of his party colleagues in Gujarat. Even senior party leader Atal Behari Vajpayee favoured a review of the project, but the BJP at the national level did not appear to have an official position on the projects, and this confusion was naturally reflected in the State government's policy pronouncements. Thus, Minister for Irrigation Shitla Sahay, sometimes definitively ruled out a reduction in height, and at other times pleaded helplessness in negotiating a

and that the people of the area wanted the dam. Whenever the prospects of World Bank financing appeared to be bleak, the government resorted to brave assertions of confidence in its ability to raise resources for the project internally. The ambiguity of the M. P. government's position, and its vacillation between truculent support for the projects and hesitant requests for height reduction, may be partially explicable in terms of the results of the parliamentary elections of 1991. The BJP did extremely well in Gujarat, winning 20 out of 25 seats. In M. P., by contrast, the Congress fared very well, winning 27 out of 40 Lok Sabha seats. The BJP posed as much of a threat to the Patel Ministry in Gujarat, as the Congress did to the Patwa Government in Madhya Pradesh. The latter could not therefore insist on fresh elections in Gujarat, for these could only be held at its own peril in Madhya Pradesh. It was thus possible for the Congress Opposition in the Madhya Pradesh Assembly to use the Narmada issue to taunt the Patwa regime, which, when it stoutly defended the project, was told that it was arguing ably on behalf of the Gujarat government, thus bringing the issue of regional chauvinism to the forefront in the political debate on the dam.

In Maharashtra, meanwhile, the task of clearing villages scheduled to be submerged was beginning. Even as the Bombay High Court restrained the Government from forcible evictions, the focus of the agitation against the SSP shifted to one of these villages, Manibeli, in Dhule district. The 74-day Manibeli satyagraha of the NBA was launched on 14 July 1991. It was provoked by notices issued on 15 May to people in the villages of Gadher and Vadgam (Gujarat), asking them to move out of their homes within five days, because it was possible that these might be submerged in the monsoon due to the Sardar Sarovar dam. The NCA's schedule of submergence of villages published in March had clearly stated that the earliest submergence would take place in 1992. In any case, the NWDT Award obliged the government to inform the people at least a year before submergence, and resettle them on land of their choice at least six months prior to submergence. Though such

---

reduction, on the plea that his government was irreversibly committed to the present parameters of the project by the preceding Congress government (*Rajasthan Patrika*, 11.7.1991).

notices had not been issued in Manibeli, it was clear that it would certainly also be submerged along with Gadher and Vadgam, being situated at a lower elevation than those villages just across the river. It was this that determined the choice of Manibeli, the first Maharashtra village to be submerged, as the location of this phase of the agitation. The mode of agitation here was to stay at Manibeli, and face the rising waters, even if it meant drowning: *doobenge, par hatenge nahin*. As more and more people came to Manibeli to join the satyagraha, the Gujarat Chief Minister issued a statement to say that submergence would not occur before 1993, and if it did, it would be due not to the dam but to 'natural floods'. His Narmada Development Minister, Babubhai Patel, said that the notices had been a 'mistake' on the part of junior officials, and that no submergence was expected on account of the dam. At the same time, the Government of Maharashtra issued a notice (undated) to say that there was a possibility of flood waters submerging the village. Villagers from Gadher and Vadgam were taken to temporary camps. At the end of July, the waters of the Narmada began to rise, but after two days of being in spate, close to the agitators, it receded.

In early August, the Maharashtra police entered Manibeli by boat, stormed Narmadayi, the symbolic hut built by the NBA such that it would be the first dwelling to be submerged, and arrested 68 villagers. The arrests continued over the next few days, and Section 144 of the Indian Penal Code was imposed on the 36 villages of Maharashtra scheduled for submergence, Medha Patkar and a few other activists were declared *persona non grata* by the district administration, and 'chapter cases' were filed against them, on charges including attacking officials with lethal weapons, rioting, and incitement to riot. Most access routes to Manibeli from the Gujarat side were also barred, and it is significant that roadblocks were manned not only by the Gujarat police, but also by employees of Jaiprakash Associates, the construction firm building the dam.

The waters, meanwhile, began rising again in the last week of August. Radio warnings were broadcast but not heeded, and after three days of rising and falling, the river eventually receded once more. Officials who attempted to enter Manibeli, as did a team from the Union Ministry of Social Welfare, were refused admission.

The Chief Engineers of Gujarat and Maharashtra, sent by the Bombay High Court to ascertain the effects of the backwaters of the dam on the village, were taken around by the Andolan, while the Additional Collector (Rehabilitation), M. S. Gill, was not allowed in. This was part of the NBA's symbolic strategy, the *gaon bandi*, of outlawing an unresponsive government.[25]

This second phase of confrontation between the anti-dam movement and the State had without doubt been the most dramatic that had so far occurred in the history of this conflict. Both the major mobilizations by the Narmada Bachao Andolan were, in an ironical manipulation of the democratic idea, countered by political mobilizations sponsored by the Government of Gujarat. The NBA's choice of an extra-parliamentary politics of protest was expressed not only in its advocacy of boycott of elections, but also in the form of the *gaon bandi* strategy of preventing government functionaries of all description from entering the villages. Equivocation by a weak government at the Centre contrasted with the determined resolve of the Government of Gujarat in proceeding with the project and mobilizing both resources and popular opinion in its favour. Even the government of Madhya Pradesh, which was paying a more exacting price for the project in terms of the extent of submergence and benefiting correspondingly less, actively engaged in the repression of activists.

Recognizing that there was intense opposition to the dam both within and without the country, and that its environmental and social consequences had still not received adequate attention from the government, the World Bank set up, in March 1991, an Independent Review Team, headed by Bradford Morse, to examine the project specifically in terms of these two parameters. The report of the Independent Review proved to be of great significance for the future of the project, and coincided with a phase in which the forces of the anti-dam movement and the State were evenly balanced in a no-win situation.

[25] In 1992, the Narmada Control Authority classified the accessibility of villages to government officials thus: Gujarat: free access and no resistance; Madhya Pradesh: no access and complete resistance in 34 villages, difficult access with moderate resistance in 99 villages, and no resistance in the remaining 60 villages; Maharashtra: no access to all 33 villages (Parasuraman, 1997: 49).

II.3 *Checkmate*

The terms of reference of the Independent Review[26] required it to consider, firstly, the measures being taken for the R&R of the displaced people, both the Project Affected Persons as well as the Canal Affected Persons;[27] and, secondly, the measures being taken to ameliorate the environmental impact of 'all aspects of the Projects'.

The Government of Gujarat reportedly feted and wooed the mission and arranged for it to meet not only with officials, but with representatives of all political parties in the State, with delegations of oustees satisfied with resettlement, and with members of the Gujarat Chamber of Commerce and Industry. This is indicative of the optimism of the Gujarat Government, and its expectation of being vindicated by the review committee. When, in June 1992, the Report of the Independent Review was published, it certainly gave a more favourable verdict on Gujarat's efforts on R&R than on those of Maharashtra and Madhya Pradesh. Yet, its reservations about the serious shortcomings of the project as a whole led to the Gujarat Government publicly announcing that the team was biased and lacked credibility. The NBA, on the other hand, initially adopted a cautious approach to the mission, but later cooperated actively with it, when assured that its terms of reference could be

---

[26] The Committee consisted of Bradford Morse, an American politician and a former head of the UNDP; Thomas Berger, a Canadian lawyer known for his work on aboriginal, environmental, and human rights issues; Donald Gamble, an environmental scientist, and Hugh Brody, an anthropologist. The Team travelled extensively in the Narmada Valley: to villages, relocation sites, the dam site; the upstream, downstream and command areas; as well as to the drought-prone areas of Gujarat. They met ministers and officials of the Government of India, as well as of the three State governments, members of NGOs, and other concerned citizens.

[27] Even as the members of the Independent Review were conducting their mission, a study of the Indian Institute of Management, Ahmedabad, commissioned by the SSNNL, on Canal Affected Persons was completed and released. This report estimated that the canal-affected people numbered 2.2 lakhs (twice the number of people being displaced by the reservoir), of whom 15,000 would become totally landless. Accordingly, it suggested a compensation package for the CAPs which would have cost the government about three times its budget for compensation. It was therefore not surprising that the Nigam first kept the findings secret, then disputed them, and eventually disowned the report.

expanded, and that the review committee would 'determine the truth regarding the project as objectively, honestly and independently as possible' (*Free Press Journal*, 22.10.1991).

In June 1992, the *Report of the Independent Review* was released and made public. The Independent Review recommended that the Bank 'step back from the Projects and consider them afresh' (xxv) as 'absence of adequate data, failure of consultation and hostility to the Project in the Narmada Valley bear on every aspect of implementation' (Independent Review: 355). The World Bank was accused of overlooking obvious evidence of non-compliance with its own policy on involuntary settlement (World Bank, 1980); its comprehensive resettlement policy for oustees generally (World Bank, 1990) and for tribals in particular (World Bank, 1991). The Government of India, for its part, had failed to adhere to the requirements of the ILO's Convention 107 on the *Protection and Integration of Indigenous and other Tribal and Semi-Tribal Populations in Independent Countries*, to which it had been a signatory since 1958. On the environmental impact of the project, the *Review* noted that environmental clearance had been given to the projects, though the information required for such clearance had thus far remained unavailable. Similarly, the hydrological data and analyses contained discrepancies, and the cumulative effects of the SSP and NSP had not been studied. Above all, the plans for the delivery of drinking water to the drought-prone districts of Kutch and Saurashtra were in the earliest stages of preparation, though this was being touted as a major benefit of the project.[28] The most serious indictment was, however, of the Bank itself:

It seems clear that engineering and economic imperatives have driven the Projects to the exclusion of human and environmental concerns. Social and environmental trade-offs have been made that seem insupportable today [ibid.: xxiv].

Despite this indictment of the project's failure to satisfactorily address the questions of rehabilitation and environmental protection,

[28] While defending the projects at the Earth Summit at Rio de Janeiro in June 1992, SSNNL Chairman C. C. Patel admitted that the costs of supplying drinking water to these areas had not yet been calculated, while Y. K. Alagh of the Narmada Planning Group argued that, even if drinking water was not included in an assessment of the project, its benefits still far outweighed its costs (*Times of India*, 12.6.1992).

the Governments of India and Gujarat and even the World Bank remained as committed, indeed wedded, to the project as before. The Bank's President, Lewis Preston made a guarded statement saying that the Bank would continue to fund the SSP, with the necessary modifications, for the continued involvement of the Bank was more likely to ensure the redressal of the problems identified by the Review team. In July, a 14-member mission of the Bank visited India, and its briefing to the Executive Directors confirmed the anxieties of the Independent Review.[29]

However, only ten weeks after the Independent Review, in a document entitled *Narmada: Next Steps*, the Bank sought to reassure the directors by claiming that significant collaborative solutions had been developed, and that the Indian Government had adopted a comprehensive set of actions in line with the Bank's recommendations, giving evidence of its seriousness of purpose in the matter. The Bank's commitment was endorsed by its Board, conditional upon the benchmarks on both R&R and environment being met within the next six months, though several of its executive directors, commanding 41 per cent of the total vote, favoured a suspension of further disbursements (Caufield, 1996: 26–7).[30]

The Bank's innocent insistence that it was subsidizing only a small fraction of the project cost ignored the fact that even this

---

[29] The mission briefing of 5 August 1992, identified several problems in R&R implementation, including bureaucratic inflexibility; insufficient staff; lack of basic resources, especially in Madhya Pradesh; lack of procedures for handling grievances; lack of reliable data; limited and ineffective consultation with the PAPs and CAPs; and poor coordination between states on the people to be resettled in Gujarat (World Bank, 1992: 2–3).

[30] Caufield's (1996) account of these events shows that the review team was furious when it saw the document justifying continued funding and support for the project, and that Morse told the directors that the document had ignored and misrepresented the principal findings of his report. In his letter to the directors, Morse wrote: 'The Bank may decide that overriding political and economic considerations are so compelling that its Operational Directives are irrelevant when decisions have to be made, about the Sardar Sarovar Project. But it should not seek to reshape our report to support such decisions' (ibid.: 27). Thus, despite the opposition of directors from the US, Canada, Japan, Germany, Australia, and the Scandinavian countries, the board voted to give India another five months to comply with the terms of the loan.

small component was the very seal of approval as far as other foreign lenders were concerned. Thus, emboldened by the World Bank's assurance of continued support, the Government of India declared that, notwithstanding the recommendations of the Independent Review, it had no intentions of reviewing the project. However, on a bilateral basis, many countries had begun to reconsider their loans and support for the project. In Sweden, reservations about the SSP were already being widely entertained. Parliamentarians belonging to several parties—the Swedish Left Party, the erstwhile Communist Party and the Greens party— argued that, as a constituent member of the World Bank consortium, Sweden had invested 2.8 billion SEK in the project, and that its participation in this ecologically destructive project should therefore be subject to public and parliamentary scrutiny. Patkar visited several countries in Europe,[31] addressing meetings and press conferences. Shortly thereafter, it was announced that two committees, one of the German Federal Parliament and another from Sweden, would visit the Narmada valley and assess the project. 34 members of the Bundestag (the lower house of the German Parliament) had urged the suspension of the Project and demanded a government statement justifying Bonn's consent to World Bank credit to the SSP. Some months later, a visit to the Narmada Valley by the Bundestag's Committee on Environment, Nature Conservation, and Nuclear Safety was not positive in its response. Japan had already suspended assistance to the project, members of the Japanese Diet had been lobbied, and the Japanese Broadcasting Corporation had shown an hour-long television programme on the environmental damage that would result from the construction of the dam. Bertrand Schneider, the Secretary-General of the Club of Rome, at a government-sponsored international seminar in Delhi, described the project as 'scandalous' (*Hindustan Times*, 9.3.1992).

Meanwhile, the resource crunch was manifest and threatening. The Bank had, pending the Independent Review, put on hold the processing of a loan instalment of $ 375 million. The Government announced in the Gujarat legislature that, prices having gone up

[31] In Stockholm, Medha Patkar was given the Right Livelihood Award, the sponsors of which wrote to the Indian Prime Minister, questioning the legitimacy of a project 'if it tramples on the cultures, livelihood and basic rights of the people' (*Indian Express*, 9.12.1991).

by 8–10 per cent, the estimated cost of the project was also up by Rs 9 crores. The Chief Minister, while insisting that the project would be completed on time, admitted that his government would be able to marshal only Rs 2900 crores in the Eighth Plan period, as against a requirement of Rs 5500 crores for the dam.[32] Nevertheless, some support for the project was forthcoming from various state agencies, most notably the Supreme Court which had been petitioned by Dr B. D. Sharma, Commissioner for Scheduled Castes and Tribes, regarding the rehabilitation of 1,30,000 people, mostly tribals, displaced by the dam. In a ruling that provided a shot in the arm for the government, the Court recognizing that it had not been asked to pronounce on the viability of the dam, nevertheless declared that it would like the work to be expeditiously completed. It however simultaneously directed the three State governments to evolve an effective rehabilitation package consistent with Article 21 (pertaining to the right to life) of the Constitution.

The focus of the anti-dam agitation, meanwhile, had once again shifted to Manibeli, provoked by the serving of eviction notices to tribals in about a dozen villages on both sides of the river. A signboard went up in Manibeli, barring entry to all government officials except teachers and doctors, signed 'By Order of the People'. A resident of the village said:

We are not rats. We are the very same people who form this *sarkar*. They touched our feet for our votes and now, in power, they threaten to uproot us [*Pioneer*, 19.1.1992].

In several upstream villages, agitated residents refused to accept eviction notices, and physically drove away the police and other officials who had come to serve them. This also happened in Manibeli, where district administration officials therefore came to the village at night, leaving a sheaf of eviction notices outside the

[32] In the wake of the demolition of the Babri Masjid in December 1992, 340 persons were killed in Gujarat in communal riots. The state government decided to give only 40 per cent of the relief compensation of Rs 2 lakhs to the families of those who lost their lives in cash and the remaining 60 per cent in the form of Narmada Vikas Patras which would mature over a period of twenty years. By this clever channelling of relief funds from the State exchequer into the dam project, the SSP was made the real beneficiary of an ostensibly humanitarian gesture (*Indian Express*, 1.2.1993).

thirteenth century Shoolpaneshwar temple, also threatened by submergence.[33] By March 1992, the Government of Maharashtra was preparing to resort to police action, despite Chief Minister Naik's assurance to the NBA that force would not be used. Twelve truckloads of police were stationed on the outskirts of Manibeli, as 178 families of the village determined not to vacate their homes. 18 families which had been given alternate land returned the papers to the revenue minister. The NBA launched a fresh round of protest in Bombay and Delhi (which extended to protest outside the World Bank offices), and also challenged the forcible evictions in the district court at Dhule.[34]

In January and February 1993, the NBA conducted a Lok Nivada (People's Referendum) in the Narmada Valley, covering 25,000 families, of which 22,593 said they did not wish to leave their homes to be resettled. Seventy-five per cent of the residents of sixty villages declared themselves ready to join the *jal samadhi*. The six-month deadline of the World Bank was drawing to a close in March, but before another embarassing review could be launched, and just two days before the expiry of the six-month period, the Government of India unilaterally withdrew from Bank funding, committing itself to implementing the project from its own resources, and to fully conforming to the R&R and environmental standards. The decision was justified by reference to India's 'self-respect', but created the apprehension that, without World Bank

[33] The people's resolve to resist this eviction was encouraged by the return of twenty families which had accepted rehabilitation, but now returned to their ancestral homes with woeful accounts of their relocation experiences. Similarly, twenty-four families from Vadgam in Gujarat, who had lived at the Malu resettlement site for three years, also trekked back to return resettlement land records to the government, and had to face a hostile confrontation with the police en route at Kevadia.

[34] Aware that forcible evictions were violative of a recent resolution of the UN Sub-Committee on the Prevention of Discrimination and Protection of Minorities (26 August 1991), which declared forced evictions to be 'gross violations of human rights', the Maharashtra Chief Minister told an NBA delegation that the police had been sent at the request of the Gujarat Government, only to protect those who wished to be resettled, because Gujarat apprehended the use of force by the NBA to prevent those who wanted to opt for resettlement. The move to the Parveta rehabilitation site in Gujarat thus continued, being described by Andolan activists as coercive eviction, and by the Government as evacuation.

funding, the one agency that could bind the government to meeting minimal standards was now removed from the scene.[35] Though Preston regretfully endorsed the decision, it appeared that it had triggered off an institutional crisis within the Bank, creating a measure of mistrust between the operations staff and the executive board.[36] Even as the NBA welcomed India's decision as a victory, legislators in the Gujarat Assembly gave way to emotion and even violence in their disappointment, such that all the BJP MLAs and one from the Janata Dal had to be suspended from the assembly for a day. In another incident in Ahmedabad, a convention on water became the target of violence because it was being attended by, among other activists, Medha Patkar.

Another, albeit shortlived if not illusory, victory for the NBA in 1993 was the Central Government's response to the monsoon satyagraha of that year in Manibeli. As Medha Patkar went on an indefinite fast, demanding an end to police atrocities in the village, Narmadayi, the symbolically named first hut due to be submerged, was razed to the ground by the police, and resistance only led to more arrests and assaults. Eventually, Union Minister for Water Resources, V. C. Shukla met the NBA for prolonged talks, and in what appeared to be a success for the NBA, it was decided to constitute a group of officials, experts, and eminent persons to evolve a reasonable solution to the controversy surrounding the project. Meanwhile, the water levels began rising rapidly, Baba Amte began an indefinite *dharna*, and the NBA prepared for *jal samadhi*. A five-member panel was immediately announced, though it promised and proved to be a committee without teeth.[37] Under pressure from Chimanbhai Patel and other

---

[35] A statement by P. A. Raj of the SSNNL lent substance to these fears: 'We will not go to the Bank again because we have to face the same music. We have to go by their standards, here we can live by our own' (*The Statesman*, 17.4.1993).

[36] Only a few months later, an internal review of the $ 140 billion loan portfolio of the Bank, by a former vice-president, Willi Wapenhans, was leaked. This review argued that internal pressures to fund and promote projects overwhelmed all other considerations, and that the 'approval culture' within the Bank resulted in almost 40 per cent of Bank-aided projects being unsatisfactory (*Illustrated Weekly of India*, 8–14.5.1993).

[37] The members of this committee were Dr Jayant Patil (its Chairman), Dr Vasant Gorwariker, Mr L. C. Jain, Professor V. C. Kulandaiswamy, and Dr Ramaswamy R. Iyer.

Gujarat politicians, Shukla reneged on his commitment, stating in the Lok Sabha that any change in the status of the project was ruled out. The NBA had been duped, and it was simultaneously duped again in Manibeli. The dam area was placed under the Official Secrets Act and the Defence of India Rules, while Kevadia was virtually a police camp. In one of the most shocking episodes in the annals of the agitation, a fifteen year old tribal boy, Raimal Punya Vasave who, along with other tribals of Chinchkhedi village, was opposing the survey of villages to be submerged, was killed when police fired to disperse the protestors.

In Kutch, the purported ultimate beneficiary of the project, the Kutch Jal Sankat Niwaran Samiti (committee for relief from water scarcity) threatened an agitation for water. Pro-dam politicians were alarmed by this, as it might strengthen the case of the anti-dam lobby, but could not allay local perceptions of neglect by the government, which was seen as heavily biased in favour of the prosperous south Gujarat areas, encouraging sugar factories and water-intensive sugar-cane cultivation, while Kutch thirsted.

At the institutional level too, the conflicts persisted. The Monitoring and Evaluation Agency appointed by the Maharashtra Government, the Tata Institute of Social Sciences, concluded a six-year study in December 1993, challenging official claims about resettlement sites. The Gujarat Government however floated bonds worth Rs 300 crores, and the attractive rates of interest offered were an index of its desperation. It even amended the Cooperatives Act of the State to enable cooperatives to invest in the issue. The Centre, for its part, announced that it would make good the shortfall created by the termination of World Bank assistance for the project.

II. 4 *Impasse*

The next and final phase in the movement against the dam began in 1994, and remains unconcluded. The two most important events that heralded it were, first, the sudden death of Chimanbhai Patel in February 1994, and second, the initiative taken by the new Congress Chief Minister of Madhya Pradesh, Digvijay Singh, in campaigning for a lowering of the height of the dam from 455 feet to 436 feet. This move was intended to save 30,000 people and 6000 ha. of land in M. P. from submergence, thereby also reducing the benefits that would have accrued to that state under the original plan, but without affecting Gujarat's share of water or power. If the first event deprived Gujarat of its most powerful and committed advocate of the dam, the second placed on the agenda an altogether new option regarding the future of the project which is even today under consideration of the Supreme Court.

This phase has seen many developments that could be construed as encouraging for the movement against the dam project. Ironically, however, these have coincided with an impasse in terms of both the stay on further construction imposed by the Supreme Court, as also in terms of a decline in the dynamism and momentum of the movement itself. The Ministry of Environment and Forests had already, in 1993, pointed out that the environmental clearance given to the project had lapsed. Even the Narmada Control Authority urged suspension of all further work on the dam, as conditionalities of environment and R&R had not been met. At the end of 1994, the report of the five-member group headed by Jayant Patil was made public on the instructions of the Supreme Court, which had been petitioned by the NBA in April. The findings of this Committee were by no means designed to make the government's case stronger. Quite to the contrary, the report questioned even the government's estimates of water availability of 28 MAF in the Narmada,[38] and suggested a reordering of water allocation priorities amongst different regions. It criticized the encouragement of sugar-cane cropping in the region by the award of licenses to sugar factories, as this would establish a water-intensive cropping pattern and create vested interests, thereby making it even less likely that water would reach the truly water-scarce areas. Thus, allocations of water to Kutch and Saurashtra should be increased and, if that were not feasible, then greater attention should be paid to localized water development schemes, if necessary through the revival of traditional water systems (Five Member Group, 1994: 42). In this way, the committee gave, to the dry regions of Kutch and Saurashtra, the priority that they were undeservedly denied in official planning. Through their emphasis on addressing the needs of these areas, the committee also implicitly provided for an alternative approach towards water management that was not wholly dependent on big

---

[38] The Government of Madhya Pradesh and others have claimed that the total water availability in the river is 23 MAF.

dams, but was also cognizant of local possibilities for watershed management and therefore more equitable patterns of water distribution. The committee asked the government for its detailed plans for the provision of water, along with the financial and administrative arrangements to implement it, and for a full list of villages and towns to be provided with drinking water benefits, (ibid.: 52). Similarly, on the question of rehabilitation, it expressed the view that the category of PAPs should be interpreted widely to cover 'every person or group directly or indirectly affected by the project in any manner whatsoever' (ibid.: 82).

Two other official reports lent strength to the NBA's case. The first of these was an inquiry by a team of Members of Parliament from Madhya Pradesh, headed by Dilip Singh Bhuria, to look into the problems of Scheduled Tribes in the state. This committee, apart from recommending that adivasi gram *sabhas* should have the power to decide on natural resource use, and place safeguards on rights relating to natural resources and common property resources, also suggested that work on the dam must be stayed and a reduction in its height effected. Simultaneously, a seven-member team of the Madhya Pradesh Legislative Assembly, headed by a former Irrigation minister of the state government, Ramchandra Singh Deo, was constituted to ascertain the post-resettlement conditions in Gujarat for those who had moved to these sites from M.P. The Singh Deo committee argued that while it was undoubtedly true that the dam would greatly benefit the state of Gujarat, the political obstinacy of its government should not be allowed to have a negative impact on the people of Madhya Pradesh. The gains of Gujarat must be secured at minimal cost to Madhya Pradesh. It concluded:

Our committee has to say, with great sadness, that the oustees of Madhya Pradesh are not being properly resettled in Gujarat. They are living in discomfort and their future is dark. The Madhya Pradesh Government should therefore endeavour to get further work on the dam stopped [Deo Committee Report, 1994: 8, trans. author].

If the formation of the Five Member Group was a reluctant sop to the NBA's protest in Manibeli in the monsoon satyagraha of 1993, the constitution of these two committees was a direct consequence of the Bhopal agitation of the NBA in October–November 1994. This *dharna* and indefinite fast was mounted against the backdrop of submergence in the monsoon of 1994, when the backwaters reached the plains of Nimar in M.P., generating fears of greater submergence without resettlement. The strongest demand of this agitation was that construction on the dam not be allowed to proceed beyond the height of 80.3 m. to Gujarat's declared objective of 110 m.

On 5 May 1995, the Supreme Court placed a stay on further construction of the dam—its middle spillway portions—beyond the height of 81.5 m. (80.3 m. plus hump) already accomplished. Since 1995, there have been several hearings, the filing of affidavits by the State governments, counter-affidavits by the NBA and, at the time of writing, the case is being heard by a Constitution Bench of the Supreme Court. In July 1996, following a Supreme Court order to the States to resolve their differences before appearing in Court, a meeting of the four Chief Ministers was convened by the then Prime Minister H. D. Deve Gowda. This meeting apparently reached an agreement to raise the height of the dam to 132.9 m. (436 ft.), with a displacement fall-out of ten to fifteen thousand families. Thus far, Madhya Pradesh had been demanding that the final height of the dam not exceed 436 ft., while Gujarat had been unwilling to accept anything less than the originally decided 455 ft. (138.7 m.). Now, Gujarat wanted immediate clearance to continue work on the dam and take it to a height of 360 feet (110 metres).[39] Even as the Attorney-General asked the Supreme Court to postpone the hearing, the four States which had been locked in disagreement for several days, suddenly arrived at an agreement, according to which the eventual height of the dam would remain at 455 feet. In the short run, it would be built to a height of 436 ft., and then pause for a period of five years, to allow time for further hydrological studies. The NBA naturally cried foul, till it was discovered that the purported agreement was basically a decision of the Prime Minister, that Madhya Pradesh was not a consenting party to the so-called agreement, and that it had expressed its disagreement with the way in which the meeting and its decisions had been falsely represented in public (*Narmada Samachar*, August 1996: 1–7; Sangvai, 1996: 2287). Rajasthan too

[39] It has been argued that, keeping in view the more realistic estimates of water availability, as also the quantum of displacement, it makes eminent sense, even on technical considerations, to review and reduce the height of the dam (cf. Raina, 1994: 774–5).

clarified that it had not accepted any such agreement (Prajapati, 1997: 694).

In the Supreme Court's hearing on 16 August 1996, the Court expressed its concern over human rights violations, as well as over the rehabilitation record of the project, and refused to revoke the stay on further construction. This position was reiterated in its ruling of 3 March 1997, and again upheld in its final hearings in April 1997, when the matter was finally referred to a five-member Constitution Bench of the Supreme Court of India. The Government has repeatedly claimed that it is unconstitutional for the Court to reopen the Tribunal's Award; that the Award in any case makes provision for the rehabilitation of oustees; and, finally, that the Court lacks jurisdiction even in the matter of implementation of the Award's provisions. On the other hand, counsel for the NBA has been arguing that judicial review is an accepted principle, and that the human rights issues as well as India's conformity to various ILO conventions on the subject, still remain important. Above all, the NBA has contested the claim of the States to simultaneously represent all interests, those of water claimants as well as of those adversely affected by the dam (*Narmada Samachar*, May 1997: 1–3). Whatever the final decision of the Supreme Court, its interim rulings have implicitly made a case for treating the NWDT Award as something that is open to renegotiation.

Through this period, the NBA's efforts have also received some support, intentional or otherwise, from external agencies. Thus, within months of filing a writ petition in the Supreme Court in April 1994, challenging the project on every conceivable ground—social, environmental, technical, economic and financial—the Andolan also mobilized support from over two thousand NGOs from 43 countries, all of whom signed the Manibeli Declaration, calling for a moratorium on World Bank funding for large dams all over the world. A year later, the World Bank's Project Completion Report on the SSP acknowledged that the Bank had violated its own operational guidelines on both environmental as well as R&R aspects, apart from having ignored the uncertainties regarding the economic rate of return projected (World Bank 1995: 2–4). This was vindication indeed for the NBA.

Meanwhile, there were significant developments in the valley. Large numbers of families which had opted for resettlement were now returning to their original homes, acutely dissatisfied with their living conditions on these allotted sites. The NBA has claimed that there are over 1000 such families from Gujarat, in addition to several hundred oustees from Madhya Pradesh (*Narmada Samachar*, May 1997: 6). In June 1995, the ARCH-Vahini also announced its withdrawal from the Committee on Resettlement of the Government of Gujarat, on account of dissatisfaction with the facilities provided for project oustees from M.P. resettled in Gujarat. Anil Patel, who has worked with resettlement programmes in the Narmada Valley since 1980, argues that the R&R bureaucracy in Gujarat was party to the scuttling of the programme, engaged in corruption and violated norms with impunity.

All our efforts to obtain corrective action were rejected by the administration. This had not happened before. In the past, the administration had often yielded to our gentle but persistent pressure, and rectified its mistakes and lapses.... Complacency, expediency, ignorance may all have played a part.... The agony of the tribals continues [Patel, 1997: 91–2].

On the negative side, however, there have been developments that have been less than favourable for the movement against the dam. The long wait for a judicial decision has led many families to wearily accept the resettlement package. Observers' accounts also suggest that the monsoon satyagraha in the years following 1994 have witnessed lower levels of participation and energy (Dwivedi, 1997: 18).

The NBA has responded to this situation in two quite distinct ways. In the Narmada Valley, it decided to reformulate the monsoon satyagraha in 1996 differently, in a mode of positive reconstruction rather than, as earlier, of protest and threats of suicide by drowning. This was done through an initiative called the Nav Nirman programme, which envisaged the large-scale planting of trees, housing, biogas, soil water conservation, small irrigation schemes, schools called *jeevanshalas*[40] (school of life), and libraries (International Rivers Network, 1996: 1). Outside the

---

[40] The *jeevanshalas* are an innovative educational experiment, in which teachers are trainers from among the tribals themselves, who have evolved teaching materials based on an emphasis on local history and geography; a life science curriculum that encourages children to respect their own health traditions and acquaints them with the flora and fauna of their own environment; and a language syllabus that seeks to conserve the vocabulary of their native dialects and teaches children to respect it (*The Hindu*, 13 April 1997).

valley, the NBA decided to forge an alliance with like-minded peoples' movements across the country, which were brought together under the banner of the National Alliance of People's Movements. The NBA is one of the most important constituents of the NAPM, which is inspired by the objective of challenging the dominant development paradigm, opposing the globalization and liberalization of the Indian economy, and working towards an egalitarian, just, secular, and ecologically sustainable society.

It is ironical that just as the tide has begun to turn in favour of the NBA, its momentum has tended to falter. This might be explained partly by the fact that, having decided to nominate the Supreme Court as the final arbiter, and having secured a stay from it, the NBA has deprived itself of opportunities to mobilize and of governmental targets to assail.[41] The decision to follow the path of litigation was not the outcome of unanimous agreement within the Andolan, which has had a long tradition of debate on the issue of whether the battle should be fought exclusively in the public arena, or also taken to courts at various levels. Partly, too, the loss in momentum could be attributed to the fatigue factor. The movement can be said to date back to the early 1980s, and in its more aggressive form has been active for ten years under the leadership of the NBA. In a later section of this chapter, the role of the NBA's position vis-à-vis mainstream political parties will be discussed, keeping in view examples of environmental movements outside India to whose success the lobbying of political parties has been crucial.

III. FOR REASONS OF STATE

The Indian state has been interventionist by design, and it is arguable that the primary impetus of interventionism, indeed its inspiring and guiding force, has been development. The state's claims to legitimacy have appealed to its commitment to developmental tasks, which have therefore come to acquire the rather exalted status of 'reasons of state'. To the extent that development wears the mantle of an important reason of state, it also gets inexorably aligned to a certain conception of the national interest. In a state that wins the spurs of sovereignty after a protracted

---

[41] The NBA does apparently recognize that this 'a fragile victory', and that 'vested interests could succeed in getting the construction work to start again' (International Rivers Network, June 1996: 1).

movement of national liberation, it is hardly surprising that the nation becomes an inextricable part of the constitution and even definition of the state. Nationhood is precisely what distinguishes the colonial state in India from the sovereign state that emerges from the ashes of colonialism: a state that is not only an arena of exciting new possibilities for Nehru and his compeers, but at the same time an entrenched bureaucratic structure that sets about defining its constitutive rules in ways that suggest a strong resemblance to, and continuities with, a superseded era of governance. It is hardly remarkable that the coincidence between development as *raison d'etat* and as national interest should also generate arguments of national security.

Like national security and national interest, development becomes an article of faith, as its purposes and consequences alike are placed outside the domain of that which can be legitimately questioned or challenged. The ideological neutrality of national security is requisitioned by development projects as both come to be seen as aspects of the paternalist protector state. It is not surprising that workers demanding better working conditions and wages on the site of the Sardar Sarovar Dam have been booked on charges of sedition and anti-national activities.

As threats to national security are branded as treachery, so too challenges to development programmes are projected as the handiwork of enemies of the nation and its progress and prosperity. The theme of nationalism has been echoed variously in criticisms of the NBA for taking its case abroad, notwithstanding the government doing the same both for fund-raising and refurbishing its external image; in the allegations of foreign funding, implying that all detractors of the dam are agents of hostile foreign states; and in the charges of sedition and anti-national activities in cases against workers demanding better working conditions at the dam site.

The 'national interest' argument has also frequently been invoked in the NVP to justify the displacement of large numbers of people rendered homeless by the construction of the dams.[42] It

---

[42] This is facilitated by the ILO Convention 107, to which India is a signatory, and which provides: 'The populations concerned shall not be removed without their free consent from their habitual territories except in accordance with national laws and regulations for reasons relating to national security or in the interest of national economic development or of the health of the said populations' (Article 12.1, quoted in the *Independent Review:* 18).

fluently translates into an argument of public purpose that enables the state to ask sections of its citizenry to sacrifice some of their rights in order that 'society as a whole' may benefit. The decision as to what legitimately constitutes public purpose is not, however, open to discussion or participation. Thus, the public purpose argument is found to be equally serviceable in justifying the expropriation of tribal persons from their land and in imposing the Official Secrets Act for reasons of state.

The imagery of the nation that is fashioned by this ideology of developmentalism bears closer examination, particularly since much of this jingoism has been furbished by the strongly parochial, even chauvinist, sentiments of subregional Gujarati nationalism. The project has been justified as being integral to the *asmita* (identity) of Gujarat, and even its dharma (religion). The fact that the people of Kutch and Saurashtra, by reference to whose acute need for water the project has been most powerfully justified, are not Gujaratis, in any sense other than the purely administrative (a decision whose soundness has been trenchantly questioned) has naturally been conveniently ignored (Patel, 1994: 1957). This Gujarat-centred discourse, oblivious to the possible disjuncture between nation and region, has tended to view any disagreement with the project as anti-national, seditious and deserving of retributive initiatives taken by citizens. This has been manifest in the civil and official witch-hunt of eminent persons from Gujarat (Mrinalini Sarabhai and P. G. Mavalankar) who signed a memorandum questioning the desirability of the project; the hysterical reaction of even the national media to the testimony of activists before a US Congressional sub-committee; the mob-violence and rampage in the NBA office in Baroda (Srinivasan, 1994: 1058–59); and the common accusation of almost all critics of the project of being traitors and agents of foreign governments. This emotional and millenarian appeal of the Narmada Project is reminiscent of the patriotic fervour whipped up by Nasser's government in Egypt in favour of building the Aswan High Dam on the river Nile. That dam, too, was made a symbol of national, even militarist, patriotism, with all criticism of it being dubbed as subversive and treacherous.[43]

---

[43] John Waterbury's study of the Aswan High Dam clearly establishes that political considerations enjoyed primacy in determining all technological

Finally, recalling the emotional frenzy of its violent destruction of the Babri Masjid, and in a macabre comparison of the dam project with its project for the Ram temple, the BJP unit in Gujarat actually coined a slogan resonant of its Ayodhya battle-cry: '*saugandh Narmada ki khatey hain, baandh vahin banayenge*' (we swear by the Narmada, we shall build the dam there) (Sangvai, 1994: 537). Not merely religious symbolism, but also religious leadership, has been deployed to serve the official purpose of justifying the dam. Thus, the Gujarat Government enlisted the support of religious leaders like Morari Bapu and Pramukh Swami, to give legitimacy to the project (Mukta, 1995: 106).

An interrogation of the state's developmental claims can proceed at two levels: the first questioning the very content and substance of a received notion of development, and suggesting alternative ways of reconceptualizing it;[44] and the second, eschewing that strategy to concentrate on evaluating the strength of the state's claims to providing equitable development through policy choices to design and execute projects such as these. It is proposed here to follow the second strategy (and to return to some of the issues raised by the first in Section VI of this chapter). As such, I begin by asking what sorts of development benefits are envisaged in the dam projects and how they are intended to be secured; whether these benefits are intended to promote equitable growth or to secure benefits only for certain sections; and who appear to be the likely beneficiaries and casualties of the projects.

It scarcely needs to be stated that a policy of increased agricultural production, especially of irrigation-intensive crops, has been central to the model of planned development adopted by India

---

choices. The political value of the dam was that it would be 'gigantic and daring…and highly visible and fittingly monumental' (1979: 99).

[44] The development debate has come a long way since the 1950s when it enjoyed primacy on the agenda of the decolonized nations and of international funding agencies. The belief that development outcomes could be evaluated purely in terms of quantifiable measures of economic growth, such as the Gross National Product, began to be challenged in the 1970s, and the following decades have seen a burgeoning of alternative conceptions, notably the movement for sustainable development (cf. Esteva, 1997). Considerably more potent is the definition of development advanced by Jean Dreze and Amartya Sen (1995: ch. 2) as the enlargement of human capabilities and the enhancement of the quality of life for all citizens.

since independence. It is, however, the so-called modern and dynamic industrial sector that has enjoyed priority on the development agenda, with its greater promise of quick growth. This overarching framework of priority for the industrial sector is reflected in the choice of strategies for agricultural development, which have tended to favour technological change and megaprojects. Thus, for the development and extension of irrigation facilities, successive five year plans have emphasized major and medium, rather than minor, irrigation works.[45] The new agricultural strategy of the mid-sixties concentrated on growth in productivity, with a focus on the better-endowed and infrastructurally superior areas of high productivity. In this enthusiasm for the dramatic results of green revolution technology, rainfed and dryland agriculture have suffered unconscionable neglect, leading to the aggravation of regional disparities, as well as poverty, ecological degradation, and recurrent drought.

Like any large multipurpose project, the Sardar Sarovar dam has many projected benefits, especially irrigation and power generation. Most visibly, however, official claims about its benefits have been couched in the language of succour, appealing to its promise

[45] This approach has its roots in the colonial policy of developing canal irrigation, which encouraged the production of cash crops like wheat, cotton, and sugarcane at the expense of the pulses and millets which were the staple food of the producers. According to Whitcombe (1971), persistent overcropping disturbed the hydrological cycle, effecting deforestation, a deterioration in fertility, and an increase in barren area. Amiya Bagchi (1973: 50) has also argued that the extension of external demand made extensive cultivation by large landowners profitable, leading to more intense exploitation of the landless among the small peasants. Irrigation is not, in any case, politically neutral, and the fact that economic merit is not the chief consideration in initiating irrigation projects is well known (Carruthers and Clark, 1981: 1). In India, too, political pressures play an important part in the planning of irrigation projects, with the benefits being reaped by politically and economically powerful regions, while tribal areas often beccome victims of such projects (Bose, 1988: 155). Not only do the rich and powerful farmers tend to have privileged access to canal water, at the expense of the tail-enders, the irrigation bureaucracy is also caught up in political competition. To pay ministers for transfers to lucrative postings, they raise money from farmers by manipulating water deliveries, and through their control over the tendering of contracts (Wade, 1990: 279).

of water for the water-scarce and drought-prone districts of Kutch and Saurashtra. Despite official protestations, there is little evidence that any serious exercise has been undertaken to plan the supply of water to these regions, a fact remarked upon by the *Independent Review*[46] in 1992, and reiterated by the Five-Member Group in 1995. On the contrary, there is evidence aplenty of how these regions have not only been systematically neglected in development planning so far, but of how they are likely to remain deprived and marginalized in the future too. Though the SSP has been repeatedly justified as 'the lifeline of Gujarat', it has been argued that Kutch and Saurashtra, being at the tail-end of the dam's catchment area, are unlikely to benefit at all, a concern that was reflected in the report of the Five-Member Group which explicitly recommended putting their needs first, to ensure that the demands of equity are met. The most optimistic projections for a date by which water could conceivably reach these areas was 2021, according to, the Chairman of the Narmada Planning Group, Y. K. Alagh (Alagh and Buch 1995: 314), and between 2020–5 for Saurashtra and Kutch, according to the *World Bank Review Mission Report* (1992).

Apart from the manifest absence of plans for water delivery systems for these areas, and the low priority that has been accorded to them over the past ten years, it is clear that supplying water to these areas would be an extremely expensive proposition, a cost that has apparently not been factored into the cost of the project as a whole (Ram, 1995: 118). Likewise, although the special needs of the predominantly pastoral population of these districts have been periodically mentioned, their livestock merits no mention even in the broad allocations suggested for the sharing of water. That is why the Gujarat Government's claim of its commitment to the project primarily to secure the needy and thirsty districts of Kutch and Saurashtra against drought has a hollow ring.

Through a peculiar utilitarian twist, the official answer to criticisms of the large numbers of people to be displaced by the project has frequently taken the form of showing how many more people are likely to be benefited by it. On the numbers, however, there has been much vacillation, and publicity material on the

[46] The *Independent Review* noted that 'the cursory treatment, of the issue in the Sardar Sarovar Projects documents appears to be out of keeping with the stated priority' (1992: 318).

project is replete with a variety of estimations of the huge numbers of beneficiaries, ranging from 28 to 30 to 40 million, and back again to 25 million (ibid.: 116). Likewise, the computation of the number of beneficiary villages fails to exclude over 200 uninhabited ones. The SSNNL has claimed:

it would benefit about 25 lac persons by way of irrigation and 295 lac persons (population projection 2021) by way of water supply. Thus SSP would benefit 320 lac persons while it would affect 1.0 lac persons. The ratio of population affected to that benefitted would be only one third per cent against all India average of 4 per cent   [Raj, 1990: 43].

Of the total of 9 MAF of Narmada waters allocated to Gujarat, 1.06 MAF have been reserved for domestic, municipal, and industrial use, of which 0.853 MAF are for drinking purposes. The utilization of the 1.06 MAF has been left to the Gujarat Water Supply and Sewerage Board and the Industries Department of the state. A GWSSB report suggests that the four cities of Ahmedabad, Vadodara, Rajkot, and Jamnagar, will account for over 40 per cent of the total drinking water from the SSP, with just two of these, Ahmedabad and Vadodara, together accounting for 25 per cent. That the GWSSB is more than receptive to the claims of these cities was indicated when it revised earlier allocations in Baroda's favour in response to a vote by the Baroda Municipal Corporation!

In 1996, the SSNNL decided to offer the Ahmedabad Municipal Corporation an assured supply of 200 m. litres everyday for twenty years, beginning 1998. The prohibitive price tag attached to this supply, fixed at Rs 256 crore in consonance with market prices, was claimed by the AMC to be unaffordable. The SSNNL, it stated, is asking for Rs 50 per 10,000 litres, while the corporation cannot pay more than Rs 5. In 1997, the SSNNL announced its plans to sell water rights to industry.[47] An aggressive marketing attempt by the industries department of the State government has already attracted many large industrial houses, including Essar Oil, Reliance Oil, Nirma, Birla VXL Ltd., and others. It is notable that most of these industries are in the chemical, petrochemical, fertilizer, steel, cement, and power sectors. The SSNNL manage-

---

[47] The imperative to sell 'water rights' is chiefly a function of the resource crunch faced by the project, and the reluctance to increase market borrowings at steep rates (Interview by A. T. Luke, Managing Director, SSNNL to *The Pioneer*, 29.8.1996).

ment has expressed confidence that, as industry has thus far been resorting to the expensive process of desalinating sea water, it would surely be willing to pay for water, and that water marketing would soon be followed by privatization of power projects (*Indian Express*, Baroda, 10.2.1997). The promise of the SSP as the only hope for the dry and drought-prone regions of Gujarat could need no further rebuttal. Perhaps in recognition of this, Chief Minister Shankarsinh Vaghela announced in February 1997 that Mehsana, Banaskantha, and Sabarkantha districts in North Gujarat would be supplied water from the Dharoi dam. He also promised to consider alternative schemes, such as the Kalpasar scheme and the Narmada pipeline scheme, to provide water to Kutch and Saurashtra. That the Sardar Sarovar Dam no longer pretends to its original justification is more than evident.

The amount of water likely to be available to quench the thirst of other areas was in any case questionable, given that a new industrial corridor is expected to develop around the main Narmada canal, the Ahmedabad–Delhi metre gauge railway line, and the eastern highway, extending the present railroad corridor to Delhi. The industries proposed are agro-businesses and export-oriented units.[48] Five sugar factories were licensed several years ago, strongly suggestive of the large-scale cultivation of sugar-cane in the command area of the main canal. This is, in fact, the key to the symbolic importance of the Sardar Sarovar Dam, for in the 1970s, facilitated by the construction of the Ukai dam, sugar-cane supplanted cotton as the most important cash crop in Gujarat. The people displaced by this dam came on to the sugar fields as seasonal labour, and the powerful landed élite, the Patidars, consolidated their economic control through a nexus with political power (Mukta, 1995: 101). It is this landed élite of central Gujarat that stands to gain—both in terms of electricity as well as the assured water supply so necessary for sugar-cane cultivation—from the SSP, and which is therefore among its most vocal supporters.

On a somewhat optimistic official estimation,[49] the SSP has the potential to irrigate 18 lakh ha. of land in 12 districts of the state,

[48] In 1991, NVDA Chairman Sharad Jain announced that at least 15 export-oriented units would be set up in the Narmada Valley, generating 20,000 jobs in the area (*Indian Express*, 29.10.1991).

[49] It has been calculated that the 75 per cent dependable flow of the river is likely to be 17 per cent less than estimated by the planners (Ram, 1995: 120).

accounting for only 14.5 per cent of the total cultivable area of 124 lakh ha. (Raj, 1990: 9). The development perspective discussed above is, unambiguously and unrepentantly, reflected in the Gujarat Government's advertised justification for the Narmada project:

The agricultural development visualized in these regions is mainly of the cash crops. The [sic] agricultural development inevitably leads to industrial development particularly agro-based industries [Mehta, 1988: 9].

And again:

After the development of Narmada irrigation system the gross irrigated ratio of Ahmedabad district will be as high as 70 per cent as compared to present 17.8 per cent only. This is obviously going to usher a green revolution in many districts, particularly Ahmedabad. Narmada development will not merely hold the decline of Ahmedabad, but will usher a new prosperity to Ahmedabad economy because of rapid agricultural development and agro-based industrial development   [ibid.: 10].

It is notable that past investments in irrigation have chiefly benefited the cement and transport industry, rather than agriculture (Paranjype, 1990: 91–2). Thus, the rate of growth in the secondary (industries) and tertiary (trade and services) sectors in Gujarat's economy has been 5.9 per cent while the primary sector (agriculture) has stagnated at 3 per cent. The enormous investment envisaged in the SSP, accounting for over 80 per cent of the state's water budget, implies that the minor irrigation sector is and will continue to be neglected. Further, it is estimated that the nature of water distributaries and their alignment is such that the major beneficiary districts will be those that are already the richest and most developed, namely Baroda, Ahmedabad, Kheda, Gandhinagar, and Surendranagar, while the eastern hill districts, including the tribal and backward areas, will receive virtually no benefits (ibid.: 307). The data on output growth rates of major crops in these districts suggests that, even as Gujarat as a whole registered a steep fall in agricultural output due to severe drought in 1984–5 and 1987–8,

---

The *Independent Review* also noted the warning in a World Bank memorandum that the irrigation potential of the project might drop by 30 per cent without the Narmada Sagar Project (*Independent Review*, 1992: 250). Adding to these evaporative losses in the canal system brings down the irrigation efficiency of the dam from 60 to 46 per cent (Ram, op. cit.).

these districts either retained their output growth rates or improved them[50] (Bhalla and Tyagi, 1989: 127–30).

The Planning Commission's approval for the SSP was significantly influenced by the case made for it in terms of its potential for mitigating drought, and alleviating tribal poverty. It has been argued, however, that of the 56 *taluka*s in Gujarat covered by the Drought Prone Areas Programme or the Desert Development Programme, only 20 stand to benefit from the dam, and of these 4 (in Kutch) will benefit marginally, continuing to suffer water scarcity in one out of every four years. Of the 70 *taluka*s in 13 districts in the SSP command area, only 20 (i.e. 28 per cent) fall in the desert or drought-prone area. Thus, 72 per cent of the command is in the rich, central plains that already have plenty of water (Paranjype, 1990: 143). The second rationale for Planning Commission approval, namely tribal poverty, is similarly infirm, as only 6.5 per cent of the total irrigation benefits will go to the tribal areas. Of the 32 tribal *taluka*s and 15 pockets supposed to benefit from the Sardar Sarovar dam, only 2 benefit to the extent of over 50 per cent, while 3 benefit between 4.8 and 20 per cent (ibid.: 145).

Power generation is another important aspect of large dams, including the SSP, which is expected to generate 1450 MW to be shared by Madhya Pradesh, Gujarat, and Maharashtra. According to the Award, M.P. would receive 51 per cent of this, in return for bearing 80 per cent of the submergence costs. Gujarat's share of 33 per cent would be substantially depleted by the energy requirement of the dam itself, particularly once all its components are in place, including the canals in Kutch and Saurashtra (Dharmadhikary, 1995: 141).

[50] Of these districts, data on output growth rates of major crops is available for four out of the five (as Gandhinagar was a later creation). This data pertains to the period 1962–5 to 1970–3 and 1970–3 to 1980–3, during which Baroda and Surendranagar improved their output growth rate category, with Baroda moving from a 0.0–1.5 per cent per annum growth rate category between the 1960s and 70s to the 2.5–3.5 per cent per annum growth rate category in the following decade. Surendranagar, similarly, moved from the 1.5–2.5 per cent growth rate category in the first decade to the 2.5–3.5 per cent category in the next. Ahmedabad remained constant in the 0.0–1.5 per cent category, while Kheda remained constant in the 3.5–5.0 per cent category. By contrast, it is notable that Kutch fell from the 3.5–5.0 per cent category (1960s–70s) to 2.5–3.5 per cent (1970s–80s) (Bhalla and Tyagi, 1989: 127–30).

It appears that the dam is favoured by a variety of intermeshed interests, including those of state and central level politicians, bureaucrats, industrialists, big farmers, and contractors. The support of the powerful Patidar lobby of central Gujarat has already been documented. Industrial and commercial interests too have been vocal in their support for the project. The Narmada Foundation Trust was established under the auspices of the Gujarat Chamber of Commerce and Industry, from whose premises it functions. In addition to sponsoring and subsidizing much of the counter-mobilization at Delhi and Ferkuwa, the Trust, along with the GCCI and the Sankat Nivaran Society, also submitted a memorandum to the Independent Review in October 1991. The people of Gujarat, it said, would never forgive the 'motivated and malicious' efforts of the 'enemies of development' to halt the implementation of the project. This would not only disrupt the economy of Gujarat, but would also compel the people of the drought-prone areas to 'come out on the streets for a new revolution (*Nav Nirman*)', (Narmada Foundation Trust, 1991: 11–12).

The personal and political commitment of the late Chimanbhai Patel to this project is quite unparalleled in the annals of development planning in India, and its possible motivations have been elegantly satirized in the poetry of Vikram Seth (1995: 337 ff.). Allegations of corruption against former SSNNL Chairman and veteran Congress politician Sanat Mehta have been rife, with one contract of Rs 80 m. having been given to a private company Gujarat Securities Limited, of which too he was the Chairman (Mukta, 1995: 103).

Among the more immediate commercial interests is, of course, that of the construction firm engaged in building the dam. Jaiprakash Associates, with its headquarters in Delhi, is the main firm contracted for this task, while the canal network is being built by Mahalinga Shetty and Co. Jaiprakash Associates were also contractors for the stadia and other sports facilities built for the 1982 Asian Games in Delhi. At that time, they were taken to the Supreme Court by the People's Union for Civil Liberties, charged with violation of labour laws. The next section will detail how Jaiprakash Associates have consistently, since 1987, denied trade union representatives and lawyers access to the residential quarters of the labourers, and have intimidated and fired workers who joined the union. They have also been known to join hands with the police in holding off protestors and engaging in violence against them.

IV. CITIZENSHIP IN THE NARMADA VALLEY

Chapter I outlined two ways in which citizenship is commonly undermined. Both these dimensions of citizenship are relevant in the context of the Narmada Valley Projects. Thus, this section will be concerned with (a) the violation of citizens' rights to organize and protest (including the right of workers to unionize) and state violence and repression, as also violence perpetrated by private agencies with the protection of state personnel; and (b) the absence of social conditions for the effective exercise of citizenship, expressed in, for instance, the marginalization of tribal groups from the mainstream economy, polity, and society, as also in the lack of an adequate policy response for the proper resettlement of all displaced persons. In the latter case, it is obvious that the interests shortchanged by the dam run into formidably large numbers and several categories of people, such as the Project Affected Persons (those who are, in official eyes, the displaced and, as such, entitled to compensation); the Canal Affected Persons (yet unacknowledged as eligible for compensation); the tribals (who are, in official eyes, 'encroachers' on forests); a large number of landless labourers, landless tenant-cultivators, sharecroppers, and the secondarily displaced.

The First Mode of Undermining Citizenship

As the developmental claims of the state have come to be challenged by the movement against the dam projects, its repressive and violent face has become increasingly manifest. Far from being the benevolent provider of development, the state has come to be seen and projected, in the Valley, as an aggressor. In fact, its most benign face here has probably been its very facelessness and even disappearance from the areas to be submerged, especially in Madhya Pradesh, as documented by the MARG studies in 1986–8. The missing state of these areas, however, reappears in a violent and intimidating incarnation in areas marked by protest and opposition to the dam. Experiences of forced evictions and police repression mounted as the agitation gathered momentum, and the US based Asia Watch published a document cataloguing human rights violations at the Narmada dam (1992).[51] The Narmada Valley has been the scene of familiar episodes of state-sponsored violations of civil liberties and democratic rights, including arrests of activists, violence against them, repeated detentions on exaggerated charges, violations of preventive detention laws (such as the right of access to family and legal counsel), the absence of information as to the charges as well as the bailability or otherwise of the arrest, and abuses in custody. Physical beatings, harassment, the forcible breaking up of meetings and demonstrations, as well as forcible evictions, have formed part of the standard state response to protest by activists. The imposi-tion of the Official Secrets Act[52] at the dam site since 1988 has been one of the most widely criticized actions of the government, even as it is justified as being necessary for the safety and security of the people living and working on the site, and of the materials lying there! (Raj, 1990: 52).

Almost every stage of the resettlement process has also been marked by violence, as forced evictions have been the norm. The government has generally defaulted on its obligation to notify evacuation six months in advance, or even to provide information about resettlement plans and dates, much less to consult the PAPs. Where some attempts at communication have been made, they are couched in highly legalistic language, and 'people have been suddenly introduced to institutions, procedures and systems which are beyond their world-view' (Bhatia, 1997: 307). As is only to be expected, fraud and corruption have become an entrenched part

---

[51] Though the Government of India has generally treated reports by Asia Watch as suspect and inauthentic, this 35-page document is, for the most part, merely a systematic compilation of reports published in the Indian press, public documents, and interviews with lawyers and activists.

[52] There are striking continuities between state response here and in a 1921 agitation against the Tata Hydroelectric Power Company's project to con-struct a dam across the Nila and Mula rivers at Mulshi Petha in Pune district. That agitation was fortuitously politicized, as Marathi 'extremist' nationalists, finding themselves upstaged by Gandhi's non-cooperation movement, seized upon the opportunity to organize resistance. The Government devised a two-pronged strategy to tackle the agitation: it persuaded the peasants to accept a generous compensation package, and also declared Mulshi Petha a prohibited area. The latter strategy enabled it to arrest some leaders of the agitation on grounds of 'criminal trespass', and complete the project.

of the resettlement process, while the people have no recourse to any mechanism for the redressal of their grievances. Forcible evictions, using threats, pressure through disinformation, intimidation and outright coercion,[53] have often been followed up by forcing those who are insecure and unable to adjust, to stay on against their stated wishes (ibid.: 310–13).

The role of Jaiprakash Associates, the construction firm, has also been controversial. In February 1987, several workers, including many drivers who were being made to work twelve hours a day, visited the General Secretary of the Vadodara Kamdar Union, expressing a wish to join it. When they returned to their camp in Kevadia colony, they were fired and ordered to leave immediately. Similarly, in September 1987, seven workers were fired for maintaining contacts with the union. In January 1988, a worker who was active in the union was assaulted by the security guards at the camp and could not persuade the local police to file a complaint. A month later, a 300-strong meeting of the union was broken up by the police. In March, when dam workers went on strike, three of them were transferred and, when they refused to accept the transfers, were arrested. They were detained separately in office rooms and alternately threatened and offered inducements. A Deputy Superintendent of Police, a Subdivisional Magistrate, and a police sub-inspector were present when one of the workers was threatened with arrest on charges of disloyalty to the state. At the point of a revolver, all three were asked to leave the camp or submit to arrest. As part of the agitation against the Official Secrets Act in January 1989, 3000 workers at Kevadia also struck work, demanding that they be allowed to meet union representatives, that the prohibitory orders under the Act be

[53] Brutality and violence have frequently characterized forced evictions in development projects. The Rihand dam (Singrauli) forced 50,000 people to flee at only 24 hours notice, as the dam gates were shut, and the waters started to rise (Singh, 1985). An investigation into the Srisailam dam on the Krishna river, near Hyderabad, discovered that over 100,000 people were forcibly evicted from 117 villages in May 1981, and though the total cost of compensation was less than 1 per cent of the total project cost, there was unfair calculation of compensation, as also corruption and delays in its disbursement. Evacuation was carried out under heavy police guard, as homes were demolished and old people physically dragged out of their homes (Goldsmith and Hildyard, 1984b: 258–9).

removed, and that the construction firm be required to abide by existing labour laws regarding minimum wages, maximum working hours, and equal pay for equal work for women (*Asia Watch*, 1992: 27).

Reasons of state have thus been invoked to justify repression of workers at the dam site, just as 'national interest' has been invoked by government and industry alike to establish the beneficial character of the project.

The Second Mode of Undermining Citizenship

The undifferentiated administrative category of Project Affected Persons includes only those who are entitled to compensation from the state. While this number has been placed at about 199,500, an estimated 140,000 Canal Affected Persons (both figures are from the *Independent Review*) are still outside the purview of official compensation, as indeed are the 'encroachers' (an official euphemism for tribal peoples living in and by the forests), the secondarily displaced, and the earliest displaced people of Kevadia in 1961. A large number of the PAPs are members of the Scheduled Castes and Scheduled Tribes, which appears to be the invariant pattern for development-induced displacement in India.[54] According to the *Independent Review* on the basis of data from government resettlement plans as well as from non-governmental organizations engaged in resettlement work, 90 per cent of the PAPs in Gujarat and 95 per cent in Maharashtra are tribal people. In Madhya Pradesh, tribals constitute 49 per cent of the people to be affected. Only 10 per cent of the CAPs are tribals, but 100 per cent of those to be affected by the sanctuary belong to this category (1992: 62).

With regard to the tribals, the important issues at stake include not only adequate resettlement, but also concerns about the rights customarily enjoyed by such communities: including the right to primary resources such as forests, pastures, and water; the rights of minority cultures; the right to traditional self-governing institutions; and even the very right of these communities to life and existence. The transformation of the tribals' relationship to

---

[54] Though tribal people constitute only 7.5 per cent of the Indian population, it has been estimated that over 40 per cent of those displaced by development projects till 1990, belong to these communities (*29th Report of the Commissioner for Scheduled Castes and Tribes*, 1990).

common property resources in nature into market relationships; the continuance of the practice of bonded labour; the criminalization of tribal communities; and the imposition of alien representative institutions are all considered to have seriously damaged the texture of the tribal way of life. The *Twenty-Ninth Report of the Commissioner for Scheduled Castes and Tribes* (1990) provides a wealth of evidence of the way in which the tribal way of life in the Narmada Valley has been impacted by economic development.[55]

The displacement of tribal people by the Narmada projects is only the last step in a process that began in the colonial period, and has continued since independence. With this displacement, the tribals are being drawn into the mainstream of national life, economic, political and cultural, but without the necessary skills needed to make their way in this new world. From their position of marginality in the Indian social structure, they are now consigned to the space at the bottom of the class structure, as labourers in agriculture, mines, and factories.

The predominantly tribal category of displaced persons, thus, is variously represented in different discourses, though it ought necessarily to be simultaneously located in each. Firstly, in relation to this project, and in official discourse, these people are classified as Project Affected Persons. The imperative of their official recognition is, of course, the citizen–state relationship, that places certain welfarist obligations on the state, even as it commands the acquiescence of the citizenry. Official discourse has, however, so far refused to take cognizance of three other categories of affected people—the Canal Affeccted Persons, the secondarily displaced,[56] and those who were displaced from the first six villages in Kevadia

---

[55] While the debate on this issue remains unresolved, proponents of the project characterize the case for the rights of tribals as an isolationist and preservationist one, and charge the Independent Review with subscribing to a romantic picture of the tribal as a noble savage. Social anthropologists too have been critical of the 'timeless, essentialist, primordialist definition of tribe' adopted by the Independent Review (Das, 1996: 1513). Assimilation may be either facilitative or coercive, but involuntary resettlement can scarcely be treated as an acceptable strategy of assimilation in the name of development.

[56] Secondary or indirect displacement refers to displacement caused not by submergence but by other associated activities related to the project, e.g., the creation of a wildlife sanctuary to make up the loss of wildlife due to submergence. In relation to the SSP, an example of secondary displacement

in the 1960s—as official recognition of these is self-evidently an expensive proposition. Similar considerations have underlain official attempts at disaggregating the total data in terms of State boundaries. Secondly, sociologists and anthropologists classify the affected population in terms of its position in the social structure, highlighting its caste and tribe affiliations. These marginal people must also, thirdly, find a place in any representation of the class structure, where they would appear at the bottom of agrarian society as landless labourers and sharecroppers. Such an emphasis is largely missing in the existing literature on the subject.

The fact remains that the affected populations may be simultaneously located in the class structure, the social structure, and the structure of power. Along all these axes—the class hierarchy, the hierarchy of social stratification or the relationship of domination and obedience between state and citizen—these groups belong to the poorest, most powerless strata, and possess little clout to ensure for themselves humane and adequate rehabilitation, much less social justice. It is this compounded deprivation that justifies the description of this category of citizens as doubly disadvantaged. Their location in the social and economic structure renders almost inevitable their position in the structure of power, as citizens who, despite political mobilizaton, have little voice in the polity to ensure for themselves better rehabilitation prospects, much less social justice. This helps to explain the inadequacy of resettlement policies and their implementation as evaluated by researchers; the modest success of tribal mobilization by the ARCH-Vahini in securing improvements in the policy on resettlement; and the powerful appeal of the Narmada Bachao Andolan and its charismatic leader, Medha Patkar, in incorporating this struggle into a larger anti-development agenda.

The rehabilitation and resettlement policies adopted by the three concerned States are in varying degrees derived from the NWDT Award of 1978, which was acclaimed as a landmark in R&R policy in India, given the historical experience of R&R in

---

is the government's decision to encourage oustees to buy land directly from landowners, with government officials helping to negotiate the transaction, and government paying for it. Many landowners, whose lands come on to the market in such situations, are absentee landlords, whose land has been worked by tenants and sharecroppers. As the land passes into the hands of owner–cultivators, the tenants and sharecroppers are thus necessarily displaced.

almost every other major irrigation project.[57] The Award departed from the conventional practice of giving only monetary compensation to landholders under the colonial Land Acquisition Act. For the first time in India, the Award provided that landed oustees would be given land for land: agricultural land of equal size for every displaced family losing more than 25 per cent of its holdings, with a minimum of 2 ha. for each family. Major sons would also receive the benefits of compensation in their own right. In addition to cash compensation for property lost, the Award also provided for rehabilitation grants, grants-in-aid, civic amenities in new or existing villages where the displaced were to be relocated, and house plots. There was, however, no special provision made for the tribal people being displaced, and the Tribunal thus ignored the customary usage of tribal people using encroached land for cultivation and grazing. This lacuna is, however, addressed both in the ILO Convention 107, and in the World Bank's policy on Involuntary Resettlement (1992), which states that

As a general policy, the Bank will not asist development projects that knowingly involve encroachment on traditional territories being used or occupied by tribal people, unless adequate safeguards are provided [quoted in the *Independent Review*: 27].

These principles were also embodied in the credit agreements between the World Bank and the Government of India, which provided that the oustees should, promptly after their displacement

(i) improve or at least regain the standard of living they were enjoying prior to their displacement; (ii) be relocated as village units, village sections or

---

[57] The past record of displacement and rehabilitation in dam projects is truly dismal. In 1985, 3000 of the 35,000 oustees of the Koyna dam, completed in 1961, had not been resettled. Oustees of the Bhakra dam who were allotted land in Haryana in 1957-9, petitioned the Lok Sabha in 1978, complaining that they had still not, after two decades, been given proprietary rights to this land. The Rengali dam in Orissa displaced over 50,000 people, who were mostly resettled on barren, uncultivable land, resulting in disease and starvation deaths. Impoverishment and a large-scale conversion to migrant labour was also the result of the Ukai–Kokrapur multipurpose project, which displaced over 16,000 families in Gujarat and Maharashtra. The displaced tribals suffered a loss of livelihood, malnutrition, a rise in alcoholism, and 95 per cent of these were seen to be living below the poverty line, as compared to 70 per cent before rehabilitation.

families in accordance with the Oustees' preference; (iii) be fully integrated in the community to which they are resettled, and (iv) be provided with appropriate compensation and adequate social and physical rehabilitation infrastructure, including community services and facilities   [ibid.: 29].

Among the three riparian states, Gujarat has the smallest number of oustees, from only 19 villages, out of a total of 297 villages to be submerged by the reservoir. However, in keeping with its status as the biggest beneficiary of drinking water and irrigation, it bears the bulk of the responsibility for the R&R of those families of Maharashtra and Madhya Pradesh who are to be displaced by the reservoir and choose to leave their home states for Gujarat. Gujarat's present policy on R&R is the product of a cumulative process of broadening, in response to pressure from NGOs like ARCH-Vahini and the World Bank, that gradually extended it to cover landless people, thus bringing within its ambit the predomi- nantly tribal people who lived by agriculture and the collection of forest produce. In subsequent years, implementation was also sought to be improved and, as government-owned land became scarce, private land began to be purchased for resettlement. The processes of site selection and resettlement were also refined, winning the government the support of NGOs like the ARCH- Vahini and the Anand Niketan Ashram, which have been closely associated with resettlement activities. However, the sites have been beset with problems, as it was gradually discovered that the particular needs, social, economic and cultural, of the oustees were not built into the resettlement programmes; a flaw stemming from the lack of research and impact assessment at the initial stages of appraisal and planning. Hence, even if relocation is achieved, the prospects of adequate rehabilitation remain troubled. Meanwhile, the problem of the CAPs, as well as of the original oustees of Kevadia, have remained unaddressed.

A study of the Gujarat resettlement experience by the Centre for Social Studies, Surat, concluded that the compensation package of the SSP was better by far than any other in India, adding this caveat: 'within the given constraints of the development para- digm—the capitalist path of growth' (Centre for Social Studies, 1997: 233). However, it particularly remarked on two aspects of the resettlement experience: the initiation of the oustees into the intricacies of the market economy, and the declining status of women. With regard to the first, the study argued that oustees were having to operate within the framework of markets in land, water, credit, and labour, and their unfamiliarity with such phenomena placed them at a disadvantage, especially in the absence of a strong supportive structure to facilitate their effective participation in these. Secondly, the dominance of the ideology of sanskritization has implied a decline in the position of oustee women and their participation in the economy.

Documenting the change in Vasava culture in the Bharuch district of Gujarat, Roxanne Hakim (1997: 164–5) echoes the anxiety of the earlier study in relation to women, pointing to an increasing gender gap and gender-based taboos. The former dependence of the Vasavas on forest produce is likely to be felt most in the area of medicine, while other visible changes include the emergence of leaders, on a non-traditional basis, to deal with the government and NGOs, and along with this a new emphasis on literacy. Another study of 19 resettlement sites in Gujarat (in 11 of which oustees from Maharashtra and Madhya Pradesh have been resettled) argues that, in none of the sites visited, could the oustees be said to have improved or regained their standard of living; the principle of relocation as village units had been systematically violated; the integration of the oustees with the host population was proving to be difficult, if not impossible; and the physical uprootment of oustees, accompanied by the fragmentation of communities, had resulted in psychological and cultural alienation (People's Union for Civil Liberties, 1995: 20–1). It concluded:

we find people who had self-sustaining occupations in agriculture and related areas have been forced into wage-labour, to work in other's lands or in urban areas. In most cases, dignified, self-respecting people with means have been reduced to diffident, shattered individuals with their communities fragmented and dispersed. The Narmada resettlement process appears to be a classic case of pauperisation and immiserization of entire self-reliant communities. In the name of development   [Ibid.: 21].

In Maharashtra, the area of submergence is located in the Satpura mountain range, where all the villages are tribal, and the now famous village of Manibeli, which became the centre of resistance to the project in 1991, is the submergence village closest to the dam site. In Maharashtra, as in Gujarat, there has been no attempt to build in the special characteristics of the tribal way of life and livelihood into resettlement policies. Indeed, Maharashtra's policy is considerably less liberal. As updated till 1992, it allocates benefits on the basis of a distinction between landed and landless oustees, privileging the former for purposes of compensation.[58] This distinction between the landed and landless oustees is meaningless to the extent that landlessness is a legally correct but factually inaccurate description of the reality. The so-called landless are landless only for official purposes, in that they do not cultivate revenue lands, but rely on traditional rainfed agriculture on 'encroached' land. Of the two affected districts of Akrani and Akkalkuwa, the villages of Akrani have no revenue land, and major sons of these villages, who constitute 30 to 50 per cent of the total oustees, thus have no status even as landless oustees, and are not entitled to any land. In Akkalkuwa, there are de facto no landless people, as those who do not own revenue lands are cultivating encroached plots of similar size and use the same forest resources for grazing as do those who have revenue lands. Loss of forest and water resources, such as grazing, firewood, medicinal herbs, fruit, vegetables, and fish are not within the purview of a compensation policy. The discrepancy between the policies of Gujarat and Maharashtra effectively implies that the 'choice' before the oustees is purely academic, and the latter's lack of inclination to broaden its policies leaves the oustees with no option but to leave for Gujarat.

An extensive study by the Tata Institute of Social Sciences, Bombay, which was commissioned as the Monitoring and Evaluation Agency by the Maharashtra government, concluded that the project had adversely affected the life-situation of the displaced. Being forced to move to Gujarat meant sacrificing important determinants of the economic and social security of the people in terms of caste, religion, language, and kinship structures. Hitherto cohesive social groups were irreversibly fragmented following the policy of 'divide and shift', triggering off serious social and political

[58] The landed oustees are eligible for the standard minimum of 2 ha. of land. Landless oustees, including major sons and major unmarried daughters of 'landed' oustees; non-regularized encroachers; landless agricultural labourers; village artisans and persons engaged in non-agricultural trades and callings, will be allotted, on a first-come, first-served basis, a maximum of one acre of irrigable land if it is available near the relocation site, and if the landless oustee moves with other oustees to the relocation site. Those unable to obtain land under this provision are eligible for a grant-in-aid. But major sons of the landless still do not qualify to get any land.

consequences. This study also noted the likelihood of the demonstration effect of the host population in terms of a decline in the position of women. Most disturbing, however, was its finding that a narrowing of the occupational base had occurred after resettlement, in which there was a greater dependence on agriculture. But the ability of agriculture to absorb people had also narrowed, and the problem of surplus labour was further accentuated by the fact that many in the host population, who had been employed as labourers by absentee landlords, now lost their jobs as the land was acquired for purposes of resettlement. Sharecroppers now became landless labourers (Tata Institute of Social Sciences, 1997: 209).

In Madhya Pradesh, as in Maharashtra, the question of compensation is centred around revenue lands, to the complete neglect of the tribal forest economies. Thus, the distinction between landed oustees and encroachers is discriminatory in its treatment of encroachers, whose traditional rights have been completely ignored. In remote and isolated tribal areas, where about 40 submergence villages of Madhya Pradesh are located, so-called encroachment is an integral part of the economic lives of people.[59] Madhya Pradesh also does not recognize major sons and landless oustees, who must perforce go to Gujarat for better compensation, even though they are reluctant to leave their lands and the social support system that sustains them. Once again, as with Maharashtra, the requirement of choice is seen to be severely compromised.

The two regions of Madhya Pradesh most affected by the SSP are the Nimar plains, which account for two-thirds of the displacement, and are occupied by peasant communities of mixed caste and tribal groups; and the Vindhya ranges, home to the Bhil and Bhilala tribal communities. Though approximately one-third of the people to be displaced in the Nimar belong to the Scheduled Tribes, they have few of the distinctive cultural characteristics of the tribal oustees from the hills. Amita Baviskar's ethnographic study of the hill adivasis of Alirajpur in Jhabua district reaffirms the developmental neglect of this region, and the fact that the tribal people

---

[59] The requirement of producing five year old receipts for fines paid to forest guards to establish the veracity and tenure of encroachment is clearly an expression of bureaucratic inflexibility. Further, the reliance placed on revenue records, and the assumption that these are entirely accurate and up to date, is unrealistic as transfers often go unrecorded for generations.

of this area have not been officially informed of their impending displacement. Of the people belonging to the fertile plains of Nimar, it is the upper-caste landowning class of Patidars which have lent crucial financial and logistical support to, and actively participated in, the Narmada Bachao Andolan's activities (Baviskar, 1995: 218–19). As members of the middle and rich peasantry, which has become increasingly articulate and assertive in Indian politics since the 1980s, the Patidars have a certain political clout. This is very likely a factor influencing the Madhya Pradesh government's decision in recent years to demand a reduction in the height of the dam, thereby reducing the area of submergence. The contradictions between the positions of the governments of Gujarat and Madhya Pradesh are thus illuminated by the contradictions between the position assumed by the Patidars of central Gujarat, as they lend aggressive support to the dam, and that of the Patidars of the Nimar plains, as they lend support to the Andolan, and simultaneously use their political power to press for a reduction in the height of the dam.

At another level, there are deep contradictions between the class interests of the Patidars of the Nimar and the politics of the Andolan. Baviskar has pointed to the fact that, even as the Patidars and the hill adivasis make common cause in the Andolan, participating together in every agitation, the Patidars are reluctant to pay anything approximating the minimum wage to those adivasis who work on their land. Equally, they are unlikely adherents to the alternative ideology of sustainable development so assiduously promoted by the NBA (ibid.: 221). Baviskar observes that the Andolan has chosen to gloss over caste and class differences, by downplaying the important role played by the numerically dominant Patidars in the movement in this region, instead showcasing that of the adivasis, because it makes for better political strategy.

Finally, among the most troubled questions relating to tribal communities that has arisen from this conflict over the dam, is that of authentic representation. Who really represents the tribals? Who speaks for them in an authentic voice? How may the rival claims of the ARCH-Vahini and the Narmada Bachao Andolan to represent the tribals be arbitrated? Anil Patel, of the ARCH-Vahini claims (1997: 91) that the tribals have already spoken with their actions, and have shown a distinct preference for good land and security of tenure, and for better access and infrastructure. He charges the NBA with keeping relevant information about resettlement from the tribals, thereby depriving them of the power to make informed choices for themselves, so that they may continue to provide support to the anti-dam programme of the Andolan. The NBA, on the contrary, has tended to see the work of ARCH-Vahini as essentially collaborative with the State, and has consciously assumed a more radical political posture, to which the interrogation of 'destructive development' is central. Within this framework of political argument, the tribal oustee is necessarily seen as a victim of development, who must be made aware of the larger processes that are at work to dispossess him. A definitive pronouncement on this conflict is hardly possible, and there is some merit in Vasudha Dhagamwar's suggestion (1997: 100-1) that for these rival organizations to make common cause would strengthen the case of the tribals in the long run, whereas the existing polarization benefits no one.

At the policy level, it is also clear that the impact of displacement in the Narmada Valley has been guaranteed to create the spiral of impoverishment described by the model developed by Michael Cernea (1995: 266-7). This model sees eight processes of displacement as converging in impoverishment: landlessness, joblessness, homelessness, marginalization (downward economic slide); increased morbidity; food insecurity; loss of access to common property; and social disarticulation. These eight processes could arguably provide an almost complete window on the problems of displacement and resettlement in the Narmada Valley. Almost all these aspects are evocatively described in a letter written by Bava Mahalia of Jalsindhi village to M.P. Chief Minister Digvijay Singh in March 1994:

You tell us to take land in Gujarat. You tell us to take compensation. What is the state compensating us for? For our land, for our fields, for the trees along our fields. But we don't live only by this. Are you going to compensate us for our forest?...Or are you going to compensate us for our great river—for her fish, her water, for the vegetables that grow along her banks, for the joy of living beside her? What is the price of this? Our livestock and the fodder—water that is essential for it—are you going to compensate for that? How are you compensating us for our fields either—we didn't buy this land; our forefathers cleared it and settled here. What price this land? Our gods, the support of those who are our kin—what price do you have for these? Our adivasi life—what price do you put on it? [Mahalia, 1994: 157-8.]

V. STATE DIFFERENTIATEDNESS AND AUTONOMY

In Chapter 1, it was argued that the state, far from being a unified and monolithic entity, is characterized by a high degree of internal differentiation. As such, there is no necessary coherence between the functioning of different wings of the state structure, or between state institutions at the local, intermediate, and national levels. It was also argued there that it is important to understand state autonomy in relation not only to strong groups in society, but also weak ones; and state capacity in terms both of what it can do, and what it can evade. This section will discuss state differentiation as it is evinced in the conflict around the Narmada Valley Projects. It will further use this example to reflect upon the nature of state autonomy and capacity in positive as well as negative terms, by examining not only the interests of which the state is not autonomous, but also those of which it manifestly enjoys autonomy; and by specifying, on this basis, not only what the state possesses the capability to accomplish, but also what it possesses the capability to not attempt.

State Differentiation

First, this section seeks to demonstrate the differentiatedness of the state in relation to the career of a single policy initiative, namely the Narmada Valley Projects, and so to identify shades of difference between diverse agencies of the state as also between state functionaries at various levels. The overarching framework, of course, has remained fairly stable for, though there have been several changes of government at the Centre, and in the States, these have not been regime changes in any significant ideological sense. The developmental and welfare goals affected by the state have remained unchanged, as an underlying consensus has prevailed on the centralizing, nation-building model of economic and political development.

Nevertheless, the absence of coherence is manifest at several levels, of which three may be identified for closer examination. These are (a) the conflicts within and between the three major organs of the central government, namely the executive, the legislature, and the judiciary; (b) the conflicts between the central and State governments, and between the States themselves; and

(c) the shifts in the position of different political parties, depending upon their status as parties of government or of opposition.

The early history of the project is, as we have seen, marked by the conflicting claims of the four affected States, to arbitrate which the Narmada Water Disputes Tribunal was appointed. Initially, its proceedings had to be adjourned as calculations of expediency led to the States submitting themselves to arbitration by the Prime Minister. When it resumed work, its terms of reference were narrowed down, once again as a result of a political consensus between the States. In 1987, the project was cleared in almost indecent haste at the behest of the then Prime Minister Rajiv Gandhi, despite the reservations of both the Planning Commission and the Ministry of Environment and Forests. On the whole, the Centre has backed the project fairly consistently, with some governments being more aggressively supportive than others. Thus, for instance, Prime Minister Deve Gowda played an important role in attempting to persuade the four states to come to an agreement and present a united face to the Supreme Court in August 1996. The premature release of a statement claiming that such an agreement had actually been arrived at naturally invited the expected disavowal from Madhya Pradesh and Rajasthan.

While the political executive has been more or less convinced of the need for the project, the same cannot be said of the permanent executive. Rumblings within the bureaucracy, and more so among its retired personnel, have been common throughout the past decade of the project's history. Fairly early on, eminent scientists like Dr M. S. Swaminathan and Dr U. S. Rao had expressed doubts about the project, as had Planning Commission member Rajni Kothari. Serving secretaries to the Union Government, S. S. Varma (Social Welfare) and S. Geethakrishnan (Environment) had pointed to the unavailability of land for resettlement and the continuance of environmental clearance respectively. Retired civil servants, including former Union secretaries B. B. Vohra and N. D. Jayal, could afford to be more outspoken, and began to publicly express their views against the dam by writing in the press and participating in anti-dam agitations, while M. N. Buch wrote in defence of the tribals. Above all, B. D. Sharma authored two (28th and 29th) extremely radical reports as the Commissioner for Scheduled Castes and Tribes, and eventually formed the Jan Vikas Andolan. His radical reports had the rather extreme effect of provoking the government to abolish, by constitutional amendment, the office of the Commissioner![60] Unpalatable findings by monitoring and evaluation agencies have been suppressed, while governmental agencies, like the Anthropological Survey of India, have simply avoided taking on studies, for fear of reporting inconvenient and unacceptable findings.

As the movement against the dam has deliberately chosen to steer an extra-parliamentary path, the NBA has not been especially energetic in lobbying Members of Parliament. Thus, as and when the projects have figured in parliamentary debates, the questions have generally been partisan rather than adversarial in tone, betraying anxiety about the completion of the project, rather than expressing reservations about it. In the years 1987–90, the period of most energetic mobilization and dramatic publicity for the movement against the dam, a total of 59 questions were asked about the Narmada Valley Projects, if questions expressing environmental concerns about big dams and multipurpose irrigation projects in general are included. Barely one-fourth of these pertained to displacement, while the rest sought information about World Bank funding, the techno–economic viability of the project, and the causes of delay in its construction, while not more than 17 of the 59 questions could be construed as reflecting any concern for the rehabilitation and environmental consequences of the projects. The ministerial responses, in turn, were mostly of a routine, bureaucratic nature, repetitively providing cursory information, answering questions in an evasive manner designed to give away as little as possible, and only to fulfil the formality of a reply. That governmental matter-of-factness can border upon insensitivity is well illustrated in the answer to a question (by MP Sudhir Roy) asking whether the NSP is likely to displace many people, including Scheduled Castes and Tribes; the number of people likely

---

[60] In 1978, a Commission for Scheduled Castes and Scheduled Tribes was established by a Government of India resolution and assigned functions similar to those of the Commissioner for Scheduled Castes and Scheduled Tribes, who was an ex-officio member of the Commission. On 1 September 1987, the Commission was reconstituted as the National Commission for Scheduled Castes and Scheduled Tribes, and the office of the Commissioner, the 'Special Officer' under Article 358 of the Constitution, was subsequently abolished by the Constitution (65th Amendment) Act, 1990.

to be affected; the damage to forest wealth and fertile lands; and whether it was true that Harsud would be totally submerged. The answer, given by Minister for Water Resources, B. Shankaranand, stated baldly and dispassionately:

(a) and (b). A population of about 1.30 lakhs, including tribals is likely to be affected.
(c) Some forest and cultivated lands will also get submerged.
(d) and (e). The Harsud town will be totally submerged.

[Lok Sabha Debates, 12.3. 1987: 256]

Till 1994, when the NBA filed a petition in the Supreme Court, it had deliberately eschewed the path of litigation on account of internal differences on its appositeness as well as timing. The misgivings about going to court have mostly centred around the possibility of an adverse judicial decision backfiring on the movement. However, in its early initiatives, the ARCH-Vahini did take recourse to the courts, as when it encouraged some tribals to move the Gujarat High Court for recognition of their rights (Patel, 1997: 72). The constituent oganizations of the NBA have also supported cases filed in the district courts of Dhule and Baroda, the bulk of which pertain to land acquisition (Ashish Kothari, Interview, 18.9.1992). Since such cases were filed by individuals whose lands were being acquired, they were interpreted as demands for better compensation, and received fairly sympathetic treatment, from the Dhule court in particular. This district court has also issued stays, and frequently extended these, on evictions. Other district level cases relate to police action against demonstrators, though here the courts have been less sympathetic towards petitioners.

In 1994, the NBA overcame its reservations about moving the Supreme Court and filed a writ petition (Writ Petition [Civil] No. 319/94, *Narmada Bachao Andolan* v. *Union of India*) challenging the project on the grounds that it was socially, economically, technically, and environmentally unviable, and not in the national interest. The case has (as discussed above in Section II.4) been recently referred to a Constitution bench of the Court. Till it is decided, the future of the dam hangs in the balance. The NBA's appeal to the Supreme Court, though an apparent departure from its earlier strategy of avoiding litigation (except in terms of backing individual litigants in local level cases), has been interpreted as being continuous with its earlier strategy, as a form of 'jury politics' which, it is alleged, the NBA has for long practised. Thus, its appeal to the Independent Review Team, its role in the constitution of the Five Member Group, its filing of a case with the National Human Rights Commission (on which the Supreme Court expressed its displeasure), are all viewed as a movement away from mass politics towards jury politics, in which the 'voice of experts and specialists get privileged as they plough through the facts and figures...[while] the voices and interests of a large segment of the local people get lost' (Dwivedi, 1997: 28–9).

It might, however, be more apposite to see this as a new stage in the history of the NBA, and one that is consonant with the very real fatigue and consequent impatience of a prolonged mass mobilization. It is also possible to view this act in the context of recent events in which the Supreme Court has been accused of 'judicial activism'. The Court is known to have been especially receptive to public interest litigations on environmental issues, and the NBA's petition could be interpreted as an attempt to capitalize on its generosity. While the court's final ruling could be favourable or unfavourable to the NBA (a risk which is no doubt recognized by its leadership), securing a stay on further construction for almost three years now is no mean achievement, and an important holding operation for a movement that is noticeably less energetic today.

The interpretation advanced above is given credence by the fact that when, in its hearing of 3 March 1997, the Supreme Court decided against vacating the stay on further construction of the dam, thereby retaining its order of 5 May 1995, there was a hostile reaction in Parliament. Fears of judicial activism and the irrelevance of Parliament were openly expressed in a debate in the Lok Sabha on 5 March 1997. Senior Members of Parliament like Sharad Pawar argued the dangers of reopening inter-State disputes and jeopardizing all Tribunal awards. While one member claimed that the Court had exceeded its jurisdiction, another said

If this kind of intervention by the Supreme Court is tolerated even after the decision of the Inter-State River Tribunal, a Pandora's box will be opened and there will be no final decision for any inter-state river dispute   [Sanat Mehta, *Lok Sabha Debates*, 5.3.1997: 307].

Cutting across party lines, parliamentarians, including two former prime ministers (Messrs. Chandrashekhar and Vajpayee), pleaded for the completion of the project, extolling its benefits, and asking the Supreme Court to reconsider its decision. This conflict between Parliament and the Supreme Court has obviously not been expressed for the first time, but the Narmada case certainly reinforced fears of judicial activism that, in other spheres, have been vexing politicians.[61]

The second level at which an absence of coherence is clearly visible is that of the conflicts between the central and State governments, and between the State governments themselves. The enormous mobilization organized by Chimanbhai Patel in Delhi, to counter the impact of the NBA-led demonstration by 300 tribals in the capital, was a landmark not only because it represented a unique unanimity between all the major political parties in the State, but more so because it was led by a State chief minister against his own party's government at the Centre.

In his campaign for the Lok Sabha elections of November 1989, V. P. Singh promised to review the scheme if the Janata Dal was voted to power.[62] However, when his attention was drawn to the fact that such promises could jeopardize his party's prospects in Gujarat, he swiftly recanted. The contradictions between public policy and electoral compulsions surfaced very quickly, as Maneka Gandhi, Minister for Environment and Forests in the V. P. Singh government was, within just a few months, faced with the dilemma

---

[61] The tension between Parliament and the Supreme Court recalls the conflict around the Tellico dam in the USA. In 1978, the US Supreme Court stopped the Tennessee Valley Authority from completing the dam, which had encountered local resistance as well as a wide-ranging campaign to save an endangered species, the snail darter, found in the river. The matter was placed in the hands of the euphemistically named 'God Committee' of seven Presidential Cabinet Secretaries, which also decided that the project was ill-conceived. Despite executive and judicial reservations, however, the Tellico dam was completed by a sleight of hand in the legislature when, in blatant violation of the rules of the House of Representatives, an existing act was amended, exempting Tellico from all federal laws and mandating its completion (cf. Chandler, 1984).

[62] In an interview, he said: 'Perhaps we will take a relook at the Narmada valley project and, instead of having one big dam, set up several small ones. But the problem is that so much money has been pumped into the project already that it may be too late to retrace it all the way. Perhaps a review can be made and some mid-path taken' (*Illustrated Weekly of India*, 20 August 1989: 17).

of defending the project in Parliament, even though she had been an enthusiastic participant in the Harsud rally herself. In Gujarat, of course, the emotional charge this project has come to possess has made it impossible for any party of opposition, including the Left parties, to survive politically unless it pays public obeisance to it. A strange politics of 'democratic' unanimity has thus been created in Gujarat, where the merest whisper of dissent cannot be articulated without adverse political and electoral consequences.

Other than in Gujarat, however, parties and politicians have been consistent in their inconsistency on this issue, depending on whether they have been in or out of office. Thus, in Madhya Pradesh, parties of opposition have, with almost predictable regularity, criticized the project, while parties of government have equally consistently supported it, and the periodic reversal of roles has caused no evident discomfiture. Thus, in 1978, Arjun Singh, as Leader of the Congress Party Opposition in the Assembly, led the Nimar Bachao Andolan but later, as Chief Minister of Madhya Pradesh, and as an influential national politician from that State, he gave it wholehearted support. His party colleague and local rival, S. C. Shukla, who alone has been consistently in favour of a reduction in height, attributes the absence of this issue from the Congress manifesto to the disagreements between himself and Arjun Singh (Interview, 4.3.1992). Thus, in Madhya Pradesh, the NVP has been a political victim of factional divisions within the State Congress. Similarly, the BJP government of Sunderlal Patwa has been unequivocally supportive of the project, despite the fact that several BJP candidates, in the election campaign, committed themselves to opposing it.[63] Within the national BJP, this issue was used by Uma Bharati as a handle against the Patwa government (*The Times of India*, 9.8.1992), while Vijayaraje Scindia threatened that she would launch a movement against the projects if the displaced were not properly rehabilitated. As already noted, BJP

[63] See Section II. 2. for a detailed discussion of the electoral promises made by BJP candidates in the assembly elections of 1990. In February 1992, Shitla Sahay, Minister for Water Resources, stated in the Legislative Assembly that though previous Congress (I) governments had wasted eleven years, his government was not prepared to waste another day in going ahead with the project. In response to environmentalist criticisms of the project, he said that trees and animals could never take precedence over 'human interests' (*National Mail*, Bhopal, 29.2.1992).

President Murli Manohar Joshi also called for a review of the project at a press conference in Indore, but retracted his statement only a week later in Baroda, on the advice of his party colleagues in Gujarat.

Thus, politicians of at least three major parties, the Congress (I), the Janata Dal and the BJP, have publicly vacillated on the projects, and the parties themselves have been internally divided on this issue, even though the political executive at the Centre and in the States has been reasonably firm in its resolve to push ahead with the projects. That this resolve has often chosen to overlook local opposition does suggest that, at least in Madhya Pradesh, more than votes have been at stake. Unfortunately, the answers indicated by robust common sense about Indian politics are neither demonstrable nor falsifiable by any test of conventional social science methodology.

At the level of project implementation, the relevant unit is the local administration, and it is notable that all administrative work relating to the project, from land surveys to resettlement and rehabilitation, has been entirely conducted by revenue officials, with no experience or expertise in rehabilitation work. Local administration has also been a focus of lobbying activity by the NBA, which has used it to ferret out documents and other vital information to supplement its own field observations.

State Autonomy and Capacity

The inordinate influence of powerful sections of the Patidar landowning class of central Gujarat, as also of industrial interests in the state, has already been detailed. The conflict around the Narmada dam projects has seen not only large-scale mobilization against the project but, quite unparalleled in the history of development activity in India, it has also witnessed enormous well-organized counter-mobilizations in an attempt to demonstrate that there are as many, if not more, people who support the dam as oppose it. The lack of autonomy of the State from powerful classes is easily inferred from the fact that these pro-dam counter-mobilizations have received political backing from the State government and financial support from commercial and industrial interests in the State. Conversely, the groups of which the State is manifestly autonomous are the persons who have been affected in different ways by the dam: the officially recognized Project

Affected Persons being only one component of this category. The Canal Affected Persons, numbering over 100,000, remain uncompensated and unrecognized. The weakest and most powerless social groups, however, are clearly the tribals whose struggle to secure official recognition as other than 'encroachers' has been prolonged and relatively unsuccessful. Such achievements as there have been on the R&R front have been largely due to the intervention of the World Bank, at the time when it was still providing financial assistance to the dam. Many have argued that the role of the World Bank in the project should not be exaggerated, given that the quantum of assistance to be provided by it was a fairly small proportion of the total cost. It is nevertheless true that, even the very minimal way in which some Bank missions sought to enforce loan conditionalities, did pressurize the Government of Gujarat into broadening its R&R policy.

On the whole, it is the tribal communities, accounting for almost all the displacement in Gujarat and Maharashtra, and approximately half that in Madhya Pradesh, which have borne the brunt of forced evictions, forcible resettlement in subhuman conditions, as well as police repression against attempted resistance. These are quite clearly not social groups that the state feels obliged to heed. As such, the state's autonomy of marginalized groups may be seen as a factor contributing to its capacity to evade its proclaimed commitment to social justice and equity.

VI. DISCOURSES OF DEMOCRACY

Three ostensibly democratic arguments have been marshalled in defense of the projects vis-à-vis the affected tribal population. First, the political argument of majoritarianism which chooses as the test of democracy, the numbers of people affected both positively and negatively, and weighs these numbers against each other. This is premised on an assumption of the essential fairness of a political system of representation, where the highest decision-making bodies are elected in accordance with widely accepted democratic procedures, and whose laws are believed to apply uniformly to all citizens.

The second argument is overtly developmentalist, though no less political than the first. This is the argument of 'public purpose', enabling the state to ask sections of its citizenry to sacrifice some of their rights in order that society 'as a whole' may benefit. That these benefits may be far removed from the lives of those making the sacrifice remains tangential. Thus, Prime Minister Indira Gandhi wrote in a letter to Baba Amte in 1983:

I am most unhappy that development projects displace tribal people from their habitat, especially as project authorities do not always take care to properly rehabilitate the affected population. But sometimes there is no alternative and we have to go ahead in the larger interest... [quoted in Colchester, 1984: 253].

While the rate of compensation may be questioned or challenged, the decision as to what can legitimately constitute public purpose is not, however, open to discussion or participation. Thus, the public purpose argument is found to be equally serviceable in justifying displacement as it is in justifying the imposition of the Official Secrets Act for reasons of state.

Finally, there is a cultural argument, with clear economic and political overtones. This argument appeals to the notion of 'the national mainstream', claiming that those who want the tribals to live as they always have, are conspiring to keep them out of the national mainstream, culturally and economically, and thus preventing them from enjoying the fruits of development.

In different ways, each of these three arguments appeals to the democratic principle: the first, through its thoroughgoing majoritarianism; the second, by invoking the notion of the public interest and the common good; and the third, by alluding to the idea of uniform application of laws and, more distantly, to the idea of equal opportunity. None of these arguments, it is significant, invokes the notion of a right to equal respect for all persons (Dworkin, 1977), including respect for diverse cultures and ways of life (Kymlicka, 1989).

The mobilization of pro-dam opinion in Gujarat, and the witch-hunt of dissenters in that State is an integral part of the cynical manipulation of democratic discourse, intended to demonstrate as much, if not more, support for the project, than the opposition against it. The strategy, adopted by the Gujarat Government, of crushing opposition and sponsoring counter-mobilization has been projected as a people vs. people confrontation, with the state playing the role of neutral arbiter. An extension of the strategy of counter-mobilization has been the use of elections to make promises reflecting the local mood, only to renege on them later. The policy equivalent of this majoritarian defence of the project, namely that there are as many, if not more, people supporting it as those opposing it, is the utilitarian argument, that draws upon statistics to prove that the beneficiary population is much larger than the displaced population, and its needs (drinking water) more basic and vital (cf. Dalal, 1989: 15). Regarding the lack of consultation, another argument has been advanced, also invoking democracy:

The Narmada projects have been debated for two generations. Elected representatives of the submergence areas sit in panchayati bodies, State legislatures and in Parliament [Verghese, 1994: 174].

While protest against the NVP has generally taken the form of non-violent acts of civil disobedience, including the boycott of State institutions and personnel, e.g., the census, elections, government officials, these deliberate acts of non-cooperation consciously invoke the democratic ideal, seeking to implicate the State in the transgression of democratic practice. At the heart of this protest is a wide-ranging conception of democracy that, even as it appeals to democratic institutions, invokes a more substantive definition of democracy than the procedural.

Medha Patkar's assertion that the ideological perspective of the NBA is a 'combination of green and red values and ideas' (1992: 282) encompasses the programmatic appeal of the Andolan, as a movement for ecological sustainability as well as socio–economic justice. Claiming to be concerned not merely with individual issues such as decreasing the height of the dam, or reducing the area of submergence, it brings into question the dominant strategy of development as a whole. To do so, it goes beyond 'insensitive' party politics, to explore the space for 'people's politics' and 'people's power' outside the ambit of parliamentary politics (*The Times of India*, 9.7.1993). The financial pullout of the World Bank from the project was in fact hailed by Patkar as proving that such a space does exist.

This interpretation of democracy is premised on a strong assertion of the rights of participation in decisions governing the lives of citizens. The right to information naturally becomes a prerequisite for such a consultative and participatory process of decision-making. It is significant, though, that the right to be consulted is asserted not merely as an abstract democratic right, but in the form of an enabling provision available in the recommendations of the

Tribunal's Award and the World Bank. The Award required that oustees be informed about the submergence at least one year earlier, and be resettled at least six months prior to actual submergence. To this, the loan and credit agreements with the World Bank added an element of choice, by offering oustees the opportunity to indicate their preference between alternative resettlement sites. The Bank has also specified among the prerequisites of a successful development plan for indigenous peoples, 'the preparation of a culturally appropriate development plan based on full consideration of the options preferred by the indigenous people affected by the project' (Operational Directive 4.20, 1991: 3). The nature of this participation and the criteria for determining its adequacy are not however spelt out.

The fact that the affected people were not informed about the submergence, much less consulted about the projects, is sufficiently well-established (Multiple Action Research Group, vols. I–V, 1986–8). The State administrations, especially in Madhya Pradesh and Maharashtra, did not notify people in advance, nor relocate them within the requisite time frame. NGOs were also denied access to the dam site by the imposition of the Official Secrets Act, and meetings of more than five people prohibited by Section 144 of the same Act. Both the right of information and the norms of consultation have thus been systematically disrespected in this, as in many other, issues. The right of association, especially the right to unionize, has similarly been undermined by a variety of means, ranging from discouragement and intimidation to outright harassment and police action. The protection of the police has, it appears, been more generously extended to the contractors for the dam, than to the workers engaged in executing the project. Even protests against work and employment conditions have thus been uniformly put down as treachery against the State, and enmity towards the nation. Nationalist discourse has been enlisted in the service of developmentalist discourse, and reasons of state have prevailed, with a callous disregard for democratic rights.

An important rights-claim expressed in the movement against the dam relates to the rights of minority cultures. The Government of India has, despite its avowed commitment to tribal welfare, neglected to adequately secure this sizeable portion of the affected population against the economic, social, and cultural effects of displacement. The 29th Report (1990) of the Commissioner for

Scheduled Castes and Scheduled Tribes[64] fundamentally questions the assumption of land as property and, following from this, of compensation as a price to be determined. For the tribal person, land is a source of livelihood in a more fundamental sense. Even were he entitled to it, which in most cases he is not, as forest lands are not covered by revenue records, could any monetary compensation be adequate to provide him with a substitute for the very basis of his life? The fact that the tribal areas in question are still outside the market economy, that the 'sale' of land is not part of the traditional tribal idiom, and that money has little use for the tribal person means that, as far as he is concerned, the taking away of his land, with or without compensation, amounts to landgrabbing. The modernizing economy and state also do not regard the traditional use of natural resources as their legitimate use: the vast untapped mineral wealth of tribal areas, for instance, is on this view a waste unless exploited for 'economic development'.[65]

The legal rules uniformly governing Indian society thus ignore the special realities of tribal life. Laws do not, most importantly,

[64] The 29th Report argued that while the displacement of tribals is an age-old phenomenon, its character has changed through history. An early form of displacement occurred when more powerful groups appeared, and forcibly took control of their lands, driving tribal communities deeper into the forests. In the colonial period, the authority of the state over natural resources came to be asserted, and natural resources, including land, got transformed from being means of livelihood into property with a commercial value attached to it. The Land Acquisition Act of 1894, which was the instrument of this transformation, was updated in 1986, and continues to be the operative law determining the extent of compensation to be paid by the state for involuntary displacement. Thus, though the argument of public purpose sets the developmental post-colonial state apart from the repressive and exploitative colonial state, the legal instrument of tribal expropriation remains exactly the same— a substantially colonial legislation (Government of India, 1990: 245-7).

[65] This attitude is echoed in the case of the Bakolori Irrigation Project in north-west Nigeria which was completed despite stiff resistance from the local peasantry, for which the latter was punished with violence, plunder, and massacre by the police in 1980. It has been argued that the commitment of the Nigerian élite to a development strategy of which big dams are an important component, is only partially explained by the 'contract-intensiveness' of such projects. There is, in addition, the fact that domestic and foreign business have a joint stake in the expansion of the market system, and a shared belief that peasant society is backward and in urgent need of modernization (Beckman, 1984: 152).

recognize the rights of tribal communities over natural resources, including land. Instead, complicated and confusing statutes govern the ownership and transfer of land, and are in any case incomprehensible to the average illiterate tribal, enabling unscrupulous officials to dupe him. Not only do laws fail to appreciate the reality of tribal economy, they ignore also the social reality of tribal life, namely the fact of the community, and not the individual, being the basic social unit. In treating individuals as separate entities, to whom alone things like rights can be attached, laws demonstrate their own irrelevance to the field of their application.

Irrelevant acts of legislation, representing alien ways of ordering social and political relationships are, however, less intrusive and penetrative than the new relationships ordained by the market economy. The alienation of the tribal from the natural resources by which he lives, has a psychological as well as economic impact. Undercutting his psychological dependence on nature, which provides him with food, firewood, medicines, housing materials, and culture, creates improverishment and has adverse effects on his health, as studies of the resettlement experience in Parveta have shown (Tata Institute of Social Studies, 1997: 203, 209). It also effects a new, irreversible and yet precarious dependence on agricultural labour, as the meagre cash compensation is quickly consumed.

The utilitarian calculus of losses and benefits in terms of numbers of people benefiting versus the number displaced has a tragic ring when applied to tribal communities, whose loss of community itself is irreplaceable, and as such ought to be non-negotiable. The fact that this loss is neither recompensable, nor brought about after dialogue and consultation, also makes it arbitrary and undemocratic. Further, it is in the nature of procedural representative democracy that the interests of a minority, even one for which the Constitution makes special provision, cannot be adequately protected. Indeed, the Indian state has been more sensitive to the demands of communities defined by religion and caste, as they have made claims to special needs such as the protection of culture or affirmative action in public employment and education. It has arguably been much less receptive to claims made by tribal communities, and considerably more invasive and predatory in its relationship towards them.

On the other hand, critics of the Andolan have argued that its articulation of protest is also inauthentic and unrepresentative, inasmuch as it is the highly educated, urban, middle-class activists who lead the Andolan and formulate its strategies, rather than the affected tribals themselves.

I maintain that adivasis (as well as non-adivasis from the Valley) do not initiate any programmes of Andolan action. Strategic and tactical decisions are taken by activists; the people of the Valley only have the power to veto what is proposed. There is a great deal of passivity with respect to decision-making. By and large, people do not raise questions about proposed programmes; they agree with what the Andolan does on their behalf.... So the structure of the Andolan is pyramidal. I accept that this may be the Iron law of Oligarchy at work, but I think a *jan andolan* must take conscious steps to change the hierarchy... so that, gradually, the middle class activist is rendered redundant [Baviskar, 1991: 96].

In Medha Patkar's perception, this is part of a democratic learning process:

You can say partly it was a trainer's role...since a trainer brings with him or her certain perspectives and knowledge along with analysis and ideology but who also has to take the trainee with him   [Patkar, 1992: 279].

She appears to envisage the role of the activist as that of a facilitator, rather than a leader. Of her early attempts to communicate with the people of the Valley, she says:

They were saying that no one has asked us anything about it, no one has told us anything about it. They felt it was unjust, and that their way of life would be snatched away from them. Such feelings and opinions were expressed in the meetings. But they never saw it clearly as a fight to stop the Sardar Sarovar Project.

So we went through a long process of three years of questioning the government on the issues which were of prime importance to them.... Once the local representative group was formed, after detailed organizational work with even a hamlet as a unit, the representatives always came out of the community, many of them who had not even seen the *tehsil* ever before. Once they went through this process and had a kind of a dialogue with the government, they understood the reality themselves. They realized how difficult it was to get true answers from the government, leave aside resettlement [Ibid.: 276–7].

The question of democracy, as it relates to the movement against the Narmada Valley Projects and the Indian state, may be assessed both in terms of the content of democracy (exclusively formal–institutional or also substantive and participatory) and in terms of modes of democratic intervention (e.g. parliamentary or extra-parliamentary). The arguments of majoritarianism and public purpose may be seen to provide alibis for the state's claim to democratic credentials, insofar as they appeal to the moral superiority of the common good as the crucial criterion for judging the merits of the enterprise. Even as state practices are openly violative of democratic norms and rights, state discourse adopts a purely formal, procedural, conception of democracy, defined in utilitarian terms.

The opposition to the dam, on the other hand, may be said to subscribe to a more substantive notion of democracy, in its appeals to the right to information, the right of participation, the right to be consulted, and the right not to have 'ways of life' destroyed. Underlying this appeal to participatory democracy is the consciousness that existing mechanisms of democracy fail to make provision even for the fundamental principle on which they are premised, namely consent. In the dominant paradigm of development, planners decide upon national developmental priorities, and the fact that these are endorsed and implemented by elected governments is considered sufficient evidence of the choice of project being democratic and representative. In Gujarat, of course, as we have seen, the project has been so politicized as to make support for it a passport to electoral success. In Madhya Pradesh, on the contrary, electoral promises to withdraw from the project have won votes, with the promises being forgotten immediately after the elections.

At the second level of analysis—that of modes of democratic intervention—it is evident that the NBA has very deliberately abstained from party politics, choosing instead the path of extra-parliamentary protest. It is arguable that the unwillingness of the NBA to intervene directly in the political process, including party and electoral politics, has been a factor inhibiting success. On its failure to lobby political parties, as opposed to individual MPs and politicians, Medha Patkar has said:

We regularly held meetings and briefed them. But it was alright as far as the questions were seen as more related to resettlement. But when it comes to questioning the project, at individual level they all agreed, many of them agreed...but when they went back to their party forums and all even started talking to their colleagues, where you know there were networks already working, and there were party influentials who, within the party, always thought of the impact it would have on their votes in Gujarat. So as far as M.P. and Maharashtra was concerned this was the problem. Every party thought of its counterpart in Gujarat.... [Interview, 24.5.1992].

In comparable circumstances, the Tasmanian Wilderness Society of Australia was successful in preventing the construction of a dam on the Gordon river in south-west Tasmania, though it had been authorized by the Tasmanian parliament after a virtual constitutional crisis and a referendum.[66] Its success was, to a considerable degree, due to its active lobbying of the Australian Labour Party, whose leader Bob Hawke committed his party to a 'no dam' platform. When the party came to power, it ordered closure of work on the dam, which was ignored by the Tasmanian government, and then enacted legislation reinforcing it. This culminated in a constitutional case between the federal and provincial government, which was only very narrowly won by the Commonwealth (Thompson, 1984).

Whether or not the NBA could have been more successful had it sought to enter the domain of partisan politics, it has without doubt been remarkably successful in placing a development issue on the national and international agenda, and in contributing to the delegitimization of the project, following the termination of international financial assistance for it. While it has periodically claimed support from the Left parties (particularly from their student wings) as well as from other radical political formations, it has not made a sustained effort to 'green' the existing political parties. Indeed, it has chosen instead to 'redden' its own agenda, by incorporating questions of social justice. The NBA's own brand of politics raises several significant questions: Can an extra-parliamentary movement transcend its single-issue focus to become a radical transformatory force in its own right? Can such an

[66] In an episode that bears an uncanny resemblance to the NBA's Jan Vikas Sangharsh Yatra at Ferkuwa, the Wilderness Society began a blockade on the Gordon river in the winter of 1982. Protestors peacefully entered land belonging to the Hydro-Electric Commission (a body, it was said, that generated as much political as electrical power!) to stop the bulldozers from coming in to the rain forest, and willingly accepted arrest for trespass. As bail was conditional upon not returning to the site, 46 protestors refused bail, and remained in jail. There were 1300 arrests, all of them peaceful, in the course of the three month blockade (Thompson, 1984).

objective be accomplished outside of party politics and the institutionalized processes of democracy? This movement is perhaps a unique instance of the extraordinary way in which extra-parliamentary protest has also been used by the state and its allies, in the form of the organization of counter-mobilizations outside the arena of the state and formal politics.

Thus, the Narmada Bachao Andolan's appeal to a substantive conception of democracy, (even as the state pretends loyalty to a procedural definition) may be viewed as a dismal signal of the difficulties that encumber a participatory notion of democracy, as even procedural aspects are routinely compromised in everyday political practice. At the same time, the countering of extra-parliamentary modes of protest both by parliamentary and extra-parliamentary means, suggests that the state itself is not altogether reluctant to enter the terrain of its challengers, to engage the opposition in combat outside the sphere of institutional democracy.

In the 1960s and 70s, the relationship between democracy and development took possession of the imaginations of political scientists, and recent years have seen a revival, arguably in a more enlightened form, of this debate, that is echoed in the controversies surrounding this project. The arguments of that earlier period—that democracy obstructs development; that democracy may have to be temporarily sacrificed till a satisfactory level of development has been achieved; or even that the two are hopelessly incompatible—find frequent expression in governmental pronouncements on this project which lament the fact that a major development effort is being obstructed. (Patel, 1995: 86). However, within a broader conception of development, civil and political freedoms and rights can be seen as instrumentally necessary for development. Development in the sense of an improvement in well-being, or, in the language of Drèze and Sen (1995), an enhancement of capabilities, cannot but be premised on the autonomy and participation of the people. In such a context, the insulation of the policy élite (characteristic of the 'developmental states' of East Asia, for instance) becomes particularly suspect. Large-scale development projects, with an essentially technocratic inspiration and directed from above by an insulated modernizing élite, are often far removed from or insensitive to local communities' needs and concerns. They tend to treat people simply as objects of the development process, become conduits of largesse for middlemen and contractors, and encourage large-scale parasitism on the state.

It is altogether appropriate, therefore, that the democratic challenge to development strategy has come to be raised at the level of political practice, rather than scholarly discourse. The interrogation of technocratic development policies has come, not from arguments of democracy *qua* democracy, but mounting protest on questions of survival, against the displacement and alienation, by development projects, of people from their habitats, cultures, and ways of life. The big question of the 1960s (is democracy appropriate for developing societies?) has given way, in the 1990s, to a new question: how appropriate is this model of development, given that it is economically inequitous, environmentally unsustainable, and politically less than democratic in its denial of the rights of equal citizenship? In India, both projects of democracy and development have suffered a myriad distortions. It could even be argued that if outcome criteria are taken as decisive, they are barely distinguishable from each other. There is an astonishing similarity between those who have benefited from, and been marginalized by, these parallel processes, such that the beneficiaries of development are also, on the whole, the beneficiaries of democracy; and the victims of development do not generally enjoy much purchase in the democratic system. Neither democracy nor development have come much closer to achieving the ideals that informed them, namely genuine equality and distributive justice.

5

Conclusion

In the preceding pages, this study has sought to plough many furrows simultaneously and across a wide-ranging field of indeterminate fertility, in an attempt to illuminate the overarching argument outlined in Chapter 1. In this concluding chapter, I seek to forge and establish links between that argument and the individual case studies, which are now also compared and contrasted with one another.

It was argued, in Chapter 1, that nationalist élites in third world societies such as India built the structure of the post-colonial state on the foundations of the existing colonial state, on which were superimposed many elements borrowed from the West. The legacy of the colonial state has resonated, to a greater or lesser degree, in all the cases examined in this volume. Thus, the legal issues raised by the Shah Bano case revolved around the interpretation of the Criminal Procedure Code of 1898, a colonial legislation partially revised in 1973. In that exercise of revision, certain clauses became so controversial that the government withdrew from its proposed amendments, and it was the interpretation of precisely these clauses that became contentious in the Shah Bano case over a decade later. In the Kalahandi case study, the continuity between the state's response to famine before and after independence is of a more general level. In the spirit more than the letter, the approach of the Famine Relief Codes formulated by various provincial governments in the colonial period has left an enduring and apparently indelible imprint on the relief codes and scarcity manuals of latter-day state governments, despite the fact that the post-colonial state is supposedly animated by a very different philosophy of welfare for its citizens. It was, indeed, the Famine Commission of 1880 that suggested giving priority to irrigation, as the most important way of protecting India against the scourge of repeated droughts (Bhatia,

1967: 197). Thus was inaugurated the colonial approach to water management, through the construction of canal irrigation systems that has been an enduring legacy of post-colonial development planning. The Narmada case, one of the most visible manifestations of this policy, also highlights the incongruity of a colonial enactment, the Land Acquisition Act of 1894 (though revised in 1986), remaining the legal instrument of expropriation of tribal people from their habitat. Of course, while striking continuities may be observed, both in terms of policy and legislative instruments, between the colonial and post-colonial state, it would not do to overstate these similarities, for a continuity in legal instruments can quite easily disguise a discontinuity of substance, as contradictions arise between colonial laws and practices, on the one hand, and modern democratic politics, on the other.

In this study, the relationship between the state, society, and democracy has been explored in relation to three specific cases, and with reference to three different aspects of state functioning, namely, welfare, secularism, and development. In a sense, these cases have illuminated the careers of welfare, secularism, and development as components of the modernizing agenda of the state of independent India. In doing so, they have also highlighted at least three modes, among a putatively wide variety, of democratic expression. In the sphere of welfare, thus, we analysed the challenge represented by the food crisis in Kalahandi district of Orissa, and the use of institutions of *parliamentary* democracy, such as adversarial politics in the legislature, a vigilant press, and a judiciary receptive to public interest litigation, to bring the issue to public notice and to demand governmental accountability. In the area of secularism, we examined the controversy generated by the Supreme Court's judgement in the Shah Bano case, and the subsequent enactment of the Muslim Women's (Protection of Rights on Divorce) Act, 1986 to assuage fears of Muslim Personal Law being undermined. This campaign belongs to the category of *para-parliamentary* politics, for the demand was largely articulated by Muslim community leadership through established channels of ecclesiastical authority, while Muslim Members of Parliament played an important, but essentially supportive and supplementary role. Finally, in relation to arguably the most contentious development project in the history of independent India, we surveyed the *extra-parliamentary* challenge mounted against the construction of the

Sardar Sarovar Dam. This movement has deliberately and programmatically eschewed partisan and parliamentary politics, preferring to tread the not always efficacious path of extra-institutional protest.

I

The relationship between the state and democracy is, as argued in Chapter 1, premised upon a certain view of state–society relations, encompassing questions of boundary, as well as of state capacity and autonomy. The evidence from the cases appears to substantiate the argument for a non-essentializing view of both state and society, and to suggest that a recognition of the heterogeneity of societal interests should be supplemented by the parallel recognition of a high degree of differentiatedness in state structures. To speak of state–society relations in an abstract, universalistic sense is to posit each as a fully and finally constituted unity, which neither arguably is. It is also to presume that this relationship, between the unified monolith of the state, on the one hand, and a more or less coherent entity, society, on the other, is necessarily competitive and conflictual. However, the internal differentiation that characterizes both encourages us to abandon such an essentialist view of state and society, as well as the cardboard model of their relationship to each other. It compels us also to reconsider the notion of boundaries in relation to our case study materials.

It has been argued that the boundaries between state and society are historically and socially constructed, and are constantly being redrawn, frequently at the instance of the state as, for example, when it seeks to enlarge the sphere of effective action for itself. In doing so, it was argued, the state is dependent, to a greater or lesser degree, on the cooperation of other forces in society. Two of the case studies authenticate this observation. In the post-independence history of India, one of the most striking examples of the redefinition by the state, of the boundary between the public and the private, is the Shah Bano controversy and the legislation in which it culminated. This enactment, paradoxically, enlarged the sphere of the private, redefining the public in a more restrictive manner. This was accomplished by legislating the abbreviation of the state's role in the area of its criminal jurisdiction, by exempting a category of citizens from its provisions, such that they may be governed by their religious personal laws. The Narmada case exemplifies exactly the obverse, insofar as it shows the state relentlessly committed to developmental intervention, regardless of its social consequences. If the retreat of the state from the project of secularism enjoys the support of a politically consequential community leadership, its invasive commitment to the project of development derives support not from the project affected people, but from powerful political and economic interests.

Both these cases also show how increasing interventionism engenders fragmentation and even a lack of coordination within state structures. The Shah Bano case was, of course, portrayed as a conflict between an unrepresentative judiciary (which lacked the legitimacy to intervene) and a democratically elected legislature (which exclusively possessed that legitimacy), and was as such exploited by the executive. The narrative of the events leading up to the enactment of the Muslim Women's Bill has shown how, only six months earlier, the government, supported by the advice of the relevant adminstrative ministries, opposed a Private Members' Bill (the Banatwala bill) seeking to accomplish a similar objective. Shifts and modifications in the official definition of secularism accordingly ensued.

The sheer size of the Narmada Valley Projects, and their location in two states has also, as we have seen, led to considerable disarticulation within state structures. The working of the Narmada Control Authority at cross-purposes with the Ministries of Social Welfare and Environment, as also the dissent voiced by individual bureaucrats at the Central and State levels, points to a lack of coordination between different policy networks. The conflicts have also manifested themselves in terms of the Centre–State relationship, as well as the relationship between States, chiefly Gujarat and Madhya Pradesh, thus straining the federal structure. The involvement of some non-governmental organizations in the programme of rehabilitation and resettlement, as well as in the task of obtaining popular legitimacy for the projects, is also suggestive of the permeability of State boundaries. However, even when recognizing the existence of boundaries between state and society, the evidence suggests the inadvisability of assuming that these are delineated either precisely or in perpetuity.

In Kalahandi, too, we noted the importance of taking a disaggregated view of the state. The national state's distance from local society enables it to assume a role of paternalistic benevolence, which is contrasted with the greater vulnerability to dominant local interests of the regional State. Both these in turn are contrasted with the direct and exploitative nature of the relationship between local society and the local state, whose functionaries routinely extract commissions for every welfare activity, and collude with local élites and powerful groups to cream off the benefits of development activity.

While questioning the simplistic and often reductionist view of state and society as unified entities, situated in a relationship of necessary opposition to each other, I also contest the exclusivist view that an explanation of politics must necessarily be either state-centred or society-centred. The multi-faceted nature of social and political processes encourages us to reject such a binary choice, and to abandon the search for the one constant and unvaryingly independent variable as the password to a methodologically accept-able and 'true' explanation of politics. At the theoretical level I countered one such influential view, that of the statist school, and my case evidence strongly reinforces this critique. If the state were indeed an independent actor, it should logically have been better able to accomplish its goals of social transformation and to effectively implement its self-ordained agenda. That is demonstra-bly not the case. The constraints that have been identified in this study relate to the democratic process, but are underpinned by societal factors of great importance, notably social and economic inequalities. At the same time, it is impossible to consider these inequalities in isolation, whether from state policies that may reinforce rather than redress them, or from the role of the state in relation to democratic institutions and processes. To exclusively privilege either the state or society is to ignore the internal complexity of both these categories, of the realities they describe and sometimes even disguise, and, of course, the irreducibility of this reality to two arbitrarily defined and mutually exclusive conceptual categories.

The case studies also suggest the inadequacy of the two rival approaches that the statist school has attacked for their society-centred bias, namely pluralism and Marxism. The pluralist perspec-tive is shown to be manifestly wanting, as the democratic political process is far from being an authentic register of all interests, much less an impartial arbiter of them. Critics of pluralism are right in pointing out that agenda-setting is as significant, if not more than decision-making in determining the locus of power in a society; and that, therefore, the understanding of power is advanced by identifying those who are actually disprivileged by a particular policy (Lukes, 1974). Shortchanged interests may thus provide vital clues to the question of power, and all the cases, especially Kalahandi and Narmada, compel our attention to the fact that, even in a formally democratic pluralist polity, the poor are voiceless and politically marginalized.

Further, my evidence suggests that explanations which hinge exclusively on the class factor do not necessarily tell the whole story. Social inequalities derive not only from class differences, but also from those of caste, gender, and community, and these may often overlap with class-derived inequalities. Shah Bano is, of course, an obvious example of gender as a source of inequality, which patriarchal interests conspired to entrench. The problem of tribal poverty in Kalahandi is also, at the same time, a problem of landless labour in the context of structural backwardness and gross inequalities, both social and economic. The prospects of tribal communities being displaced from the Narmada Valley similarly suggest that caste-derived inequalities are extendable into and in turn reinforce class-derived ones. The complexity of society, as it is fractured along several axes—class, caste, gender—and sometimes along more than one axis simultaneously, makes it an analytical imperative not to adhere dogmatically to any one line of division as the sole or most crucial determinant of the political process.

Having established that state and society are not constituted as internally coherent, unified entities, and that neither has the definitive prerogative of constituting the other, we proceed to a consideration of state capacity and autonomy. Democracy is a significant mediation here, as the democratic process provides clues to how and why state responses are layered and differentiated. It illuminates a variety of societal interests, some of which are effective in keeping the state committed to its goals of social transformation, while others are woefully ineffective in doing so. The state's commitment to development in the Narmada Valley is clearly an example of the former, while its role in Kalahandi may be seen to reflect a certain ambivalence on its part to the question of welfare. To speak of state capacity in relation to state objectives is therefore a far more complex exercise than is generally supposed.

The state's capacity to accomplish its goals, on the one hand, and its autonomy of dominant interests in society, on the other, should be defined positively as well as negatively. We need to know not only what the state possesses the capability to accomplish, but also what it possesses the capability to not attempt. Likewise, we need to identify not only the interests of which the state is not autonomous, relatively or otherwise, but also those of which it manifestly enjoys autonomy.

Turning again to the case study materials, we observe that the lack of a substantive commitment to welfarist goals suggests the autonomy of the state from marginalized groups, such as landless tribals, who are politically unorganized and unrepresented in any but the most formal sense. It is hardly surprising, then, that the state manifests a capacity to evade the problem of structural poverty, while providing relief and development funds that can buy political quiescence and are not without advantage for dominant local interests.

The Shah Bano case suggests state collusion with the stronger, and more politically articulate, interests within the Muslim community: those of the male clergy. When the state acts so as to reinforce patriarchy, it not only undermines gender claims to equal rights but also the need of Muslim women divorcees for economic security. Its capacity to jettison its self-ordained project of secularism is partly a function of its autonomy of the affected interests, and partly that of the beholdenness of the regime to the powerful political leadership of the community.

In relation to the Narmada Valley Projects, the state remains enthusiastically committed to its developmental goals despite a multiplicity of deterrents, including the withdrawal of foreign assistance; the strictures of the World Bank on the rehabilitation of displaced persons; the controversial nature of the ecological and social consequences of the project; and, above all, a powerful movement of opposition that includes those affected by it. State capability to push ahead despite these obstacles is clearly a reflection of the ineffectuality of shortchanged interests, and even today Government counsels are putting forward a strong case for the vacation of the stay imposed by the Supreme Court on the construction of the dam.

Thus, in Kalahandi, the state's autonomy from the marginalized classes enables it to renege on its avowed goal of providing welfare;

in the Shah Bano case, its political dependence on the Muslim community leadership renders it too weak to defend the secular project, much less the cause of women's rights; while in the Narmada Valley, its lack of autonomy impels it to act so as to subserve powerful political and commercial interests. The capacity to not implement goals, as much as to implement them, is thus a function of both autonomy and its absence.

II

It was argued in Chapter 1 that there are broadly two types of institutional factors that inhibit democratization, some of which are external to the state, while others are internal to it. The cases selected for study in this volume can naturally throw light on just a few of these, and only a more comprehensive study of *all* political and policy issues could offer evidence of each. Of the first category, three types of factors were identified, foremost among them being the way in which the public realm is defined. As discussed earlier, at least two of our three cases afford illustrations of this. In the Shah Bano case, the public realm is at once redefined and circumscribed. The redefinition of the public realm occurs as the protection earlier afforded to personal law, against uniformity imposed by the civil law of the state, is now also extended to criminal law. Its circumscription is not merely a formal matter of rewriting laws, but has important consequences for Muslim women divorcees, and their lien on the state. An important aspect of their existence is removed from the state's jurisdiction, and placed exclusively under that of patriarchal structures, justified in the name of cultural community. This act of renunciation on the part of the state is a double-edged weapon: on the one hand, it offers protection and security against the threatened hegemony of a Hindu majority society, but on the other, it serves to deny some citizens of their right to appeal for justice even under the criminal law.

If the Shah Bano issue shows the state willingly acquiescing in the abridgment of its own domain, the state's assertion, in the Narmada issue, of its exclusive claims over the domain of planning, shows exactly the opposite. Here, the state as the controller and manager of the public agenda, refuses to recognize public participation in development issues as legitimate. As development takes on the character of *raison d'etat,* its technocratically determined content is deemed non-negotiable and emphatically not open to public contestation. Indeed, disagreement with it is tantamount to a subversion of development planning, as sanctified by the early practice of such processes. While some have taken the view that development planning should take place exclusively within the framework of the Planning Commission (Alagh, 1994), others have argued that the way in which planning was constituted as a domain outside politics, made it, through its legitimizing role, an instrument of politics itself (Chatterjee, 1997a).[1]

The second institutional factor identified pertains to the dependence of the state on the process of capital accumulation, and its protection of the long-term interests of capital. While industrial policy in this period would no doubt afford better examples of this, our cases do provide some, albeit limited, evidence. Thus, in Orissa, legislative committees and judicial commissions alike have commented on the widespread corruption in government departments in Kalahandi, and the collusion of officials with contractors, traders, and moneylenders to create an intermeshed web of exploitation of the poor and vulnerable. The sanctioned irrigation schemes, on the other hand, have been so located as to benefit the extended family of the former ruler and other *gauntias*. The Mishra Commission pointed to the connivance of the prosperous and powerful former *gauntias* with moneylenders and officials to usurp the lands of the poor tribals. It also commented on the corruption, fraud, and leakages in the administration of development funds intended for 'poverty alleviation'. The out-migration of the people, in search of wage labour in other states, has been surreptitiously organized by labour contractors, and clearly not for philanthropic reasons, and the same applies to the sale of young women into brothels in Hyderabad and Bombay.

In the Narmada projects, too, it is evident that the protection of the commercial interests of both the industrialists and the landowning Patidar class of central Gujarat has been an influential factor in creating support and mobilizing public opinion in favour of the projects. These classes have been loud in their acclaim for the dam, and have sponsored and funded the political mobilizations

---

[1] 'It was in planning above all that the post-colonial state would claim its legitimacy as a single will and consciousness—the will of the nation—pursuing a task that was both universal and rational—the well-being of the people as a whole' (Chatterjee, 1997a: 279).

to express support for it against its detractors. Allegations of corruption and rent-seeking have also, not surprisingly, been rife. On the other hand, recent developments suggest that the social justification of the project is now being pushed into the background with the arrival, in Gujarat, of several large corporations, and the decision of the Sardar Sarovar Narmada Nigam Limited to sell water to these industries at competitive rates.

Thirdly, the decline of political parties is a truism of political practice in almost all parts of the world. In India, this decline has been well-documented by scholars, especially with regard to party organizations at the local-level (Kohli, 1990), and our cases provide only tangential evidence for this. In Kalahandi, it was the Opposition parties which, taking their cue from a vigilant regional press, brought the crisis to the Legislative Assembly. The immediate official response was, of course, to deny that hunger of famine proportions had occurred, and a motion sponsored by the opposition Janata Party, seeking a probe into the situation, was defeated in the Legislative Assembly. It was not before some months that the Congress (I) government of the state partially conceded the demand for an investigation, arguably pressured more by adverse reports in the media than by the opposition. In 1991, following the confirmation of some starvation deaths by the Mishra Commission Report, Prime Minister Narasimha Rao sent his Minister of State for Agriculture, K. C. Lenka to Kalahandi. Lenka suggested a revival of the ADAPT scheme, which had lapsed when the Janata Dal came to power in Orissa in 1990. This visit provoked the Orissa Panchayati Raj Minister Damodar Rout to also visit Kalahandi, alleging politicization by the Union Minister, and that the money spent under the ADAPT scheme had been misappropriated by the previous Congress government of the state! The apportionment of blame by rival political parties to one another imparts a certain partisanship to the problem of welfare, which tends to impact policy formulation and implementation in the longer run.

On the Narmada issue, the movement against the dam has maintained a distance from the party political process, partly following a deliberate extra-parliamentary strategy, and partly because its experiences with party pledges of support have always ended in betrayal. Agitations such as these are notoriously used by political parties in the short run, but abandoned as soon as they become politically inconvenient. It is notable that, in recent years, protest on development issues has tended to be expressed through social movements and non-party political formations in general, rather than through the party political process. Correspondingly, developmental issues, and the controversies surrounding many of them, are virtually absent from the election agendas of political parties.

In the debate on the Muslim Women's bill, though the Opposition parties in Parliament were extremely vocal in their protest, the Government's majority enabled it to enact the legislation anyway. It is notable that the party of Government, the Congress (I), had itself, only a few months earlier, and for the same reasons, rejected a private members' bill, which was in content barely distinguishable from the legislation subsequently sponsored and enthusiastically defended by it.

Of the three factors internal to the state, the increasing concentration of power in the executive branch of government is easily demonstrated in relation to all three cases. Kalahandi was rewarded with three Prime Ministerial visits between 1987 and 1993 (in addition to one ministerial and secretarial visit each to report to the Prime Minister on its condition). The most visible policy response too was personalized, with schemes such as Operation Salvage and ADAPT being announced by the Prime Minister himself, even as the local adminstration claimed lack of knowledge of these! The outcry against the Muslim Women's Bill was also largely attended to by Prime Minister Rajiv Gandhi personally, in a series of meetings with women's groups and members of the intelligentsia. Even in the drafting of the legislation, Muslim community leadership interacted directly with the Prime Minister, and the role of Muslim citizens, women, and members of the Congress Party was limited. The Prime Minister had assured the Opposition that he would take it into confidence, but it was taken by surprise when the Bill was tabled in the House without any prior notification. The Narmada Valley Projects, similarly, have throughout been dependent upon Prime Ministerial support: from the first decision of the concerned chief ministers to let the Prime Minister determine the quantum of water available and the proportion of its distribution, through Rajiv Gandhi's personal initiative in approving the project through hastily secured clearances, to H. D. Deve Gowda's controversial attempt to project a 'consensus' between the States with a view to persuading the Supreme Court.

Secondly, the fusion of the executive and legislative power has been greater than that of judicial power with either of the other two branches of government. Parliamentary discussions on Narmada and Kalahandi have been rare of occurrence and perfunctory in nature. In the debate on the Muslim Women's Bill, by contrast, the opposition's participation was considerable, both in numbers and intensity. This episode highlights, however, the facility with which a parliamentary majority can ensure the passage of a legislation to which the executive is firmly committed. The Shah Bano case and the Narmada issue have both been represented in terms of a conflict between the legislature and the judiciary. On the Narmada issue, most recently, the Supreme Court's mainte-nance of its stay on the construction of the Sardar Sarovar Dam in 1997, provoked a voluble and hostile reaction against that court in the Lok Sabha, uniting senior politicians across what otherwise appear to be the most immovable and rigid ideological fault-lines. The parliamentary debate on the Muslim Women's Bill is also replete with references not only to the incompetence of the Supreme Court to legislate on religious matters, but also to the illegitimacy of that Court, as a nominated body, assuming the functions that should be rightfully performed only by an elected body. We saw, however, that even in the aftermath of the Act, many High Court benches have delivered progressive judgements in maintenance cases of Muslim divorcees, by appeal to the absence of a retrospective clause in the Act. In Kalahandi, too, while a succession of House Committees of the Orissa Legislative Assem-bly sought to gloss over the reasons for the scarcity and its extent, it was the Orissa High Court's intervention, taking *suo moto* cognizance of a press report, that resulted in the appointment of the Baidyanath Mishra Commission and, following from this, in its forthright condemnation of the district administration, and its award of compensation to the families of those who had suffered starvation deaths, as established by the Mishra Commission.

Chapter 1 also identified some constraints on democratization imposed by societal factors, and all three cases examined in this book have demonstrated the overlap between economic and social inequalities. Thus, in Kalahandi and the Narmada Valley, the social exclusion of the tribal has coincided with his/her economic exclusion, both of which have tended to translate into political powerlessness. In the Shah Bano case, it is the coincidence between cultural/community identity, on the one hand, and gender identity, on the other, that has contributed to the political marginality of Muslim women as the state and patriarchy work in tandem. It is in recognition of these forms of political exclusion, filtered through caste, religion, and gender as well as through economic disadvantage, that I have spoken of the category of doubly disadvantaged citizens. If the category of the disadvantaged citizen includes all those who live below the poverty line, the category of the doubly disadvantaged citizen includes all those whose situation is characterized by economic precariousness as well as at least one other form of social disprivilege, whether this stems from caste or religion or gender identity. It is in this sense that I have chosen to characterize as doubly disadvantaged citizens the tribals of Kalahandi district who are vulnerable to hunger, the tribals of the Narmada valley who are vulnerable to displacement, and the divorcees of the Muslim community who are economically vulnerable as regards their post-divorce maintenance.

Citizenship indeed lies at the heart of democracy, and has been posited here as its very test. I have discussed two ways in which citizenship may be, and commonly is, undermined. The first of these is when the state fails to ensure the enforceability of the constitutionally guaranteed rights of equal citizenship. This refers to the violation of the formal rights of citizenship enjoyed by citizens, and compared to the many examples of this brought to public notice by the civil rights movement in the country, our cases afford relatively few instances. The incidents of state repression and violence at the Sardar Sarovar dam site belong to this mode of undermining citizenship, as does the failure of state personnel, such as the police force, to protect citizens from privately perpetrated violence. The fact that the National Human Rights Commission has seen fit to investigate the occurrence of starvation deaths in Kalahandi and a few other districts in Orissa, suggests a broadening of the definition of human rights that is entirely appropriate.

Nevertheless, the primary focus of this study has been on the second mode of undermining citizenship, which refers to the social conditions that make possible the effective exercise of citizenship rights. While it would be clearly inappropriate to have too stringent a definition of these conditions, the presence of social relations of exploitation, embedded in traditional hierarchies, and often overlapping with sharp economic disparities, obviously militate against such an exercise of citizenship rights. On the other hand, the universal availability of education, health, and basic welfare provisions are enabling provisions for citizenship and, if we add to these access to information, we are well on the way to creating an informed citizenry, equipped to exercise its political rights in an enlightened manner and able to call its democratically elected government to account.

The three cases here have each exemplified a substantial way in which the effective exercise of the equal rights of citizenship is hampered, if not denied. The Shah Bano case illustrated the way in which the Muslim woman's rights of cultural community were privileged over her identity as a citizen as, through an emphasis on her filiative identity as a Muslim, her affiliative identity as a woman was altogether denied any space. Her access to the state, mediated through a filter of community control, was further limited as the state willingly acquiesced in the rewriting of law such that the criminal law, hitherto uniformly applicable to all citizens, was edited to exclude some citizens from its purview. This category of citizens was thus rendered unequal vis-à-vis men; a predominantly Hindu society; and other women who continue to have recourse to the criminal law in regard to maintenance.

The Kalahandi case, likewise, underlined the threefold exclusion of the tribal citizens of that district: from the economy, as landless, and even bonded labour; from society, as mostly scheduled tribes and castes; and from the polity, as a result of the first two. With *dalits* and tribals accounting for 84 per cent of the agricultural labour force of Kalahandi district, the overlap between these social groups, on the one hand, and landless agricultural labour, on the other, is unmistakable. Equally significant is the low literacy rate, of between ten to fifteen per cent, among these groups. These are of course merely statistical indices of deprivation, that conceal the multiple levels of exploitation that reinforce and sustain them. As such, the conditions for effective citizenship can hardly be claimed to be present. Twelve years after the first reports of starvation deaths, the destitution of Kalahandi was investigated by the National Human Rights Commission which, in February 1998, stated that 'the possibility of deaths having occurred owing to prolonged malnutrition and hunger, compounded by diseases, could not be ruled out' (National Human Rights Commission, 1998: 8). Indeed, it attributed 17 out of the 21 deaths investigated in Kalahandi, Naupada and Bolangir to such cases.

Finally, the Sardar Sarovar Dam, as we have seen, is calculated to displace a very large number of people, many of whom remain officially unrecognized as deserving of compensation. This latter category includes the Canal Affected Persons, the tribal peoples designated as 'encroachers', the secondarily displaced and the earliest displaced people of Kevadia. Over 90 per cent of the oustees in Gujarat and Maharashtra are tribals, while 40 per cent of those in Madhya Pradesh belong to this social group. The significance of displacement, as discussed earlier, lies not merely in the physical uprooting and relocation of people, but the loss of their community ties as they are scattered across disparate resettlement sites, and the loss of a unique way of life which is heavily dependent on the natural resources of the forest for everything from the construction of their homes to their food and medicines. These citizens, like those of Kalahandi, may be simultaneously located in structures of economic and social stratification, both of which contribute to their position in the structure of political power. For these disadvantaged citizens, too, the conditions for the effective exercise of citizenship rights appear to be conspicuous by their absence.

III

Finally, an important strand of argument in this study has attempted to examine discourses of democracy emanating from the state,[2] as well as from different forms of resistance to it. A state that derives legitimacy, at least in part, from its democratic credentials, can manifestly not be seen to be undemocratic, even if many of its practices are profoundly so. The discourse of democracy, as it is expressed through resistance, encompasses a

---

[2] This apparent incongruity is easily explained with reference to the origins of the democratic project in India after 1947. As the reins of the newly independent state passed into the hands of the former nationalist leadership, democracy was a central component of the nationalist ideology now coming to fruition. Hence, the argument that democracy in India was 'a gift from above' ignores the fact of its being the product of a consensus negotiated in the course of the struggle for freedom, subsequently given institutional form by a nationalist élite.

wide variety of associated concepts such as rights, justice, equality and freedom. On the other hand, discourses of democracy emanating from the state are frequently manipulative, ranging from expedient majoritarianism to cynical utilitarianism. These discourses thus vary greatly, and invoke entirely different ingredients of the democratic ideal or, even when they invoke the same principle, e.g., representation, do so in entirely different ways.

As is only to be expected, it is the procedural aspects of democracy that are most often invoked by the state, while the discourses of resistance usually appeal to the more substantive promise of the democratic ideal. This distinction, earlier discussed in Chapter 1, is a commonplace of democratic theory, but frequently if ever employed to illuminate differences in discursive aspects. The first, procedural view is a minimalist, institutionalist, and even instrumentalist conception of democracy, which interprets it as the organizing principle of the polity. On this account, the desirability of democracy vests entirely in its fairness as a decision-making procedure; the opportunities for representation it provides to its citizens through the electoral process; and the accountability of leaders that it is theoretically supposed to facilitate. In this conception, then, democracy is essentially a mechanism for arriving at common decisions, one which says little or nothing about why we consider democracy inherently desirable.

The second conception of substantive democracy invokes the richness, complexity, and meaningful substance of the democratic ideal. Democracy is viewed as a value that should imbue and permeate all spheres of social life and social relations, and this is why other social and political values, such as rights, justice, liberty and equality, have a natural moral and philosophical affinity with it. On this view, there are values and principles meant to be realized by democratic institutions, and political–institutional arrangements that can help us achieve these are an important element, but not the whole, of the democratic concern. To reduce democracy to a matter of devising the fairest possible decision-making procedure is thus to undermine it most profoundly.

State discourses of democracy invoke components of the democratic idea fairly selectively, and therefore not always consistently. In the parliamentary debate on the Muslim Women's Bill, I identified five strains in the argument from majoritarian representative democracy, which were repeatedly deployed by the government and its spokespersons in Parliament. These arguments appealed, variously, to the superior and sovereign right of Parliament as a representative institution (as opposed to a nominated Supreme Court bench) to legislate; the assertion of the majoritarian principle as the fairest procedure for decision-making, justifying the Congress majority's right to enact the bill; the subtle but unmistakable identification between the state and the majority community, which is advised legislative restraint in the matter of the personal law of the minority Muslim community; the supposed wishes of the minority, as represented by its community leadership, and the claim that between ninety and ninety-nine per cent of Indian Muslims supported this legislation; and, finally, that the state needs to be concerned with the protection of the minority as a whole, and not with Muslim women, who constitute a mere minority within a minority.

Even as this appeal to the principles of representative democracy proved serviceable for the justification of patriarchy, assisted by both the state and community leadership, it was, in turn, under-pinned and facilitated by a conception of rights as collective rather than individual. The assertion of the rights of cultural community was answered by a discourse of protection masquerading as recognition of rights, and generated a conception of justice that upheld the right of self-determination of a cultural community, to the complete exclusion of any putatively conflicting claims of gender justice. Above all, the privileging of the rights of cultural community, and their validation by the state, resulted in a curiously paradoxical situation, as the liberal discourse of represen-tative democracy was rendered complicitous in the violation of the individual rights of equal citizenship as well as the more specific claims of gender justice. A right to maintenance for an indigent divorcee remains unrecognized, even as her rights to cultural autonomy are secured.

Finally, in the Narmada Valley, the conception of democracy invoked by state practices is unabashedly majoritarian and utilitar-ian. Its majoritarianism is expressed in the statistical equations that are adduced to establish that the number of those who are adversely affected by the project is far smaller than that of those who stand to be benefited by it. Thus, the somewhat dubious promise of drinking water for Kutch and Saurashtra translates into an enormous beneficiary population of over 25 m. people which is offset against a population of 100,000 displaced persons (both official estimates). This argument has been extended in the political practice of state-sponsored mobilizations, to demonstrate that the numbers of those supporting the dam are no less than the numbers of those opposing it. In both these senses, democracy is reduced to a game of majorities and minorities, defined in numerical terms, though not by ascriptive identity or community affiliation, as in the Shah Bano case. State discourses of democracy in the Narmada Valley are thus exclusively located within a formal, procedural interpretation in which democracy is a game of numbers played out in much the same manner as heads are counted in an electoral system.

As opposed to this, the discourses of resistance invoke a much stronger conception of democracy. The movement against the dam projects appeals to a participatory ideal of democracy, in which people have a right to information and to be consulted about development plans likely to affect their lives. It also asserts, on behalf of the tribal oustees, a set of cultural rights to a way of life, and the associated material rights to the natural resources, in and by which they have always lived. Above all, it proclaims the right to protest, eschewing both the paths of violence and of parliamentary party politics, and following an essentially Gandhian strategy. All these claims are underpinned by a conception of justice which, even as it is critical of the inequalities and disparities engendered by the dominant model of development, astonishingly makes no claims to redistributive justice.

The story of Kalahandi may be, and has been, interpreted as a resounding success for the institutions of adversarial democracy. The fact that the earliest reports of starvation deaths were brought to public notice by the print media, and then pressed by the Opposition parties in the State legislature, has added credence to this analysis. What is missed, however, is the fact that none of this pressure was authentically representative. It was the voicing of protest on behalf of, rather than by, the affected people. State discourses of scarcity have generally adopted the language of succour and charity, rather than that of welfare rights or entitlements. As such, the administrative view of the scarcity-affected population is characterized by a benevolent paternalism. This is facilitated by the adoption of a manipulative approach to the social facts of hunger or starvation, which are translated into the technical language of drought-relief as purely physical and natural phenomena, so as to minimize political responsibility. The language of democracy is as far removed from the state's policy response as the experience of democracy is from the lives of the affected citizens. Claims to rights and justice find no space in an invisible vocabulary of protest.

IV

As they mediate state–society relations, democratic institutions play the role of filters, providing access—though often restricted—to the state. This is almost an auxiliary and adjunctive role, for it is the salience of the groups in question that is expressed through the democratic process, which proves to be serviceable to some interests, but closed to others. Often, organized interests find voice, while the politically unorganized poor have to be mobilized to extra-institutional protest (as in the Narmada Valley), or else do not protest at all (as in Kalahandi). There is, thus, paralleling the unorganized sector in the economy,[3] what may be described as an unorganized sector in the Indian polity. Many organized interests, even of the disadvantaged, enjoy some voice, if only at election time when they are assiduously courted as conveniently pre-aggregated stocks of valuable political currency (or 'vote banks' in everyday parlance). On the other hand, groups such as the tribals of Kalahandi, have largely subsisted on the margins of the polity, and have not forged a political identity in the same way. Women, particularly those belonging to the poorer classes or ethnic minorities, are victims of similar political disablement. Despite its size, this unorganized sector of the polity is exceedingly vulnerable.

A fundamental shortcoming of Indian democracy is its inauthenticity and unrepresentativeness. Despite the clamour of celebration that attends every election ritual, and the tributes paid to the vibrancy and resilience of Indian democracy, there is cause for concern in that intermediaries are crucial to this democracy, not just as brokers of votes, but also to represent the needs of the vulnerable. That the hungry of Kalahandi or Muslim women

[3] It has been suggested that the unorganized sector of the economy accounts for 90 per cent of the workforce, which suffers from welfare and employment insecurity (Rudolph and Rudolph, 1987: 21, 370).

divorcees did not represent their own cases is not accidental. That it took a group of middle-class activists to energize the movement against the Sardar Sarovar dam in the Narmada Valley is also not surprising. Conditions for democracy, even of the formal, procedural kind, have not been consolidated, facilitating the state's unchallenged deviation from its own avowed purposes and projects. It thus becomes possible for the state to pay only token attention to the demands of welfare; to compromise secular principles and deny its Muslim women citizens equal rights; and to answer challenges to its development strategy by resorting to technocratic arguments.

The ambivalent and even contradictory responses of the state to these claims suggests that it is not one or another form of democratic articulation that predisposes the state to act or respond in a particular, predictable manner. The conventional exercise of assessing the efficacy of democratic processes from state response is clearly an inappropriate, and even sterile, way of approaching the question. It is after all the substantive content of the challenge, in terms of which specific interests it threatens, not excluding reasons of state, that prejudices state policy. Of the three examples discussed here, two represent demands to give effect to the state's agenda of welfare and secularism. The third example, from the Narmada Valley, questions the state's agenda by interrogating the content of its project of development. In the first two cases, the state's agenda has not been effected, chiefly because the state manifestly enjoys autonomy from the numerous, legally enfranchised but politically marginal, mass of affected citizens. In the third case, the anti-development mobilization is relatively ineffectual in obtaining state recognition for its demands, in the face of formidable state and commercial interests.

I have argued that the understanding of power must encompass the importance of agenda-setting, As such, the power of the state must surely be understood in terms of its ability to not merely implement a policy, but also to place certain goals on the agenda and to revise and transform them periodically, which it does through its interactions with society. It is clear that the Indian state's project of social transformation, as expressed through its developmentalist or welfarist goals, is not above bargaining and compromise. It is closed only to democratic negotiation by vulnerable categories of citizens. In its attentiveness to some interests, the public agenda is permissively open and vastly inclusionary, while towards other, less influential ones, it remains severely exclusionary. The core projects of the state are thus rendered differentially open to negotiation. As with almost any other resource, that is not a problem of too little or too much democracy, but of its selective availability.[4]

The ultimate test of a successful democracy should surely be its ability to determine, or at least influence the agenda of the state. Disputation about the ends and goals of a society is an intrinsic part of the democratic project. To accord sacrosanctity to the agenda adopted by the state at a given moment in its history is to leviathanize democracy. As in Hobbes, this anoints the principle of consent, only to withdraw it after its first exercise (authorizing the sovereign to act on behalf of the subjects) is completed. If electoral politics are an adequate guarantee of continuous consent, and the public agenda of a society cannot be perennially open to negotiation, is there any pragmatic centre to be found between these two extremes of democratic practice? When the formal conditions provided for participation by citizens in a democratic polity are precluded from being realized, as they manifestly are in all the cases examined in this book, that agenda must be reopened to take account of the legitimate needs of the socially vulnerable and politically marginalized. The needs addressed in all three cases are fundamental as they call for security and basic sustenance, for life itself. Expressed as rights, they represent variously the right to food, the right to a way of life of one's choice, and the right not to be rendered destitute. Other forms of rights-claims by groups,

---

[4] Atul Kohli (1990) has argued that democratic mobilization and the expansion of political participation are factors contributing to the crisis of governability in India. Thus, the inability of the state to effect its declared agenda is attributed to the logic of democracy which, by enhancing participation, also leads to a multiplication of demands on the state, as the controller of scarce resources. Similarly, Lloyd and Susanne Rudolph (1987) have shown how pressures from a variety of demand groups have diminished the autonomy of the state and rendered it simultaneously 'weak–strong'. More recently, Pranab Bardhan (1993) has argued that democracy engenders parochial conflict and constrains economic development. Thus, the problems of conflict management by the state are compounded, now that the conflict is no longer between members of the dominant proprietary coalition, but includes also 'turmoil from below' (Bardhan, 1984: 82).

such as the demand for caste-based affirmative action or self-determination on the basis of religion, speak to the state from a position of strength. Couched as threats, they compel the state to garner its energies to address their demands. The rights claims articulated in the context of this study, however, present no serious threat to the state. They point, rather, to the failed promise of 1947, to the violation and compromise of the rights guaranteed in 1950 to evade those promises, and to the lack of voice in the continuously profluent refashioning of the state's agenda.

References

OFFICIAL DOCUMENTS

A. Government of India

Census of India (1991), Series 19, Orissa: Provisional Population Totals, Paper I of 1991, Supplement.

Commissioner for Scheduled Castes and Scheduled Tribes (1988), *Twenty Eighth Report*, 1986–7.

———— (1990), *Twenty Ninth Report*, 1987–9.

Government of India (1958), *Fourteenth Report of Law Commission of India*, Ministry of Law.

———— (1974), *Towards Equality: Report of the Committee on the Status of Women in India*, Department of Social Welfare.

———— (1978), *Report of the Narmada Water Disputes Tribunal*, vols I–V.

National Human Rights Commission (1998), Proceedings, Case No. 37/3/97–LD, Chaturanan Mishra, Union Minister of Agriculture (Complainant), New Delhi.

Rajya Sabha Committee on Petitions (1988), Hundred and Sixth Report on the Petition signed by Shri Chittaranjan Mandal of Orissa pertaining to improper use of funds meant for poverty alleviation programmes leading to Starvation deaths in undivided districts of Kalahandi, Bolangir and Koraput in Orissa, Presented on March 31, 1998, Rajya Sabha Secretariat, New Delhi.

Report of the Central Study Team on Koraput and Kalahandi (1992), Ministry of Agriculture, September.

Report of the Five Member Group set up by the Ministry of Water Resources to Discuss Various Issues Relating to the Sardar Sarovar Project (1994), vol. I (Report) and App. II, New Delhi.

Report of the Indian Famine Commission 1901 (1979), rpt. by Agricole Publishing Academy, New Delhi.

B. State Governments

Government of Bihar (1978), *Bihar Famine Report*, 1966–7.

Government of Gujarat (1991), *Compilation of Government Resolutions for Rehabilitation and Resettlement Policy for Oustees of Sardar Sarovar Project*, Narmada Development Department.

Government of Madhya Pradesh (1991), *Narmada Sagar Project: Rehabilitation and Resettlement Plan*, Narmada Valley Development Authority.

———— (1992), *Sardar Sarovar Project: Action Plan of Rehabilitation and Resettlement of Oustees of Madhya Pradesh*, Pts I and II, Narmada Valley Development Authority.

Government of Orissa (1980), *Orissa District Gazetteer: Kalahandi*, Gazetteers Unit, Department of Revenue.

———— (1988), 'White Paper on Drought Situation in Orissa 1987–8', Revenue Department.

———— (1990), *District Statistical Handbook 1989–90: Kalahandi*, District Statistical Office.

———— (1992), 'Memorandum Presented to the Central Team on its Visit to Study the Reported Distress Conditions in Koraput and Kalahandi Districts', Sept. 26–Oct. 1, Special Relief Commissioner.

———— (1993a), *Economic Survey 1992–3*, Directorate of Economics and Statistics.

———— (1993b), *District Statistical Handbook: Kalahandi*, Directorate of Economics and Statistics.

Madhya Pradesh Legislative Assembly (1994), *Report of Members of the Madhya Pradesh Legislative Assembly on the Resettlement in Gujarat of Persons Displaced by the Sardar Sarovar Project*.

Orissa Legislative Assembly (1986), *Thirty Fifth Report of the Committee on Estimates*, 1985–6.

———— (1987), *Committee of the House on Drought and Other Natural Calamities*, Interim Report.

———— (1988), *Committee of the House on Drought and Other Natural Calamities*, Second Interim Report.

Report of the Baidyanath Mishra Commission (1991), 'Inquiry into Original Jurisdiction Cases No. 3517 of 1988 and No. 525 of 1989', High Court of Orissa, Cuttack.

Report of the Orissa States Enquiry Committee (1939), Cuttack.

C. *Parliamentary Debates and Judicial Pronouncements*

Lok Sabha Debates.

Rajya Sabha Debates.

All India Reporter for Supreme Court and High Court cases.

D. *The Hindu to the List of Newspapers*

Free Press Journal, *Hindustan Times*, *Indian Express* , *M. P. Chronicle*

(Bhopal), *National Mail* (Bhopal), *Patriot, Pioneer, Rajasthan Patrika, Statesman, Telegraph, Sunday Observer, Times of India*

E. Periodicals

Economic and Political Weekly (EPW), India Today, Illustrated Weekly of India, Muslim India, Narmada (newsletter of the Narmada Bachao Andolan), *Narmada Samachar, Sunday*

BOOKS AND ARTICLES

AGNES, FLAVIA (1994), 'Triple Talaq Judgement: Do Women Really Benefit?', *Economic and Political Weekly*, vol. XXIX, no. 20, 14 May.

AHMAD, IMTIAZ (ed.) (1983), *Modernization and Social Change among Muslims in India*, Manohar, New Delhi.

ALAGH, Y. K. (1994), App. II (3) to the *Report of the Five-Member Group of the Ministry of Water Resources to Discuss Various Issues relating to the Sardar Sarovar Project.*

———— and D. T. BUCH (1995), 'The Sardar Sarovar Project and Sustainable Development' *in* Fisher (ed.).

ALAMGIR, MOHIUDDIN (1980), *Famine in South Asia*, Oelgeschlager, Gunn, and Hain Publishers, Inc., Cambridge, Mass.

ALFORD, ROBERT R. and ROGER FRIEDLAND (1990), *Powers of Theory: Capitalism, the State and Democracy*, Cambridge University Press, Cambridge.

All India Congress Committee (1969), *Resolutions on Economic Policy, Programme and Allied Matters* (1924–69), Indian National Congress, New Delhi.

ALTHUSSER, LOUIS (1971), *Lenin and Philosophy and Other Essays*, Monthly Review Press, New York.

ANVESHI LAW COMMITTEE (1997), 'Is Gender Justice Only a Legal Issue? Political Stakes in UCC Debate', *Economic and Political Weekly*, vol. XXXII, nos 9–10, 1–8 March.

APPADURAI, ARJUN (1984), 'How Moral is South Asia's Economy? A Review Article', *Journal of Asian Studies*, vol. XLIII, no. 3, May.

ARNOLD, DAVID (1979), 'Looting, Grain Riots and Government Policy in South India, 1918'. *Past and Present*, no. 84.

———— (1984), 'Famine in Peasant Consciousness and Peasant Action: Madras 1876–8', *in* Ranajit Guha (ed.), *Subaltern Studies III*, Oxford University Press, Delhi.

———— (1988), *Famine: Social Crisis and Historical Change*, Basil Blackwell, Oxford.

ASIA WATCH (1992), *Before the Deluge: Human Rights Abuses at India's Narmada Dam*, vol. 4, 15, New York.

AUSTIN, GRANVILLE [1966], (1976), *The Indian Constitution: Cornerstone of a Nation*, Oxford University Press, Bombay.

BAGCHI, AMIYA KUMAR (1973), 'Foreign Capital and Economic Development in India: A Schematic View', *in* Kathleen Gough and Hari P. Sharma (eds), *Imperialism and Revolution in South Asia*, Monthly Review Press, New York.

BAILEY, F. G. (1963), *Politics and Social Change: Orissa in 1959*, University of California Press, Berkeley.

BARBER, BENJAMIN (1984), *Strong Democracy: Participatory Politics for a New Age*, University of California Press, Berkeley and Los Angeles.

——— (1990), 'Symposium on the State and Economic Development, *Journal of Economic Perspectives*, vol. 4, no. 3, Summer.

BARDHAN, PRANAB (1984), *The Political Economy of Development in India*, Oxford University Press, Delhi.

——— (1993), 'Symposium on Democracy and Development', *Journal of Economic Perspectives*, vol. 7, no. 3, Summer.

BAVISKAR, AMITA (1991), 'The Researcher as Pilgrim', *Lokayan Bulletin*, 9:3/4, May–Aug.

——— (1995), *In the Belly of the River : Tribal Conflicts over Development in the Narmada Valley*, Oxford University Press, Delhi.

BECKMAN, BJORN (1984), 'Bakalori: Peasants versus State and Industry in Nigeria', *in* Goldsmith and Hildyard (eds), 1984b.

BEHURA, N. K. and P. K. DAS (1991), 'Effect of Drought on Health Condition and Nutritional Status of People', *in* Nayak and Mahajan.

BHALLA, G. S. and D. S. TYAGI (1989), *Patterns in Indian Agricultural Development: A District Level Study*, Institute for Studies in Industrial Development, New Delhi.

BHATIA, B. M. (1967), *Famines in India*, Asia Publishing House, Bombay.

——— (1988), *Indian Agriculture: A Policy Perspective*, Sage Publications, Delhi.

BHATIA, BELA (1997), 'Forced Evictions in the Narmada Valley', *in* Drèze, Samson, Singh (eds).

BILGRAMI, AKEEL (1994), 'Two Concepts of Secularism: Reason, Modernity and the Archimedean Ideal', *Economic and Political Weekly*, vol. XXIX, no. 28, 9 July.

BLOCK, FRED (1980), 'Beyond Relative Autonomy: State Managers as Historical Subjects', *in The Socialist Register* 1980, The Merlin Press, London.

BOSE, ARUN (1989), *India's Social Crisis*, Oxford University Press, New Delhi.

BOSE, PRADIP KUMAR (1988), 'Political Economy of Irrigation: A Note', App. 10 in Claude Alvares and Ramesh Billorey, *Damming the Narmada*, Third World Network, Penang, Malaysia.

BRASS, PAUL R. (1986), 'The Political Uses of Crisis: The Bihar Famine of 1966-7', *Journal of Asian Studies*, vol. XLV, no. 2, Feb.

BRENNAN, L. (1984), 'The Development of the Indian Famine Codes: Personalities, Politics and Policies', *in* Bruce Currey and Graeme Hugo (eds), *Famine as a Geographical Phenomenon*, G. Reidel Publishing Co., Dordrecht, Holland.

BUCH, M. N. (1991), 'And all the Boards did Shrink', Lokayan Bulletin, 9:3/4, May–Aug.

BURKE, EDMUND [1774], (1975), 'Speech to the Electors of Bristol', *in* B. W. Hill (ed.), *Edmund Burke on Government, Politics and Society*, Fontana/The Harvester Press, Glasgow.

CAMMACK, PAUL (1989), 'Bringing the State Back In: A Polemic', *British Journal of Political Science*, vol. 19 (2).

CARRUTHERS, IAN and COLIN CLARK (1981), *The Economics of Irrigation*, Liverpool University Press, Liverpool.

CAUFIELD, CATHERINE (1996), *Masters of Illusion: The World Bank and the Poverty of Nations*, Macmillan, London.

CENTRE FOR SOCIAL STUDIES, SURAT (1997), 'Resettlement and Rehabilitation in Gujarat', *in* Drèze, Samson, Singh (eds).

CERNEA, MICHAEL M. (1995), 'Understanding and Preventing Impoverishment from Displacement: Reflections on the State of Knowledge', *Social Action*, vol. 45, July–Sept.

CHANDLER, WILLIAM U. (1984), 'The Tellico and Columbia Dams: Stewardship and Development', *in* Goldsmith and Hildyard (eds).

CHATTERJEE, PARTHA (1997a), 'Development Planning and the Indian State', *in* Partha Chatterjee (ed.), *State and Politics in India*, Oxford University Press, Delhi.

——— (1997b), 'Beyond the Nation-State? Or Within?', *Economic and Political Weekly*, vol. XXXII, nos 1-2, 4–11 Jan.

CHEN, MARTHA ALTER (1991), *Coping with Seasonality and Drought*, Sage, Delhi.

CLAESSEN, HENRI J. M. and PETER SKALNIK (eds) (1978), *The Early State*, Mouton, The Hague.

COLCHESTER, MARCUS (1984), 'An End to Laughter? The Bhopalpatnam and the Godavari Projects', *in* Goldsmith and Hildyard (eds) (1984b).

COSSMAN, BRENDA and RATNA KAPUR (1996), 'Secularism: Bench-Marked by Hindu Right', *Economic and Political Weekly*, vol. XXXI, no. 38, 21 Sept.

CURRIE, BOB (1993), *Food Crisis, Administrative Action and Public Response: Some General Implications from the Kalahandi Issue*, Ph. D. thesis, University of Hull, UK.

——— (1996), 'Laws for the Rich and Flaws for the Poor? Legal Action and Food Insecurity in the Kalahandi Case', *in* John Toye and H. O'Neill (eds), *A World Without Famine*, Macmillan, London.

————— (1997), 'Power, Legitimacy and Hunger: Re-examining the Link between Democratic Governance and Food Security', Paper presented to the ECPR Joint Sessions of Workshops, Bern.

DALAL, LALIT (1989), *Namami Devi Narmade*, Sardar Sarovar Narmada Nigam Ltd., Gandhinagar.

DAS, VEENA (1996), 'Dislocation and Rehabilitation: Defining a Field', *Economic and Political Weekly*, vol. XXXI, no. 24, 15 June.

————— (1997), 'Cultural Rights and the Definition of Community', *in* Martin Doornbos and Sudipta Kaviraj (eds), *Dynamics of State Formation: India and Europe Compared*, Sage Publications, New Delhi.

DEN UYL, DOUGLAS J. (1993), 'The Right to Welfare and the Virtue of Charity', *Social Philosophy and Policy*, vol. 10, no. 1.

DERRETT, J. DUNCAN M. (1968), *Religion, Law and the State in India*, Faber & Faber, London.

DE WAAL, ALEXANDER (1989), *The Famine That Kills*, Oxford University Press, New York.

DHAGAMWAR, VASUDHA (1997), 'The NGO Movements in the Narmada Valley: Some Reflections', *in* Drèze, Samson and Singh (eds).

DHARMADHIKARY, SHRIPAD (1995), 'Hydropower at Sardar Sarovar: Is it Necessary, Justified and Affordable?', *in* Fisher, (ed.).

D'MONTE, DARRYL (1985), *Temples or Tombs? Industry versus Environment: Three Controversies*, Centre for Science and Environment, New Delhi.

DRÈZE, JEAN and AMARTYA SEN (1989), *Hunger and Public Action*, Clarendon Press, Oxford.

————— (eds) (1990), *The Political Economy of Hunger*, vol. I–III, Clarendon Press, Oxford.

————— (1991), 'Public Action for Social Security: Foundations and Strategy', *in* Ehtisham Ahmed, Jean Drèze, John Hills and Amartya Sen (eds), *Social Security in Developing Countries*, Clarendon Press, Oxford.

————— (1995), *India: Economic Development and Social Opportunity*, Oxford University Press, Delhi.

DRÈZE, JEAN, MEERA SAMSON and SATYAJIT SINGH (eds) (1997), *The Dam and the Nation: Displacement and resettlement in the Narmada Valley*, Oxford University Press, Delhi.

DUNCAN, GRAEME (ed.) (1989), *Democracy and the Capitalist State*, Cambridge University Press, Cambridge.

DUTT, ROMESH C. [1900] (1985), *Famines and Land Assessments in India*, B. R. Publishing Corporation, Delhi.

DWIVEDI, RANJIT (1997), 'People's Movements in Environmental Politics: A Critical Analysis of the Narmada Bachao Andolan in India', Working Paper Series no. 242, Institute of Social Studies, The Hague.

DWORKIN, RONALD (1977), *Taking Rights Seriously*, Duckworth, London.

EMBREE, AINSLIE (1992), *Utopias in Conflict: Religion and Nationalism in Modern India*, Oxford University Press, Delhi.

ENGINEER, ASGHAR ALI (ed.) (1987), *The Shah Bano Controversy*, Orient Longman, Bombay.

———— (1995), 'Let Indian Muslims Not Repeat the Mistake', *Economic and Political Weekly*, vol. XXX, no. 49, 9 Dec.

ESTEVA, GUSTAVO (1997), 'Development', *in* Wolfgang Sachs (ed.), *The Development Dictionary: A Guide to Knowledge as Power*, Orient Longman, Delhi.

EVANS, PETER, THEDA SKOCPOL and DIETRICH RUESCHEMEYER (eds) (1985), *Bringing the State Back In*, Cambridge University Press, Cambridge.

FISHER, WILLIAM F. (ed.) (1995), *Toward Sustainable Development: Struggling Over India's Narmada River*, M. E. Sharpe, New York.

FRIETAG, SANDRIA (1990), *Collective Action and Community: Public Arenas and the Emergence of Communalism in North India*, Oxford University Press, New Delhi.

GALANTER, MARC (1989), *Law and Society in Modern India*, Oxford University Press, Delhi.

GALLIE, W. B. (1956), 'Essentially Contested Concepts', Proceedings of the Aristotelian Society, 56.

GHOSE, AJIT KUMAR (1982), 'Food Supply and Starvation: A Study of Famines with Reference to the Indian Sub-continent', *Oxford Economic Papers*.

GILL, M. S. (1995), 'Resettlement and Rehabilitation in Maharashtra for the Sardar Sarovar Narmada Project', *in* Fisher (ed.).

GOLDSMITH, EDWARD and NICHOLAS HILDYARD (1984a), *The Social and Environmental Effects of Large Dams*, Sierra Club Books, San Francisco.

———— (eds) (1984b), *The Social and Environmental Effects of Large Dams: vol. 2: Case Studies*, Wadebridge Ecological Centre, UK.

GREENOUGH, PAUL R. (1982), *Prosperity and Misery in Modern Bengal: The Famine of 1943–44*, Oxford University Press, New York.

HADENIUS, AXEL (1994), 'The Duration of Democracy: Institutional vs Socio-Economic Factors', *in* David Beetham (ed.), *Defining and Measuring Democracy*, Sage, London.

HAKIM, ROXANNE P. (1997), 'Resettlement and Rehabilitation in the Context of "Vasava" Culture', *in* Drèze, Samson and Singh (eds).

HALDON, JOHN (1993), *The State and the Tributary Mode of Production*, Verso, London.

HALL, STUART (1984), 'The Rise of the Representative/Interventionist State', *in* Gregor McLennan, David Held and Stuart Hall (eds), *State and Society in Contemporary Britain*, Polity Press, Cambridge.

HANIFF, NIESHA Z. (1983), 'Muslim Women and the Minority Mentality', *in* Imtiaz Ahmad (ed.).

HANN, CHRIS (1996), 'Political Society and Civil Anthropology', Introduction to Chris Hann and Elizabeth Dunn (eds), *Civil Society: Challenging Western Models*, Routledge, London.

———— and ELIZABETH DUNN (eds) (1996), *Civil Society: Challenging Western Models*, Routledge, London.

HARRELL-BOND, BARBARA, EFTIHIA VOUTIRA and MARK LEOPOLD (1992), 'Counting the Refugees: Gifts, Givers, Patrons and Clients', *Journal of Refugee Studies*, vol. 5, no. 3/4.

HASAN, ZOYA (1989), 'Minority Identity, Muslim Women Bill Campaign and the Political Process', *Economic and Political Weekly*, vol. XXIV, no. 1, 7 Jan.

HSIAO, KUNG-CHUAN (1979), *A History of Chinese Political Thought*, trans. F. W. Mote, Princeton University Press, Princeton, N. J.

Independent Review, Report of the (1992) Sardar Sarovar, Resource Futures International, Ottawa.

INTERNATIONAL RIVERS NETWORK (1996), *Narmada International Update*, 3 June.

JAYAL, NIRAJA GOPAL (ed.) (1987), *Sidney and Beatrice Webb: Indian Diary*, Oxford University Press, Delhi.

———— (1994), 'The Gentle Leviathan: Welfare and the Indian State', *Social Scientist*, vol. 22, nos 9–12. Sept.–Dec.

———— (1997), 'The Governance Agenda: Making Democratic Development Dispensable', *Economic and Political Weekly*, vol. XXXII, no. 8, 22–8 Feb.

JESSOP, BOB (1990), *State Theory: Putting Capitalist States in their Place*, Polity Press, Cambridge.

KAUTILYA (1987), *The Arthashastra*, ed. L. N. Rangarajan, Penguin Books, Delhi.

KAVIRAJ, SUDIPTA (1991), 'On State, Society and Discourse in India', *in* James Manor (ed.), *Rethinking Third World Politics*, Longman, London.

———— (1996), 'Civil Society in India?', Paper presented at Seminar on Civil Society, Public Sphere and Organization Behaviour: Approaches to the Study of State–society Relations in the Non-Western World', University of Oslo, April.

KHALIDI, OMAR (1993), 'Muslims in Indian Political Process: Group Goals and Alternative Strategies', *Economic and Political Weekly*, vol. XXVIII, nos 1–2, 2–9 Jan.

KHAN, MUNIZA RAFIQ (1993), *Socio-Legal Status of Muslim Women*, Radiant Publishers, Delhi.

KOHLI, ATUL (1987), *The State and Poverty in India: The Politics of Reform*, Cambridge University Press, Cambridge.

———— (1990), *Democracy and Discontent: India's Growing Crisis of Governability*, Cambridge University Press, Cambridge.

———— (1993), 'Democracy Amid Economic Orthodoxy: Trends in Developing Countries', *Third World Quarterly*, vol. 14, no. 4.

KOTHARI, ASHISH and RAJIV BHARTARI (1984), 'Narmada Valley Project: Development or Destruction?' *Economic and Political Weekly*, vol. XIX, nos 22–3, 2–9 June.

KULKE, HERMANN (ed.) (1995), *The State in India 1000–1700*. Oxford University Press, Delhi.

KYMLICKA, WILL (1989), *Liberalism, Community and Culture*, Clarendon Press, Oxford.

LAITIN, DAVID (1985), 'Hegemony and Religious Conflict: British Imperial Control and Political Cleavages in Yorubaland', *in* Evans et al. (eds).

LATEEF, SHAHIDA (1983), 'Modernization in India and the Status of Muslim Women', *in* Imtiaz Ahmad (ed.).

LEFTWICH, ADRIAN (1993), 'Governance, Democracy and Development in the Third World', *Third World Quarterly*, vol. 14, no. 3.

———— (1995), 'Two Cheers for Democracy? Democracy and the Developmental State', *in* Leftwich (ed.), *Democracy and Development*, Polity Press, Cambridge.

LOCKE, JOHN (1963), *Two Treatises of Government*, (ed.) Peter Laslett, Cambridge University Press, New York.

LOKADRUSTI (1991), *Hunger and Underdevelopment: Is There a Way Out for Kalahandi*, A Workshop Report, Kalahandi, Orissa.

LUDDEN, DAVID (1985), *Peasant History in South India*, Princeton University Press.

LUKES, STEVEN (1974), *Power: A Radical View*, Macmillan, London.

MACIVER, R. M. [1926] (1969), *The Modern State*, Oxford University Press, Oxford.

MACPHERSON, C. B. (1966), *The Real World of Democracy*, Clarendon Press, Oxford.

MAHALIA, BAVA (1994), 'Letter from a Tribal Village', *Lokayan Bulletin*, 11.2/3, Sept.–Dec.

MAKINSON, DAVID (1988), 'Rights of Peoples: Point of View of a Logician', *in* James Crawford (ed.), *The Rights of Peoples*, Clarendon Press, Oxford.

MANN, MICHAEL (1988), 'The Autonomous Power of the State: Its Origins, Mechanisms and Results', *in* his *States, War and Capitalism*, Basil Blackwell, Oxford.

MANOR, JAMES (ed.) (1991), *Rethinking World Politics*, Longman, London.

MATHUR, KULDEEP and NIRAJA G. JAYAL (1993), *Drought, Policy and Politics in India*, Sage, New Delhi.

MEHTA, S. S. (1988), *Sardar Sarovar Project: A Boon to Gujarat*, Sardar Sarovar Narmada Nigam Ltd., Gandhinagar.

MIGDAL, JOEL (1988), *Strong Societies and Weak States: State–Society Relations and State Capabilities in the Third World*, Princeton University Press, Princeton, N. J.

MIGDAL, JOEL (1994), 'Introduction: Developing a State-in-Society Perspective', *in* Joel Migdal, Atul Kohli and Vivienne Shue (eds), *State Power and Social Forces: Domination and Transformation in the Third World*, Cambridge University Press, Cambridge.

MILIBAND, RALPH (1975), 'The Problem of the Capitalist State', *in* Robin Blackburn (ed.), *Ideology in Social Science*, Fontana/Collins, Glasgow.

MILLER, DAVID and LARRY SIEDENTOP (eds) (1983), *The Nature of Political Theory*, Clarendon Press, Oxford.

MISHRA, R. N. (1984), *Regionalism and State Politics in India*, Ashish Publishing House, New Delhi.

MITRA, SUBRATA (1991), 'Desecularising the State: Religion and Politics in India after Independence', *Comparative Studies in Society and History*, vol. 33.

MODY, NAWAZ (1987), 'The Press in India: The Shah Bano Judgement and its Aftermath', *Asian Survey*, vol. XXVII, no. 8, Aug.

MOHANTY, BIDYUT (1992), 'Drought and Patterns of Migration in Western Orissa: A Case-study of 1987–8 Drought in Kalahandi District', mimeo, Delhi.

MOHANTY, MANORANJAN (1990), 'Class, Caste and Dominance in Orissa', *in* Francine Frankel and M.S.A. Rao (eds), *Dominance and State Power in Modern India*, vol. II, Oxford University Press, New Delhi.

MOORE, JR. BARRINGTON (1966), *Social Origins of Dictatorship and Democracy*, Penguin Books, Harmondsworth.

MUKTA, PARITA (1995), 'Wresting Riches, Marginalizing the Poor, Criminalizing Dissent: The Building of the Narmada Dam in Western India', *South Asia Bulletin: Comparative Studies of South Asia, Africa and the Middle East*, vol. XV, no. 2.

MULTIPLE ACTION RESEARCH GROUP (MARG) (1986–8), *Sardar Sarovar Oustees in Madhya Pradesh: What Do They Know?* vols I–V, Delhi.

MUNSHI, K. M. (ed) (1967), *Indian Constitutional Documents*, vol. I. Bharatiya Vidya Bhawan, Bombay.

NAOROJI, DADABHAI (n.d.), *Memorandum on a Few Settlements in the Report of the Indian Famine Commission, 1880*, G. A. Natesan & Co., Madras.

Narmada Foundation Trust, Sankat Nivaran Society and Gujarat Chamber of Commerce and Industry (1991), 'Memorandum to World Bank Independent Review Mission on Sardar Sarovar Projects', Ahmedabad.

NAYAK, P. K. and ANIL MAHAJAN (eds) (1991), *Human Encounter with Drought*, Reliance Publishing House, New Delhi.

NETTL, J. P. (1968), 'The State as a Conceptual Variable', *World Politics*, vol. XX, no. 4, July.

NOZICK, ROBERT (1974), *Anarchy, State and Utopia*, Basic Books, Inc., New York.

O'BRIEN, DONAL B. CRUISE (1991), 'The Show of State in a Neo-Colonial Twilight : Francophone Africa', *in* James Manor (ed.), *Rethinking Third World Politics*, Longman, London.

OLLMAN, BERTELL (1992), 'Going Beyond the State?', *American Political Science Review*, vol. 86, no. 4, Dec.

O'NEILL, ONORA (1986), *Faces of Hunger*, Allen & Unwin, London.

PANDEY, GYANENDRA (1990), *The Construction of Communalism in Colonial North India*, Oxford University Press, Delhi.

PARANJYPE, VIJAY (1990), *High Dams on the Narmada: A Holistic Analysis of the River Valley Projects*, INTACH, Delhi.

PARASHAR, ARCHANA (1992), *Women and Family Law Reform in India*, Sage Publications, New Delhi.

PARASURAMAN, S. (1997), 'The Anti-Dam Movement and Rehabilitation Policy', *in* Drèze, Samson and Singh (eds).

PAREKH, BHIKHU (1993), 'The Cultural Particularity of Liberal Democracy', *in* David Held (ed.), *Prospects for Democracy*, Polity Press, Oxford.

PARRY, GERAINT and GEORGE MOYSER (1994), 'More Participation, More Democracy?', *in* David Beetham (ed.), *Defining and Measuring Democracy*, Sage, London.

PATEL, ANIL (1997), 'Resettlement Politics and Tribal Interests', *in* Drèze, Samson and Singh (eds).

PATEL, C. C. (1995), 'The Sardar Sarovar Project: A Victim of Time', *in* Fisher (ed.).

PATEL, JASHBHAI (1994), 'Is National Interest Being Served by Narmada Project?', *Economic and Political Weekly*, vol. XXIX, no. 30, 23 July.

PATHAK, ZAKIA and RAJESWARI SUNDAR RAJAN (1989), 'Shahbano' *Signs*, vol. 14, no. 3.

PATI, BISWAMOY (1990), 'What Went Wrong for the Congress?', *Economic and Political Weekly*, vol. XXV, nos 7–8, 17–24 Feb.

PATKAR, MEDHA (1992), 'The Strength of a People's Movement', Interview with Dunu Roy and Geeti Sen in *India International Centre Quarterly*, vol. 19, nos 1–2.

People's Union for Civil Liberties (1995), *Conditions of Resettlement Sites in Gujarat: The Effects on Human Rights of the Displaced due to the Sardar Sarovar Project*, Baroda.

PLANT, RAYMOND, HARRY LESSER and PETER TAYLOR-GOOBY (1980), *Political Philosophy and Social Welfare: Essays on the Normative Basis of Welfare Provision*, Routledge & Kegan Paul, London.

POULANTZAS, NICOS (1975), 'The Problem of the Capitalist State', *in* Robin Blackburn (ed.), *Ideology in Social Science*, Fontana/Collis, Glasgow.

PRADHAN, JAGADISH (1993), 'Drought in Kalahandi: The Real Story', *Economic and Political Weekly*, vol. XXVIII, no. 22, 29 May.

PRAJAPATI, ROHIT (1997), 'Narmada, the Judiciary and Parliament', *Economic and Political Weekly*, vol. XXXII, no.14, 5–11 April.

PRZEWORSKI, ADAM et al. (1995), *Sustainable Democracy*, Cambridge University Press, Cambridge.

PUBLIC INTEREST RESEARCH GROUP (1993), *Alternative Economic Survey*, 1992–3, Delhi.

RAINA, VINOD (1994), 'Sardar Sarovar: Case for Lowering Dam Height', *Economic and Political Weekly*, vol. XXIX, no. 14, 2 April.

RAJ, P. A. (1990), *Facts: Sardar Sarovar Project*, Sardar Sarovar Narmada Nigam Ltd., Gandhinagar.

RAJASHEKHAR, D. and V. VYASULU (1990), 'The Credit Delivery System and the Development Process: The Case of Kalahandi, A Backward District in a Backward State', mimeo., Institute for Social and Economic Change, Bangalore.

RAM, N. (1990), 'An Independent Press and Anti-Hunger Strategies: The Indian Experience', *in* Drèze and Sen (eds) vol. I.

RAM, RAHUL N. (1995), 'Benefits of the Sardar Sarovar Project: Are the Claims Reliable?', *in* Fisher (ed.).

RAO, C. H. HANUMANTHA (1988), *Unstable Agriculture and Droughts*, Vikas, Delhi.

RAO, R. S. (1995), *Towards Understanding Semi-Feudal, Semi-Colonial Society* (Studies in Political Economy), Perspectives Publications, Hyderabad.

RAWLS, JOHN (1972), *A Theory of Justice*, Oxford University Press, Oxford.

'Resolution of the Janata Party National Executive', 29–30 March, 1997.

RUDOLPH, L. I. and S. H. RUDOLPH (1987), *In Pursuit of Lakshmi: The Political Economy of the Indian State*, Orient Longman, Bombay.

RUDOLPH, SUSANNE HOEBER (1987), 'State Formation in Asia: Prolegomenon to a Comparative Study', *Journal of Asian Studies*, vol. 46, no. 4, Nov.

RUESCHEMEYER, DEITRICH, EVELYNE HUBER STEPHENS and JOHN D. STEPHENS (1992), *Capitalist Development and Democracy*, Polity Press, Cambridge.

SAINATH, P. (1996), *Everybody Loves a Good Drought*, Penguin Books, Delhi.

SANGMPAM, S. N. (1992), 'The Overpoliticized State and Democratization: A Theoretical Model', *Comparative Politics*, July.

SANGVAI, SANJAY (1994), ' "Nation", Nationalism and Mega Projects', *Economic and Political Weekly*, vol. XXIX, no. 10, 5 March.

———— (1996), 'CM's Meeting on Narmada Dam: What Did Not Happen', *Economic and Political Weekly*, vol. XXXI, no. 34, 24–31 August.

SCOTT, JAMES C. (1976), *The Moral Economy of the Peasant: Subsistence and Rebellion in Southeast Asia*, Yale University Press, New Haven.

SEN, AMARTYA (1982), *Poverty and Famines: An Essay on Entitlement and Deprivation*, Oxford University Press, Delhi.

———— (1995), 'Food and Freedom', *in* Stuart Corbridge (ed.), *Development Studies: A Reader*, Edward Arnold, London.

SENAPATI PHAKIRMOHANA [1917] (1985), *My Times and I*, trams. John Boulton, Orissa Sahitya Akademi, Bhubhaneshwar.

SETH, VIKRAM (1995), 'The Elephant and the Tragopan' in *Beastly Tales From Here and There*, reproduced in *The Poems 1981–94*, Viking, New Delhi.

SHAIKH, FARZANA (1991), *Community and Consensus in Islam: Muslim Representation in Colonial India, 1860–1947*, Cambridge University Press in association with Orient Longman, Bombay.

SHETH, PRAVIN (1994), *Narmada Project: Politics of Eco-Development*, Har-Anand Publications, Delhi.

SINGER, PETER (1972), 'Famine, Affluence and Morality', in *Philosophy and Public Affairs*, vol. 1, no. 3.

SINGH, SATYAJIT K. (1985), 'From the Dam to the Ghettos: The Victims of the Rihand Dam', *Economic and Political Weekly*, vol. XX, no. 40, 5 Oct.

SINGH, K. SURESH (1975), *The Indian Famine 1967: A Study in Crisis and Change*, People's Publishing House, New Delhi.

SINGH DEO, J. P. (n. d.), 'The Philosophy Behind the Alleged Sale of Children in Khariar', Mimeo.

SKINNER, QUENTIN (1989), 'The State', *in* Terence Ball, James Farr and Russell L. Hanson (eds), *Political Innovation and Conceptual Change*, Cambridge University Press, Cambridge.

SKOCPOL, THEDA (1985), 'Bringing the State Back In: Strategies of Analysis in Current Research', *in* Evans et al. (ed.).

SMITH, ADAM (1937), *The Wealth of Nations*, Edwin Canna (ed.), The Modern Library, New York.

SOM, REBA (1992), 'Jawaharlal Nehru and the Hindu Code : A Victory of Symbol over Substance?', no. XXX, Occasional Papers on Perspectives in Indian Development, Nehru Memorial Museum and Library, Delhi.

SORENSEN, GEORG (1993), 'Democracy, Authoritarianism and State Strength', *European Journal of Development Research*, vol. 5, no. 1.

SRINIVASAN, BINA (1994), 'Dissent and Democratic Practice: Attack on NBA Office', *Economic and Political Weekly*, vol. XXIX, no. 18, 30 April.

STOKES, ERIC (1989), *The English Utilitarians and India*, Oxford University Press, Delhi.

Tata Institute of Social Sciences (1997), 'Experiences with Resettlement and Rehabilitation in Maharashtra', *in* Drèze, Samson and Singh (eds).

THOMPSON, E. P. (1971), 'The Moral Economy of the English Crowd in the Eighteenth Century', *Past and Present*, no. 50.

THOMPSON, PETER (1984), 'Saving Tasmania's Franklin and Gordon Wild Rivers', *in* Goldsmith and Hildyard (1984b).

TITMUSS, RICHARD M. (1987), 'The Gift of Blood', *in* Brian Abel-Smith and Kay Titmuss (eds), *The Philosophy of Welfare: Selected Writings of Richard M. Titmuss*, Allen & Unwin, London.

TORRY, WILLIAM I. (1986), 'Drought and the Government–Village Emergency Food Distribution System in India', *Human Organization*, vol. 45, no. 1, Spring.

VERGHESE, B. G. (1994), *Winning the Future: From Bhakra to Narmada, Tehri, Rajasthan Canal*, Konark Publishers, Delhi.

WADE, ROBERT (1990), 'Employment, Water Control and Water Supply Institutions: India and South Korea', *in* W. Gooneratne and S. Hirashima (eds), *Irrigation and Water Management in Asia*, Sterling Publishers, New Delhi.

WASHBROOK, DAVID (1981), 'Law, State and Agrarian Society in Colonial India', *Modern Asian Studies*, vol. 15, no. 3.

WATERBURY, JOHN (1979), *Hydropolitics of the Nile Valley*, Syracuse University Press, New York.

WEINER, MYRON (1983), 'The Wounded Tiger: Maintaining India's Democratic Institutions', *in* Peter Lyon and James Manor (eds), *Transfer and Transformation: Political Institutions in the New Commonwealth*, Leicester University Press, Leicester.

WEINER, MYRON and JOHN OSGOOD FIELD (eds) (1975), *Electoral Politics in the Indian States: Three Disadvantaged Sectors*, Manohar Book Service, Delhi.

WHITCOMBE, ELIZABETH (1971), *Agrarian Conditions in Northern India*, vol. I. Thomson Press, Delhi.

———— (1993), 'Famine Mortality', *Economic and Political Weekly*, vol. XXVIII, no. 23, 5 June.

WORLD BANK (1990), 'Operational Directive 4.30: Involuntary Resettlement', 29 June, Washington, DC.

———— (1991), 'Operational Directive 4.20: Indigenous Peoples', 17 Sep., Washington, DC.

_____ (1992), 'India: Sardar Sarovar Projects : Mission Briefing to the Executive Directors', 5 Aug., Washington, DC.

———— (1995), 'Memorandum to the Executive Directors and the President on the Project Completion Report on India—Narmada River Development (Gujarat)', 29 March, Washington, DC.

WORLD WILDLIFE FUND—INDIA (1986), *Dams on the Narmada (Vol. 1: The Official View; Vol. 2: The People's View)*, New Delhi.

ZURBRIGG, SHEILA (1996), 'Evolution of Colonial Famine Policy in South Asia, 1880–1940', Paper presented at the conference on Asian Population History at Taipei.

Index

memo No. 1652

20/2/2001